M000085408

THE SINGULAR
GENERATION

THE
SINGULAR
GENERATION

Wanda Urbanska

DOUBLEDAY & COMPANY, INC.

GARDEN CITY, NEW YORK

1986

Library of Congress Cataloging-in-Publication Data
Urbanska, Wanda, 1956–
    The singular generation.
    1. Single people—United States—Attitudes.
2. Young adults—United States—Attitudes.   I. Title.
HQ800.4.U6U72 1986   305′.90652   86-4553
ISBN 0-385-19264-9

Copyright © 1986 by Wanda Urbanska
ALL RIGHTS RESERVED
PRINTED IN THE UNITED STATES OF AMERICA
FIRST EDITION

To my parents,
Edmund Stephen Urbanski
and
Marie Olesen Urbanski
whose convictions and courage have inspired many.

ACKNOWLEDGMENTS

So many people have helped to launch and see this project through to completion. I would like to thank Elaine Markson for her enthusiasm, support and creativity in nurturing the book when it was little more than a half-baked idea, and Geri Thoma for her practical advice and good cheer throughout. Sally Arteseros, my editor at Doubleday, deserves immeasurable credit for her careful, first-rate editing and constant encouragement. Barbara Broadhurst has been a devoted editor, even sacrificing time off during the holidays to move this project forward. I would like to thank Kate Medina and Stephanie von Hirschberg for their early support and work on this book.

I would like to give special thanks to my dear friend Liz Brody, who offered up editorial advice along with a bottomless supply of fruit drinks during the hot months of '84 and '85. And to my in-laws, Sam and Miriam Levering, for their warm hospitality during my research trip and the rewrite period. I'd like to thank everyone all over the country for their friendship and hospitality, especially Krysia Lindan, Ronald and Clare McLaughlin, Rhonda Gainer, Phil and Marilyn Wellons, Kate Kelley and John Shobe, Ruth and John Kelley and countless others who clipped articles, made phone calls, offered ideas and time and went out of their way to contribute to the project.

At the Los Angeles *Herald Examiner,* I am grateful to Mary Anne Dolan and Linda Hasert for helping to launch the series of articles that evolved into this book. Thanks and gratitude also go to Georgia Jones, Andrew Jaffe, Mary Rourke, Ellen Hoffs, Peggy Schmidt, Tison Lacy, Anne Thompson, Alex Ben Block, Benjamin Mark Cole, Tony Gittelson and the late Colleen Demaris for their friendship and assistance. My sister, Jane Robbins, deserves credit for selecting and helping set up my home computer and my mother, for her insights and thoughtful suggestions all along. At Harvard University, I would like to thank Monroe Engel for his long-standing commitment to the teaching of writing and his example to many of us, and also Adams House for use of its guest suite and the Signet Society—a refuge and resting place. Thanks also go to Howard Meyer, Barbara Lauren, George Plimpton, Carolyn Anthony, Jan Harayda, David Platt and Kent Ward for encouraging my work back when. This book began to emerge during the countless interviews donated by hundreds of people throughout the country. I thank them for their trust and the confidence into which they took me.

Finally, I would like to thank my constant companion and husband Frank Levering for his exacting criticism and continuous support (except during Dodger games). He shared the trying times of the project along with the triumphant ones.

Contents

Preface

This is a book about my generation: young adults in their twenties in the 1980s. Certain themes seem to reverberate in our lives, despite our diversity—namely, a palpable anxiety about life, a difficulty in making commitments to personal relationships, a strong motivation to make it on one's own and a reluctance—or inability—to embrace the future. This book provides a context within which to understand a generation the members of which have too often been stereotyped as narrow-minded careerists and self-serving conservatives. In assessing my generation, I try to bridge the considerable gap that exists between the reality of our lives and how we're perceived.

I spent the past two years traveling the country, interviewing hundreds of young adults in their workplaces, homes and college campuses. I spoke with parents, educators, writers and other experts. I visited San Francisco; Seattle; Greensboro and Mount Airy, North Carolina; southwestern Virginia's Carroll County; New York City; Cambridge, Massachusetts; Orono, Maine; Austin, Texas; Tulsa, Oklahoma; and Springfield, Missouri; before returning to my home in Los Angeles. I spoke with countless others via telephone and mail.

As a composite portrait of my generation gradually began to emerge, I became convinced that the word "singular" best describes us. Beneath our neat, polished and seemingly conservative exteriors is an evolving mind-set that is more radical than one might suspect. We are singular—the first generation of Americans who aspire to be self-sufficient at some primary level and who, almost instinctively, commit ourselves to a lifelong, dynamic relationship with ourselves. We do not see this commitment as excluding ties with others (though in some cases it has that effect), but rather as enhancing them.

The desire to know ourselves and to express our uniqueness is paramount among our priorities, and we are willing to sacrifice a great deal to these ends. What we singulars seek in ourselves and admire in others is stability through single-mindedness of purpose. This makes sense at a time when natural resources are diminishing, real wages are dwindling—especially for the young—and there is heightened anxiety on the international political and military fronts.

As other generations have been marked permanently by war and its aftereffects, our generation has been shaped by the divorce epidemic that moved rapidly through the ranks of our parents' marriages, decimating almost half of them. In part, our drive to be singular is a reaction to this instability.

I believe the singular persona will give my generation its historical character, just as the beat did for the fifties, the hippie did for the sixties and the "me-oriented" narcissist did for the seventies.

The ethos of each new generation rarely falls conveniently into the ten-year slot that defines that decade. Early signs of the singular impulse can be traced back to 1977, when Robert J. Ringer astonished and horrified many with his runaway bestseller, *Looking Out For # 1*. Christopher Lasch's more erudite *The Culture of Narcissism* (1979) provided a thorough critique of a developing self-centered society. And *Habits of the Heart* (1985), a multidisciplinary study of individualism and commitment in American life, issued a stern warning against the dangers to society of " 'ontological individualism,' the idea that the individual is the only firm reality." A growing self-centeredness is the most frequently cited characteristic of our time, but the litany of repetitious indictments against it fails to acknowledge or understand the new reality with its positive components. These changes and their underpinnings are the focus of *The Singular Generation*.

The singular impulse of the 1980s governs women as well as men, religious and ethnic minorities as well as Protestant Anglos. Obviously the singular credo has not taken hold with equal intensity in every social sector or geographical grid, but it is a growing reality almost everywhere in the country. Although this book attempts to characterize an entire generation, it most precisely describes those individuals on the cusp of change—those people who portend future change. To that end, some of my interviewees might seem extreme, but I include them because I believe they are riding a new wave.

My objective throughout has been to concentrate on the big issues with which young adults in the eighties are grappling, those areas that contribute to the singular generation's particular identity and point to the internal changes in our thinking. Trends and countertrends take place contemporaneously, and often the media rage of a particular moment or a surprising statistical shift can belie the more fundamental movements. I try to stay with the underlying currents of change.

Each of the book's twelve chapters—with the exception of the first and the last—deals with one of these significant areas.

Work has become the centerpiece of our lives, edging out family, marriage and even love as our overriding concern and radically recasting our priorities.

With its declining numbers, *marriage* has become an option—not an obligation—for both sexes. At the same time, a new ethos is emerging among married couples, that is, each partner should be self-sufficient or singular *within* a marriage.

For singulars, a *new integrity* between the sexes, based on the premise of self-security, fulfillment and friendship, is emerging. This new model is fast rendering old rules and roles between the sexes obsolete.

The body is to the eighties what the head was to the sixties: a means of self-expression and escape. Singulars have come to view our bodies as our most important natural resource, through which we can define not only our physicality but also our individuality.

Singulars are *political hybrids* who promise to usher in a new era in politics. We are becoming aware that our "generational" interests are aligned with an emerging neoconservative or neoliberal philosophy (the two are actually quite close) that is liberal on social issues—for example, minority and women's rights, social liberties—but conservative on government spending.

We've become *homebodies,* gathering color-coded record collec-

tions and state-of-the-art electronic equipment to perfect our domestic domains. In the home, as elsewhere, the singular generation is most comfortable focusing on the small picture—the
arrangement of our living rooms rather than the state of the
world.

Parenting is now viewed as a life-style choice, not a necessity
for the well-rounded adult. As a result, singular parents are volunteers in the truest sense. If we decide to have children, we bring to
our jobs a heightened appreciation for a child's individuality as
early as infancy.

Fun is so elusive in the eighties that we have become purposeful
in its pursuit, trying to schedule it into our lives. We mimic bygone eras, playacting the good times; we set ourselves up in pleasure domes of high-tech entertainment equipment in which we
direct the action—watching, hearing and recording what we
want, when we want.

The quest for *spirituality* in our lives has grown greater as our
international and interpersonal insecurity has intensified. Singulars are searching out and, in many cases, adopting a self-styled,
eclectic, spiritual dimension through traditional religions and secular channels alike.

The real danger of nuclear war and corresponding levels of fear
—*"the deep shadow"*—have driven members of the singular generation, like turtles, into our shells in search of sanity. As a result,
we have difficulty commiting ourselves to our personal or collective future.

The singular generation is still young, but what will lie in store
for us as we enter middle age and beyond has its roots in our
present reality. We seem quite different from the young adults
who came before us, to whom we are inevitably compared and
who seem to be so well understood in retrospect. We are a generation that, as yet, has not called much attention to itself. But by
scrutinizing this generation, at this point in time, we will be better
able to predict and prepare for a future we will all share.

THE SINGULAR
GENERATION

CHAPTER 1

The Singular Generation

A LEGACY OF INSECURITY

The singular generation is the product of the most turbulent epoch in American history. Born in the late fifties and sixties, we grew up in the sixties, seventies and eighties, a time in which every given was subject to revision—the sanctity of marriage, the expectation of upward mobility, the military and domestic indomitability of the United States, even the certainty that life on Planet Earth would continue. As a result, the singular generation is the most insecure generation in recent history.

Growing up, our emotional nerve endings were more attuned to the devastation of divorce than the security of marriage. We were better versed in the politics of sexism than the harmony between the sexes. The perimeters of our imaginations were defined by the grim prospect of worldwide nuclear annihilation, not the sense of a better tomorrow. And if the world somehow did manage to hold together until we reached old age, we learned that the planet's natural resources would most likely be depleted, polluted or decimated by the time we got there.

Young adults in our twenties hail from what Catholic theolo-

gian Henri Nouwen calls "ethically ambiguous, morally up-
rooted" backgrounds. We grew up with the disgrace of Vietnam
and Watergate and the chaos of divorce, not the stability of the
Eisenhower presidency and two-parent families. We grew up with
the odd urgings of the Moonies and the terror of political terrorism and airline hijackings, not the certainty of church on Sunday
and American supremacy. We grew up with punk rock and MTV,
not the Lennon Sisters and "Father Knows Best." Even the nour-
ishments of our youth were less substantial somehow than those
of just a short decade or two ago. We are a generation raised on
Jack-in-the-Box hamburgers and Diet Pepsi, not home cooking
and whole milk.

Without anything about which to feel secure, the singular generation has had a hard time planting our feet on the ground. At
some fundamental level, we have never learned how to trust—in
love, in marriage, in children and even in the religious and secular
institutions in which our predecessors once laid their faith.

As a result, young adults have embraced what I call the singular persona. Unable to count on other people or outside institutions to provide stability, we singulars look for it within ourselves.
The search for strength and security is our central obsession and
runs through our generation. It crops up everywhere—from our
resolve to strengthen our bodies, to our zealous pursuit of professional achievement, to a thirst for power and control on the job
and off it, to our need to build stable homes.

Many of us have turned to conservative politics and patriotic
rhetoric in an attempt to restore the America that our parents
once knew. We want desperately to believe in a strong America so
that we, too, can feel strong. To bolster our personal sense of
security, some of us wear military combat fatigues and support
military buildup programs.

Singulars try to live for ourselves, believing that no one can
really live for, or through, another human being. We live in the
present because our future seems so ominous and out of reach.
The lack of a secure future—or any future at all—is the singular
generation's greatest insecurity. Because we cannot visualize our
collective future, we have narrowed our scope of vision to the
small picture—our lives, our homes, our careers, our bodies and

our hobbies. We are tense, intense, mistrustful, perpetually ill at ease. We are tentative, phlegmatic, struggling for self-esteem. We are hardworking, conservative and pragmatic. In many cases, the world of work so dominates our lives that we don't even know how to relax.

Singulars are private and inverted. We clamp headsets to our ears, as if we were self-contained units, recirculating sound within the closed system of our psyches, shutting out the noise of the world in the process; by contrast, young adults of the sixties turned their stereos up loud, blaring their message out to the streets. The aviator glasses so popular right now resemble blinders, a leather strip blocking our peripheral vision, fixing our focus almost into tunnel vision. As for our hair, the solitary tail juts down below the rest of the hairline, just one small lock from the head of hair begging for attention.

DOWNWARD MOBILITY

At the center of our changing profile and our overarching insecurity is the fact of downward economic mobility. My generation is the first generation of young Americans in recent history whom the experts say cannot expect to do better than—or even as well as —our parents financially.

According to an April 1985 report in *The Wall Street Journal,* for young families headed by a person between the ages of twenty-five and thirty-four, after-tax income declined 2.3 percent from 1961 to 1982—a staggering loss when you consider that just 29 percent of the wives in that age group worked outside the home in 1961, as against 62 percent in 1982. What this means is that the average young, two-paycheck family of the eighties is making less than the one-paycheck family of the early sixties.

In constant 1984 dollars, the median income of year-round, full-time male workers aged twenty-five through thirty-four fell from a recent peak of $26,470 in 1973 to an estimated $21,607 in 1984—a startling plummet of 18.4 percent—before taxes. For female year-round full-time workers, the drop was 4 percent, the figure reflecting improving opportunities for women but still apparently declining in terms of the bottom line. These numbers are based on reports from the Census Bureau and other government agencies.

The economy's shift to a service and information base—with industries that generally pay lower wages—from a higher-waged industrial base has advanced this downtrend. Higher taxes, an enormously higher Social Security tax burden, the skyrocketing cost of both owning and renting a home and the increasingly common two-tier wage system that discriminates against the newly hired are other factors contributing to our inability to achieve the standard of living of our parents.

As the overall standard of living of young Americans declines, young adults, teenagers and children are more likely than ever before to live below the poverty line. "The median age of the American below the poverty line is now 23.4 years, whereas it was 45.8 years as recently as 1966, according to the Census Bureau," said an October 1983 report in *The Wall Street Journal.* This "youthening" of poverty is due in part to the fact that the standard of living of older Americans actually *expanded* during the seventies. The interests of retirees living on Social Security and fixed pensions have been fiercely guarded by such powerful lobbies as the American Association of Retired Persons.

Ironically, forecasters predict that the Social Security system that young Americans are so heavily subsidizing today will collapse before our generation ever makes use of it.

Young adults have just begun to recognize and speak out for our political interests. In December 1984, Americans for Generational Equity (AGE), a watchdog group protecting and lobbying for the interests of the young, was founded in Washington, D.C.— the first of its kind. AGE president Paul Hewitt says that current government spending policies and the ballooning federal deficit are "mortgaging away" not only our generation's future but that of our children and grandchildren. He predicts that as we move into the late eighties and nineties, neoconservative and neoliberal political leaders will emerge to champion the cause of the young.

Our generation's downward mobility has expanded our general jitters and added fire to our intense drive to succeed. Just as the hippies of the sixties made a stand for contemplative and idealized values at a time of prosperity and economic expansion, singulars are trying to buck the tide and achieve prosperity at a time when the economic outlook is grim.

It's easy to see why the hero of our generation is the self-styled entrepreneur who succeeds despite difficult economic times. He or she is upwardly mobile, self-sure and supremely singular.

THE NEW "YOUNGERLY"

As the singular generation, as a whole, moves downward economically, youth is losing its place on the pedestal it has occupied for so long. America is becoming less and less a youth culture, at a time when the stigma against old age seems to be diminishing.

A look at fashion trends provides visual confirmation. In the sixties, almost every age group dressed "young," including the young; businessmen adopted the open-neck-shirt look and grandmothers wore short skirts. Today young fast-trackers prefer to wear the gray flannel, pinstripes and pearls once associated with the middle-aged. Even fashion models let their wrinkles show, and for the first time, it's fashionable to be forty. What's more, among singulars, the look and shape of one's body—over which one has some control—has become more important than the composition of the face, over which one has little control.

In recent years, to be young was to be carefree and to have the world at your feet; to find ready employment, to have discretionary income, to be in your physical prime and to be comfortable with your probable future. But today it's the middle-aged—and even the retired—who have more disposable income. They are more likely to own their own homes, to be physically fit and healthier than were their predecessors.

"The glitter is off the Baby Boom," writes Judith Langer, a New York–based marketing research consultant, in a report for advertisers trying to reach the over-fifty consumer. "The Baby Boom was once the darling of the media, but these people, it turns out, just don't have the disposable income of older Americans."

Not only is the stature of youth generally diminishing, but some of today's downwardly mobile young adults are even assuming some of the least attractive traits of yesterday's elderly. Indeed, one small segment of young adults today—what I call the new *youngerly*—are dependent on their parents for financial and emotional sustenance and support on into their twenties, and sometimes beyond.

SINGULAR MIND-SET

There has been a fundamental shift toward voluntary single status in the singular generation, a change that has come about without much acknowledgment. According to the Statistical Abstract of the United States, the percentage of never-married individuals in their twenties and thirties has gone up sharply in recent years. In 1960, the number of never-married males aged twenty-five to twenty-nine was 20.8 percent of the population, versus 38.2 percent in 1983. The percent of never-married females in the same age group was 10.7 percent in 1960 and 24.8 percent in 1983. Among males aged twenty to twenty-four, in 1960, 53.1 percent had never married; by 1983, that number jumped to 73.2. Among females aged twenty to twenty-four, in 1960, the percent of those who'd never married was 28.4, versus 55.5 in 1983.

At the same time, the number of single individuals, including never-married, divorced and widowed, has leapfrogged. In 1960, according to figures from the Current Population Report's "Marital Status and Living Arrangements," 39.3 percent of males aged twenty to twenty-nine were single; by 1983, that number had jumped to 59.6 percent. In 1960, the number of single females of that age group was 21.8 percent; by 1983, that number had reached 46.8 percent.

This dramatic shift toward the single state is a bellwether of the entire singular generation, influencing our relationships and even our marriages. The increasing tendency to see ourselves as single units is one of the most striking changes of our time.

As the single life-style grows in numbers and acceptance, with an increasing proportion of our population choosing or remaining "forever single," the "singular" mind-set—one in which marriage is secondary, not central, to our lives and our status in life—is growing even faster. We are either marrying later, not staying married or not marrying at all.

If we do marry, singulars are increasingly likely to bring to our marriages an I-am-me-and-you-are-you attitude. We feel that two people enter marriage as individuals and stay that way, rather than becoming one new unit together. A weak marital partner, who unduly clings to the marriage for a sense of self or who assumes too much of his or her identity from a spouse, is frowned upon by the singular generation.

Singulars approach a new marriage much as we might plan to open a new business—with an eye toward problem-solving. We see the big wedding as the starting point of an ongoing dialectic, not the threshold to everlasting bliss. Implicit in the contract is the understanding that if it does not work out, it is in both partners' interests to call it quits, just as you would close a business that was consistently losing money.

Likewise, we singulars are having fewer children, later in life, or none at all. Once again, this is due to our increasing tendency to see ourselves as single units and not as families; to our emphasis on our own careers and financial well-being, not on future generations.

Marriage is no longer based on the till-death-do-us-part premise, and thus, in our search for security, provides no real sanctuary. As the divorce rate reached the 50-percent mark of all American marriages in the 1980s and even higher in some areas, marriage began to take on the aura of semi-permanence.

Despite this change, my generation finds the myth of everlasting marriage—with its loving extended families and happy children—far more attractive than the singular reality. Indeed, everlasting marriage is the unfulfilled wish-fantasy of the eighties, the way that cosmically satisfying sex was in the sixties.

Shrewd advertisers and members of the media are picking up on this unresolved tension between idealized marriage and singular reality, and are selling the marriage and family fantasy. A current TV commercial for Ritz crackers depicts a young woman showing off her new engagement ring to the family. Her father takes her fiancé under his wing for a tête-à-tête. In celebration, they break out the Ritz. President Reagan's hugely successful 1984 TV reelection advertisements similarly exploited the marriage theme. A number of spots portrayed brides embracing older relatives, to show that the generations are in harmony, that tradition is continuing. These campaigns are effective because we buy the image of marriage and children while not rushing into it or sticking with it ourselves.

The singular generation is still emotionally attached to the old values because they are part of the secure past—not the more sordid present and terrifying future. But we have moved on unwittingly, without acknowledging the change.

MARR AND WILLIAM

I have been able to identify distinctive characteristics in perception, motivation and behavior that set the singular generation apart from our predecessors. What follows is a portrait of Marr (short for Marilyn) and William, two composite singulars whose thoughts and behavior I've drawn from the hundreds of interviews I've had with young adults from across the country. They illustrate generally what is on the minds and in the hearts of my generation.

Marr and William are young, driven professionals in their midtwenties who live and work in a major metropolitan area. Since graduating from college, they've become more and more enmeshed in the web of work. Shop talk engages them—gossip about the boss, the politics of the workplace, who gets raises and how. They sometimes dream about spectacular professional feats to put on future résumés, or even a day when they won't need résumés because the headhunters will come after them.

Marr cultivates a business edge, consciously breaking from her mother's warm, accommodating style. At work, Marr tries not to adapt too readily to others, to know her own mind before she speaks it. When Marr's parents divorced and her mother started looking for outside employment, Marr became especially intense about her career. Marr has vowed that when she marries, she will never let her work slip.

She believes that job satisfaction is the key to personal fulfillment and feels that it's essential to devote a substantial amount of time in your twenties to finding what you're best suited for, to becoming psychically sound and financially and personally self-sufficient. Marr generally spends fifty hours a week at the office and often takes her work home with her at night. She put her name on her college's referral file; when new graduates come to town, she takes them to lunch and digs into her address book to give them job-hunting leads. She remembers how important that kind of help was when she started out.

Marr faithfully reads *Savvy* and *Working Woman* magazines to stay on top of the trends. When she was in high school, she gave her mother a subscription to *Ms* magazine. But Marr no longer finds feminism compelling: Not that she doesn't believe in its principles; rather, she finds it has no meaning in her life. Marr is not discriminated against on the job or anywhere else, really, she believes, because she won't let herself be; she looks out for herself. And she hates to admit it, but in the last election, she didn't even vote.

Currently Marr splits the rent in a two-bedroom apartment with a roommate. The place is special—two bathrooms, a fireplace, elaborate molding—things you don't see in newer apartments. The rent is commensurately high, but Marr doesn't see any way around it. Having a nice home, with her own bathtub to sink into every night, is a top priority, a way of nurturing herself.

William lives in his parents' sprawling five-bedroom house on the outskirts of the city. Their place is actually more than a house, it's a spread, with a pool and tennis courts and a maid who comes in three times a week. William's mother raised the three children and then went back to work. Since his parents don't really need the space anymore, they have found a condominium and asked William to move out.

William actually planned to leave eventually, but not just yet. First he wanted to save enough money to seed an entrepreneurial venture for himself. But he hasn't saved much yet, having put most of his money into buying a new Honda Accord and taking exotic vacation trips. William hit on the scheme of opening a fix-your-own-bicycle center, borrowing on the frame-it-yourself concept, where people could come in and learn the craft of bike repair for themselves. He will be a good businessman, he thinks, because he's a "people person." But if he's serious about getting this off the ground, he may have to forgo vacations and take a second job.

When William was growing up, he never had to do without. There was tennis camp every summer, then an expensive private college. But in his junior year, it hit him: "I'm not necessarily going to make the money that my father did; in fact, I probably won't. Unless I become a millionaire, I will not be able to afford to own the house I grew up in."

It was at this point that William started to fixate on making money, on being able to achieve a life-style that suddenly seemed fleeting. He began to see himself as conservative, breaking with what he views as his family's kneejerk liberalism. In college, he did the surprising: He registered Republican.

The first few times Marr and William went out, he picked up the check, but they both felt awkward about it: Would he appear cheap if he didn't grab it? Would she appear strident and un-feminine if she made a play for it? Once they had established a relationship, she began to pull her own financial weight. It simply didn't make sense to pad her bank account while his was receding.

Perhaps because they both feel so pressured at work to be responsible, to perform efficiently and thoroughly, in their private lives, they still think of themselves as kids. For fun, William and Marr take weekend trips, see odd old movies, try to discover offbeat, out-of-the-way places. Once they took a class in making taffy and began to joke about going into the taffy-making business together. They could make their fortune that way, just as Famous Amos and Mrs. Field made their millions on cookies. It would start with a little taffy cart and end up in *The Wall Street Journal.* Business, business; it always came back to business.

Marr never used to see herself as attractive. In high school, she considered herself about a 5 on the scale with 10 as perfect. But at about the time she decided to change her name from Marilyn to Marr (for the sharp, jarring sound and the fact that it gave her an edge), she discovered aerobics. For a while, she treated aerobics as a kind of religion. During one exam period, she gave up sit-down meals, surviving on nuts and yogurt and pints of coffee, but she would not skip her aerobics class. Once she took command of her body and started to feel attractive, her whole world turned around.

Always naturally athletic, William works out, too. But his latest passion is "good threads." He spends more than he should on clothing, having discovered how the right clothes enhance his image. His garments are looser, brighter and more expressive than anything his father ever wore, and William likes the feeling of freedom this gives him.

Though Marr and William have been "seeing each other" for about ten months, neither knew at the beginning whether theirs was a friendship or a romance. They got to know each other for several months before they began to sleep together. In fact, when they first met at a college networking cocktail party, they were both there to pick up business cards, not potential lovers.

When they first made love, Marr was just as ready as William. Before it happened, they talked it out, concerned that their friendship might be threatened if the sex didn't work; both vowed that that wouldn't be the case. They even bared their weaknesses before going to bed: He confessed to having a thicker penis than normal, and she admitted to being slow to reach orgasm.

If William and Marr do not remain together—if the relationship doesn't ultimately "take," or if their careers move them in different directions—it's likely that their friendship will survive. Respect has already been established, and they may ultimately decide that they make better friends and business allies than lovers and potential mates.

The difference in gender does not form any great chasm between them, because they see each other first as individuals, not as male and female. Indeed, Marr and William are more like each other than they are many members of their own sex. Ambitious, career-oriented and determined, they respect the value of money and hard work, of honesty and fair play.

Occasionally Marr's friends tease her: "When's he going to pop the question?" But, in fact, they all know the big question is not marriage but whether there is enough between them to keep the relationship going. In the eighties, when unmarried relationships are no longer illegitimate, having a steady lover/companion of the opposite sex is in itself a nod toward tradition.

Once when they went away for the weekend, William said to Marr, "Do you realize if this had been twenty years ago, we'd probably be planning our wedding right now?"

"You're what my mother would have called a good catch," she responded. And they laughed together, realizing how different things were back when their parents were starting out.

If Marr and William do decide to marry, they will bring to their marriage a new set of values, trying not to duplicate patterns set by their parents.

Marr is Catholic and William is Protestant, and they would both hold with their faith. They might flip a coin to decide in whose church to marry, or else ask both a priest and a minister to officiate. Neither would convert to the other's religious tradition, but they are open to "borrowing" from both.

William finds his parents' Presbyterian faith less compelling than the motivational programs that his company sometimes offers. Though Marr grew away from the Catholic faith in her teens, these days she has found herself going to an occasional Mass. She likes the ritual but is skeptical of the dogma. But when she attends a service, she wears a nice dress, stockings and pumps.

If they married, Marr would not take William's last name, feeling that in keeping her own, she would retain her personal identity. And William seconds her opinion. He once surprised his buddies by saying that he wouldn't marry a woman who wanted to take his name because if she wanted to keep her own, he'd know she was strong.

At this stage in their lives, Marr and William rarely come into contact with children, and when they do, they find it a special treat. As for having their own, it is a fantasy that they both relish. Occasionally Marr imagines a little girl whom she could raise to be strong and independent from day one. William would like to have two children one day—a boy and a girl. Though they are still in their mid-twenties, it's hard to imagine when that day would be.

If they were to have a baby, it's likely that Marr would stay at home for a short while following the birth, before hiring a nanny or enrolling the child in day care and returning to her job. It's likely that Marr and William would view their baby differently from the way their parents viewed them in infancy. William and Marr would look for the baby's particular, individual characteristics from the moment of birth. It's also much more likely that they would stop at one child.

TOWARD A NEW AGE

A new generation is coming of age in America. The last vestiges of the laid-back, relentlessly liberal-minded and idealistic youth vanished with the 1984 presidential election, when eighteen-through twenty-five-year-olds voted to reelect Ronald Reagan in numbers greater than the older voters. We voted for him because he seemed to represent our financial interests and because he stands for an image of America that we fear is too quickly vanishing. In 1984, it became clear that the sixties generation was gone for good, replaced by the new singular generation.

Almost without exception, members of my generation feel a strong need to establish an individual identity, to forge a particular path. Work is our lifeblood, whatever our job. As singulars, we are dead set on cultivating a lifelong relationship with ourselves. Even when we move in with mates or marry, even when we have children, we are determined to carry our particular singular identity forward into the future.

Our decade is an epoch of transition. Singulars stand between a traditionalism that is both alien and appealing to us now—having reality in our collective mythology but only a fleeting grip on our formative life experience—and a singular future that is difficult to visualize and comprehend.

The singular generation has absorbed the shock of a changing culture, and we carry on the only way we know how. Though no new social order has yet become preeminent, within our relationships, a new integrity is emerging, one in which we grant to those with whom we relate their own singularity. It is a nonpossessive, other-oriented form of support, which allows for an increasing variety of personal choices: from the traditionalist, to the eclectic, to the militant single. Within this new context, it's easy to see why marriages are dwindling in number, but quality marriages are on the upswing.

The singular mind-set is just now emerging as a major force, and its prominence will expand as the singular generation grows into maturity.

CHAPTER 2

The Entrepreneurial Spirit

> My work ethic tells me, "Make a lot of money; make a lot of money, you'll be happier." And the real me says, "Well, it's fine to make a lot of money, but the most important thing in life is to love what you do for a living."
>
> —Denise Andrews, twenty-four,
> Seattle, Washington

THE NEW WORK ETHIC

Singulars do not work to live, we live to work. We pour our passion into our jobs and define ourselves through them. Our careers are our babies that we nurture, investing seemingly endless supplies of time and money in them. We work twelve-hour days, weekends and, if needed, pull all-nighters to advance our careers. We put our personal relationships on the back burner, accepting weekend marriages, cross-country romances and the single state. We postpone getting married and having children; we neglect family and friends and even the pursuit of pleasure—all for the sake of this sacred entity called the career.

A new work ethic has arisen with the singular generation that holds that work is the centerpiece of the good life, that a commitment to your career is a commitment to yourself, that you must be effective in your job in order to be a complete person. Singulars have reclaimed the Protestant work ethic and put our own stamp on it. We believe that hard work is its own reward and that slothfulness is contemptible.

Singulars are zealous careerists, but not without good reason. We are entering the workplace at a time when America's economy is making a transition from a higher-paying manufacturing base to a lower-paying service, information and high-technology base. Since the early seventies, there has been no real wage growth for the average worker in this country, and the average real income for young workers has actually declined. For a variety of reasons and in a number of ways, my generation is carrying more than its share of the load for the economic woes of the society as a whole.

At least in part, the singular generation's work ethic represents a resistance to these factors and a vow to surmount them. Indeed, succeeding at work has become the acid test of personhood among singulars, a kind of heated competition that separates the wouldbes from the ares. Those of us who have good, growth-oriented jobs or who are earning real money or who are deriving personal satisfaction from our work are the elites of my generation, carrying with us that special flush of success.

In this hierarchy, the entrepreneurs stand imperially at the top, while those who work for a paycheck and live for the weekend, investing nothing of themselves in their jobs, rank closer to the bottom. The real "losers" of our generation, however, are those who shun the work world altogether; they either live off someone else—a parent, a lover, a spouse—or are blissfully unemployed. Because they don't work, such individuals have little standing among singulars.

On first meeting someone, singulars will invariably say, "What do you do?" not "How do you do?" Learning what a stranger does, to our way of thinking, is the best window into who he or she is. Indeed, what we do for a living has all but eclipsed our nonwork identities.

The entrepreneurial impulse gives the singular generation its work identity, and it is one of my generation's most promising vital signs. Characterized by single-mindedness of purpose, willingness to take risks, strong instincts and self-motivation, the entrepreneur is the individualist of the business world. He is the ultimate singular, because he derives both money and pleasure from doing it "his way." Singulars who are not entrepreneurs are "entrepreneurials." We view our careers as our personal ventures and are charged by, integrally connected to and almost in love with our work.

Singulars ride our careers full-throttle, feeling the thrill of a challenge, the darkness of defeat, relishing on-the-job growth, enjoying clout, authority and a modicum of autonomy. As the elite of our generation, singulars are steeped in the entrepreneurial spirit—even when working for someone else.

One such individual is Rhonda Gainer, who, at twenty-eight, makes twice her age in salary as advertising director for a $500 million leading men's designer clothing firm in New York. Rhonda is "challenge-, not money-driven," she says, and like many singulars, eventually plans to go into business for herself. But for now, she is learning everything she can on someone else's time.

The first year Rhonda was at her present job, she was a one-woman show, working seventy to eighty hours a week, developing a major national advertising campaign, setting up new business systems in her department and, because she had no secretary, typing her own letters. It was a monumental challenge for Rhonda to plan, execute and produce the ad campaign on a low budget and without supervision, since she'd never done one before. ("I even bought the ties," she says.) That same year she also wrote, directed and produced a promotional film for the firm in a foreign country. And she managed to pull it all off.

That first ad campaign proved to be a great success—even more successful than her second one, in which she was able to delegate more work to others. The first campaign was also far more thrilling to Rhonda, because she was blazing a trail in virgin territory. "I've done a lot of firsts with no experience," says Rhonda proudly.

Rhonda appraises her professional talents as coolly as if she were evaluating a new garment. "I am independent, a self-starter and an excellent idea generator." She also describes herself as confident and calm during job interviews and when speaking in public or giving TV interviews. But "I have no wit," she admits.

Rhonda still has much to learn on her job, and she will stay only as long as her work remains challenging.

"I could see getting bored," she says. "It could become a systematic routine: You think of another idea and another location and you go do it. I don't understand people who do these things twenty years in a row."

Rhonda is too passionate about her work—and puts too much of herself into her job—to let the fires at work smolder and die out. Holding down a boring job for any length of time is no more acceptable to Rhonda than making love to a man who doesn't attract her.

Part of keeping the passion alive involves taking risks. Not long ago, Rhonda's new boss came ranting and raving into her office. She had hired a photographer for an ad layout without first consulting him. He demanded that she fire her photographer and hire one he recommended. Prior to this new boss's arrival, it had been Rhonda's prerogative to select photographers. Rhonda calmly pointed this out to him and refused to fire the photographer she had selected. In so doing, she risked antagonizing her new boss, but she won the bet. The boss has since accorded her a new level of respect, and he actually complimented the photo series when it was finally submitted.

Such victories have helped build not only Rhonda's career, but her sense of self. Though she is still in her twenties, Rhonda already reminisces about her professional accomplishments the way ex-athletes talk about their glory days on the football field.

One of her greatest feats was landing her first job out of college. Rhonda had been attending a communications seminar at the Waldorf-Astoria Hotel in New York City during the spring of her senior year when she spotted the Colgate-Palmolive Building across Park Avenue. From a pay phone, she placed a cold call to a Colgate vice president, asking him if he would interview her while she was in the city. He agreed to see her the next morning.

When Rhonda arrived for the interview, the vice president was in the midst of a meeting with a representative from a major ad company. On a lark, the vice president invited Rhonda to join them. "We'll both interview you," he kidded.

Rhonda held her own in the company of these two middle-aged male executives and managed to wow them. They were especially impressed with her résumé, which folded into a pamphlet and which she'd had typeset in red on a beige background. "They looked at that résumé and teased: 'She's done more than we've done in thirty years here,' " Rhonda recalls. " 'She's going to take my job,' one said." Rhonda received a job offer for an untitled position in the sports-recreation division in the mail a week later.

WORK AS AN "ALTERNATIVE" WORLD

In our never-ending search for security, work provides a kind of refuge. For singulars, a job becomes an all-consuming way of life, a reality unto itself with distinct requirements, goals, benchmarks of achievement and tangible rewards. Work today is rather like school, a closed system in which otherwise ordinary events and interactions assume heightened importance, bearing charged emotions. The work world provides us with an attractive alternative to the larger world, which seems so precarious, overwhelming and out of control. If we can't accept the fact that each one of us is a potential hostage to a terrorist hijacking, we can face the prospect of the office Xerox machine breaking down. If we can't comfort an angry, unhappy parent, we can appease a demanding boss by putting in a couple of hours overtime. If we can't bear to think about the future in a global sense because it is so much at risk, we can draw up a plan for our own particular career. In fact, the only part of the future that singulars can visualize or think about is the future of our careers.

"I'm optimistic about the future in the micro sense," says twenty-eight-year-old Tony Gittelson, a New York film crew veteran and screenwriter. "I feel hopeful about my writing, my day-to-day life, but in a macro sense, it seems like things are going from bad to worse."

Work provides security in the form of a paycheck at a time

when the generation as a whole is downwardly mobile economically. The better we do on the job, the greater a financial buffer we can build against an uncertain economy. Developing our professional reputations is also money in the bank, because it positions us for even better next jobs.

But most important, employment enables us to be self-supporting, which is one of the singular generation's fundamental tenets. We believe that the best form of security comes from being able to take care of ourselves.

On the job, we study strategies for survival and advancement, rehearsing work behavior with close friends, coaching each other about when to speak up, when to keep quiet and when to take a risk, the way our parents' generation maneuvered to put the moves on members of the opposite sex. We are driven perfectionists who would rather skip lunch than be late with an assignment. In our dream jobs, we have clout, autonomy and are self-directed if not our own boss.

When asked what was the worst thing, short of death or disability, that could befall her, twenty-three-year-old Claire Haberman of New York City responds without hesitation: "Ruining my job record. Doing something that would affect my getting another job."

For male and female singulars alike, being blackballed from the world of work would be the worst possible fate.

THE DIFFUSION OF THE WORK ETHOS

Work's dominion over us has become undeniable, and its ripples have spread far and wide, affecting diverse sectors of our lives. Old rules about work behavior have fallen by the wayside, such as the notion that we can banish personal emotions from our professional lives. Work models have spilled over into our private lives, and even our fantasy lives are migrating to the workplace.

Complaining of a disappointing sex life, one singular says, "If you don't feel good about yourself at work, how can you feel good about yourself at home?" Not long ago, we might have said just the reverse.

For many singulars, our place of employment has become our home, our co-workers our "family" and our performance and standing on the job, our main source of happiness and feelings of self-worth. Psychologists and experts in work behavior are increasingly factoring in the personal emotional baggage of individuals who are in conflict at work. Given the fluid nature of eighties relationships, work is often the most stabilizing element in our lives. Because we're spending more time at work and investing more of our emotions in our jobs and relationships with co-workers, employers are having to discard such obsolete ground rules as Never mix business and pleasure. Most businesses are softening time-worn restrictions against hiring and keeping on married and unmarried couples; and they're looking the other way when employees date.

Moreover, the work ethos is increasingly coloring our off-the-job experience. "Everything I do is work related somehow: the parties I go to, the people I see for dinner," says Carole Markin, a twenty-eight-year-old Los Angeles producer. "Every minute of my weekend is scheduled. I have to put my errands on a calendar or they won't get done."

Prenuptial contracts, like startup company agreements, are increasingly common. A singular marriage more closely resembles a heterogeneous business partnership than the old model of a homogeneous coupled unit. Within marriage, both partners strive for parity, trying to balance what they bring into a marriage with what they take out of it. Household budgets are run on cost-accounting models. And today's young women, like yesterday's young men, feel we must prove ourselves professionally before we enter into marriage.

WORK AS FANTASY

Work has even made its way into our fantasy lives. We singulars confer onto the work world a mythology akin to the one previous generations reserved for romantic love. We believe there is that one magical, mystical job out there that is just right for us, that will draw out our particular talents and display them to advantage. All we have to do is find—or create—it.

That one right job, we believe, will bring us security, fulfillment, even happiness.

"If I could be on a board of directors—the only woman among fifteen men—I'd be happy," says twenty-four-year-old Manhattan secretary Joanne Mahoney. What her fantasy is *not* is as revealing as what it is. It does not involve falling in love with a millionaire, or winning the New Jersey state lottery or reveling in the pleasures of matrimony and motherhood. It does not involve other people except as admiring bystanders. Rather, it casts Joanne as a corporate leading lady, dressed the part in an expensive tailored suit and conducting herself with the decorum of a woman who calls her own shots. It is a quintessentially singular fantasy set in that boardroom in the sky.

When Wendy, a twenty-one-year-old Washington, D.C., coed, told her parents' friends of her ambitions to become a TV anchorwoman, one said, "Why, honey, you're pretty enough to be an actress." Wendy said she had not the slightest interest in acting; it was broadcasting or bust.

Indeed, TV broadcasting has supplanted acting as a singular job fantasy, especially among females, because newscasters look to us like take-charge professionals. From their command posts behind the camera, they relay the day's events to the world in a crisp, upbeat manner. Actresses, by contrast, seem to be at the beck and call of every director and producer who might potentially cast them. And even if the relationship remains aboveboard, it still smacks of unprofessionalism.

Singulars fuel our job fantasies by soaking up the anecdotal histories of successful entrepreneurs the way our parents did the lurid details of movie stars' lives. We are more interested in what makes Lee Iaccoca and Steven Jobs tick than in what's behind Sean Penn and Darryl Hannah. The entrepreneur, we believe, has the courage of an astronaut, the imagination of an artist and the concentration of a surgeon.

THE CAREER CLUB FOR BOTH SEXES

Work, of course, has always been important. But never before has an entire generation organized itself around the principle that work should come first. Never before have both sexes felt compelled to prove themselves in the workplace. Almost without exception, singulars are preoccupied with launching or busily engaged in promoting a career. Of all the females interviewed for this book, only a few expressed the desire to stay home and be homemakers—but only while nursing infants or rearing small children. Singular women simply no longer consider marriage to be a profession. The powerful, strings-pulling executive has taken the place of the pampered sex kitten as the sexual magnet of the singular generation, the kind of woman who is herself a good catch.

"All men talk about these days," grouses one young magazine editor, "is how much money their wives or girlfriends make."

Female singulars are often the most zealous careerists, because we are the newest initiates into the career club. Like new immigrants, women tend to be the hardest workers, so eager are we to prove our mettle, so conscious are we of our mothers with their half-victories lurking in the shadows. Those of us who want families often do double duty in our twenties to establish our careers before facing the inevitable compromises of motherhood.

Singular males can be just as competitive, recognizing the distance they must travel even to catch up with their fathers' level of achievement, much less surpass it. Relative to middle-aged men, young male adults have lost tremendous ground in just a generation. "As recently as the mid-1950s, the average fully employed man in his early 20s earned 73 percent as much as the average fully employed man 45 to 54," said a 1985 report in *The Wall Street Journal.* "But by 1983, that ratio had dropped to a mere 50 percent."

What's more, the margin of young males' wage advantage over young females has also declined. And the influx of competitive young women into the workplace has intensified the heat for landing and keeping a good job, and advancing up the ladder. Singular men who want to achieve above and beyond the norm are thus driven to unprecedented levels of hard work.

DOWNWARD MOBILITY

A variety of economic factors has caused social critics to call us the first generation of *downwardly mobile* Americans since World War II. The entrepreneurial spirit of the singular generation is at least in part a healthy response to real market conditions.

Job opportunities for new college graduates began to shrink during the seventies, at a time when the Baby Boom was delivering its millions into the work force. In fact, one out of every five college graduates in the seventies was forced to accept a job that did not require a college degree. These unlucky fifths snatched positions from high school graduates, who, in turn, were faced with increasingly high unemployment rates. This trend has worsened in the eighties, and college is no longer a guaranteed ticket to success.

There has been no real wage growth in this country since 1973, and the average wages for new entrants into the workplace have been dropping ever since. Heavy industrial jobs—the kind traditionally protected by trade unions—continue to decline in number, while lower-paying jobs are expanding. Steelworkers, for example, average $13.36 an hour, while those who assemble electronic components make just $7.17 an hour.

To the further financial detriment of young adults, two-tier wage systems, which protect the interests of employees with seniority at the expense of the newly hired, are becoming an increasingly common and accepted practice in many industries. In 1984, the U.S. Postal Service adopted such a system, whereby existing workers received a 2.7 percent increase in wages over a three-year period over and above inflation; this program is financed by paying newly hired workers $5,000 less per year. The so-called "A" and "B" (or two-tiered) wage scales exist at most major airlines.

Overall rates of unemployment have stayed higher in recent years, especially among the young. And a multitude of industries are paring their full-time staff rosters. During increasingly common job layoffs, the young are the first to go as we tend to be the newest hired.

"In a sense, we have had a depression in this country, but we've just given it over to young people," says Paul Hewitt, president of Americans for Generational Equity.

The government has contributed to the economic woes of young adults by heaping on a tax load that's heavier than ever. In 1986, the regressive Social Security tax will take 7.15 percent of every dollar earned by an employed person—up to a certain ceiling—regardless of how low one's income. (For a self-employed person, the rate is *12.3 percent* of earnings; this rate will hit *15.3 percent* by 1990.) By contrast, when today's sixty-five-year-olds first entered the job market in the thirties and forties, the Social Security tax was less than 1 percent of their annual earnings. Federal and state income taxes and other taxes have increased as well.

In addition, the cost of housing—both rental and homeownership—has been steadily rising.

Economists point to a growing gap in this country between high and low incomes and an overall depression in average wages, with some forecasters predicting the eventual demise of the middle class. Naturally, young adults, who have not gotten a foothold of their own in the middle class, would be the first victims of the fallout.

The downwardly mobile pinch is felt acutely by the low-income young, who are slipping below the poverty line at alarming rates. These unlucky members of the new "youngerly," who are either unable or unwilling to find employment or who work but cannot subsist independently, face worsening conditions.

But no young adults are immune to the effects of downward mobility; not even those in, or preparing for, traditionally high-paid professions like medicine and law.

"When we entered medical school, we were told we were entering a chosen profession, that we'd made it, but I think that's no longer true," says Lynn Brittony, a twenty-six-year-old third-year medical student at the University of Pennsylvania in Philadelphia. "It will be difficult for us to find jobs. It used to be that you could pick an area of the country where you wanted to be, and you'd have no trouble practicing there. No more."

Lynn's decision to select radiology as her medical subspecialty was in large part a strategic one. "A radiologist's services will always be needed," explains Lynn. "The studies they do, such as MRI scans and CAT scans, will be cost-saving for medicine. It's a good profession to go into because of that."

A SPARE EMPLOYMENT LANDSCAPE

Twenty years ago, it was hard to find doctors like Lynn, trained at prestigious medical schools, who would deign to go into such an "unglamorous," service-oriented subspecialty. But a new, more spare employment landscape has forced singulars to become more dogged in our search for work: exploring new paths, digging deeper along existing ones and clamping down harder.

Like entrepreneurs, singulars are scrappers without compunctions about using whatever tools we can find that will help us along, whether that means wearing a wardrobe to reinforce a chosen image or dipping into Daddy's bank account.

If we're on the great job hunt, which for many of us is a perennial condition, we prepare our résumés meticulously, network with business contacts, study *The Wall Street Journal* and spend our Saturdays at career-enhancement seminars. On college campuses, we queue up in front of college placement offices—sometimes overnight, stretched out on sleeping bags—to sign up for coveted job interview slots. We set goals for ourselves and strategize about positioning ourselves on this job and the next. Toward the goal of establishing ourselves professionally, we pull out all the stops.

Twenty-two-year-old Melissa Stephens moved to what initially seemed to her an undesirable location for the right first job. Melissa, who grew up in Greensboro, North Carolina, had become accustomed to life in the fast lane while summering in Ghana and training with North Carolina National Bank in Charlotte. She had to think hard before accepting the job as commercial branch manager of Mount Airy's NCNB.

But in so doing, the Phi Beta Kappa graduate from the University of North Carolina at Chapel Hill put the long-term interests of her career above the short-term life-style she prefers. Though no longer just a stone's throw from cultural events, good movies, good shops and dear friends, Melissa decided that the stint in Andy Griffith's real-life hometown fits into her five-year plan.

"There's nothing wrong with being a big fish in a small pond," she says. However, she's quick to point out that Mount Airy does not fit into her ten- and fifteen-year plans.

In order to stay afloat, many young adults are moonlighting, taking on two and sometimes three jobs to put together an adequate income. Free-lance work—a variation on entrepreneurship in which one's "company" is simply one's own goods or services —continues to be an attractive option for many singulars, who work out of the home.

Some of us are turning to quarters that were not considered desirable just a dozen years ago. The armed services, with their college scholarships, vocational training programs and jobs with good pay and benefits, have become increasingly popular among young adults. Service jobs in restaurants and offices are abundant today, but they are little more than a stopgap measure to the end of establishing a fulfilling and lucrative career. Likewise, the temporary staff business, which traditionally provided fill-in office help, has now become a staple in the employment world. Though the pay is reduced and comes without benefits, temporary work offers the flexibility of a no-strings free-lance arrangement.

Employment experts say that the increasingly common "sequential career" phenomenon, in which workers change careers a number of times in the course of their employed lives, will grow in the future. Singulars will have to be attuned to the changing marketplace and open to new options in order to keep up.

REVERENCE FOR THE ALMIGHTY DOLLAR

Just as entrepreneurs need money to capitalize their businesses, singulars need money to capitalize our careers. Money is both a measure of success on the job and a tool for promoting our professional objectives: It takes money to dress well, to drive a reliable car and to buy a membership to the right health club. What's more, against the current of downward mobility, just maintaining a decent standard of living is costlier now than before.

It is no longer hip to be poor. Even the artists and free spirits of the eighties hold a new, more reverent attitude toward the Almighty Dollar.

"I'm not embarrassed to say I'd like to make some money," says Lani Lindsey, a twenty-four-year-old Springfield, Missouri, waitress–cum–video artist, by way of contrasting her feelings with those of her thirty-four-year-old live-in boyfriend, who's had to battle guilt over his high earnings. "John is embarrassed he is making so much money."

Some of us believe that the route to security lies in accumulating assets. Jeff Miller, a Winston-Salem, North Carolina, pharmacist, is currently working seventy-eight hours a week at a drugstore chain in order to collect two and a half salaries, or a take-home pay of between $1,000 and $1,200 per week. "At this age, I'm farther ahead than most," says Jeff, now twenty-five. He has invested some of his earnings in video-game machines and now owns twenty-five, which are valued at between $2,000 and $3,000 apiece. He also has a fat savings account and title to several vehicles.

Denise Andrews, who earned almost $22,000 annually for two years working as an apprentice ship diesel mechanic on the Seattle Harbor, shares Jeff's hunger for monetary and material acquisitions. After being laid off from her job, she enrolled in the University of Washington to earn her degree in business. Ten years from now, Denise would like to be earning $30,000 in today's dollars, to own "a decent piece of land in eastern Washington" and to be involved in a women's sports company—either teaching mountaineering, kayaking or rock climbing or producing large-scale women's sports events.

"Money makes the world go round," says Denise, who grew up in New Jersey the child of factory-worker parents and would like to better her lot. "From my background, I have a definite desire to be comfortable, if not wealthy."

While singulars acknowledge the value of money, most of us view it as a means to the end of enhancing our careers, not an end in itself.

"Being rich is not a big thing in my life," says Joanne Mahoney, the New York secretary. "Being good is. I want to be good at what I do, and successful, and have people say 'Wow.' "

Even Denise Andrews, with her desire for upward mobility, would have to concur. "The most important thing in life is to love what you do for a living." However, she quickly adds, "I don't want to make $7,000 a year and be a potter."

Singulars will make financial sacrifices if we believe that they are shrewd career moves.

Not long after graduating with distinction from the University of Texas at Austin, Alicia Daniel, now twenty-three, received two job offers, the less desirable of which paid twice the salary of the more desirable.

Alicia accepted the job in the business office of *The Texas Observer* for about $7,500 and turned down a $15,000-a-year job writing brochures for the gas and electric company. "I can live fairly inexpensively," she says. "The freedom, the intellectual stimulation the job at *The Texas Observer* provides me, being able to work with intelligent people, the variety of creative outlets, is more important to me than money." In addition to her duties in the business office, Alicia is able to review books for the *Observer*, hobnob with visiting authors and luminaries and learn more about professional writing. Her financial sacrifice could prove to be a financial investment when she looks for her next job.

Obsession with money often abates as our work becomes intrinsically satisfying, as our adrenaline pumps up every time we go to work in the morning.

Vance Rose, an Austin, Texas, wine seller, grew up wanting

nothing more than to become rich. But after he opened his own wine shop and began to derive fulfillment from it, he noticed that his interest in money began to wane.

"The most satisfying thing about my business is not the amount of money I take out of it. It's when I walk down the street and I hear people who don't know me say, 'You ought to go into Vintages [his shop] and buy wine from them; they really know what they're doing over there.' That's more than any paycheck can do for you."

THE ENTREPRENEURS

It's not only spirited and fashionable to be an entrepreneur, but for singulars, entrepreneurial ventures and new startup businesses are likely to offer some of the best opportunities around.

According to Dun & Bradstreet, in 1980, 533,520 new businesses incorporated in America; by 1984, that number had jumped to a record-breaking 634,991. A 1985 report in *Inc.* magazine puts the number of new jobs created by such new ventures over the past ten years at 20 million. Membership in the Association of Collegiate Entrepreneurs, which started in 1983 with 7 member colleges, jumped to more than 170 in 1985, *The Wall Street Journal* reports. In 1985, 250 colleges and universities offered courses in entrepreneurship, compared to just 16 in 1970, according to *Inc.* And studies indicate that the cream of recent MBA crops are increasingly electing to go into business for themselves, either immediately upon graduation or after a few years of work experience.

Kate Kelley and John Shobe created an opportunity for themselves out of thin air; in the classic entrepreneurial sense, they found a niche and filled it.

The Missouri couple had just taken up scuba diving when they decided to vacation in North Carolina. While looking for a guidebook to inland freshwater dive spots in the Tarheel State, they discovered that no such guide existed—for the entire United States. So they decided to publish one themselves.

Though they were employed at Kate's family's furniture business in Springfield at the time, they hankered to find work at which they could put themselves to the test and from which they could derive real satisfaction. To that end, they staked their entire savings account and then some on this risky entrepreneurial venture.

They set up Divesport Publishing out of their home and divided the labor, with Kate as writer and John as researcher/production coordinator. Kate quit her job at the furniture warehouse to devote her time to the book, while John continued to earn a paycheck, giving evenings and weekends to the book. Eighteen months and $30,000 later, they had five thousand copies of *Diver's Guide to Underwater America.* "We pushed ourselves as far as we could go," says Kate. "It was the only time I've ever done my best."

"We could have been stuck with five thousand books," says Kate, "and how much debt." But their instincts paid off: The book was reviewed widely, receiving favorable notices in such key publications as *Library Journal.* The Waldenbooks chain placed an order. The first edition sold out. John was able to quit his job, and the two devoted all their time to putting out an expanded second edition of the book. They've since turned their attention to developing new diving books, having issued an updated version of their book.

THE ENTREPRENEURIAL MYSTIQUE

Entrepreneurs are the mythic heroes of our time because they have money and independence that they have secured for themselves. They can thumb their noses at the rest of the world, we believe, because they are not as dependent on it as others.

Those of us who do not work for ourselves make a habit of comparing ourselves against the entrepreneurial ideal—and generally coming up short.

"I think that if I had the risk-taking ability, I'd do fine in whatever my own business would be, because I'd give so much time to it," says Katie Eastment, personal manager for the chairman of Goodmeasure Inc., a Cambridge, Massachusetts, management-consulting firm. "I give enough time to somebody else's business, so it would be golden if I had the right idea and were working for myself."

During the "Organization Man" fifties, most everyone would have been quite satisfied to be in Katie's shoes, holding a secure $24,000-a-year position, in which she's respected and appreciated. So why then does Katie depreciate herself for not going it alone?

In part, the nature of Katie's work—scheduling appointments and promoting the career of her boss—underscores her position on the sidelines, rather than out in the field where the "real work" takes place. Like many other singulars, Katie does not believe she is pushing her work identity "to the max." She is now considering going back to school to get her MBA, a credential she believes would move her closer toward the entrepreneurial ideal.

It is especially important for Katie to find fulfillment at work because work is the center of her life. She does not have a relationship with a man, and she states matter-of-factly that she's preparing to live her life alone—although she'd prefer not to. Because she is single, the quality of her work life is the quality of her life.

Katie's feelings are also a reflection of the entire generation, which values those qualities common to most entrepreneurs, such as an ability to control one's own destiny and to maintain flexibility.

1. Being your own boss. A recognition shared by many entrepreneurs and entrepreneurials is that they were cut out to work for themselves and that this alone can be more important than the kind of work they do.

Even though twenty-seven-year-old Rob Fulop is an established computer consultant and video game designer with enormous ambitions, he says that he'd rather leave the industry altogether than become a cog in a corporate wheel or a chip in a corporate circuit board.

"Fantasize that video games and computers don't exist anymore, for some reason," says Rob, who's based in Palo Alto, California. "The Surgeon General decides that they cause brain damage, and that's it. Then fine, I can support myself playing poker—I've done it. Or I can sell pizza by the slice in San Francisco. I'd have a gourmet lunch wagon called Le Lunch, with quiche and a good salad bar. I don't want to be a middle manager at Hewlett-Packard when I'm thirty-five."

Currently Rob's interest is focused on developing nonviolent, interactive entertainment products for children that allow them to create their own story on a video screen. A Winnie-the-Pooh game, for instance, might involve one child controlling Winnie's movements and another controlling the bear's, and together they create a kind of moving cartoon. Eventually Rob would like to become "the Steven Spielberg of video games" and someday design "interactive movies."

For the time being, however, he earns most of his income from consulting with companies about their computer needs.

Rob came to know his entrepreneurial soul through the corporate route. Right out of college, he was hired by Atari to design home video games. Several of his games hit pay dirt for the company, and he won national recognition for his work. However, Rob soon tired of the big-company bureaucracy and felt he was not being properly remunerated for his contributions. He and his boss left Atari and formed another company; but it, too, grew unwieldy, and when Rob felt squeezed out of the financial decision making, once again, he left.

2. Freedom. On an impulse one Sunday night, Los Angeles businessman Nelson Friedman hopped a plane and flew to Las Vegas for the evening. "I called the girl who opens up my shop for me. I said, 'I'm not going to be in tomorrow until late afternoon.' I went crazy in Las Vegas," says Nelson, the twenty-nine-year-old owner of Nelson's, a gourmet cheese and food shop in West Los Angeles. Such a trip is an occasional indulgence; more frequently, "I'll go to the beach for the day or drive up the coast."

He relishes just knowing that on any given day, he can fly the coop—any day "except at Christmastime, when there are no breaks."

3. Turning a passion into paid employment. While studying business at University of Southern California, Vance Rose took a part-time job at a wine shop in Beverly Hills and fell in love—with the business. "I was loving it. I was drinking more wine than I ever had before, drinking better wine, learning what the business was all about."

Having experienced no such glowing feelings about his studies, Vance returned home to Austin, Texas, without diploma in hand but with an entrepreneurial scheme in mind: opening an upscale wine store that would cater to the city's growing population of young professionals.

Vance found a historical cellar location to renovate in a seedy but improving section near downtown Austin. He developed a business plan, targeting the moderate- to upper-income, $4- to $14-a-bottle customer and emphasizing personalized attention. He was able to attract an experienced partner, and, with the help of his family's backing and connections, managed to sell twenty-six "units" in the venture, raising a total of $300,000 within thirty days.

"I love wine, that's why I'm in this business," says Vance, who has good reason to indulge his passion. "I learn something every time I drink a glass of wine. If you walk into my store and want to buy a bottle of wine from me, I go to the rack and say, 'Here is this bottle of 1982 Meursault. I had it two weeks ago with dinner. It's a hundred percent French Chardonnay. It has a really interesting, exotic, creamy, lemon, butter, citric spiciness to it with a rich, fat, round taste and long aftertaste. It would be great with a rich seafood dish.' "

4. An ability to be versatile. The challenge to some entrepreneurs is figuring out what the rage of the moment is going to be, jumping on it fast and moving on as soon as it shows signs of fading.

"The new elite is a group of well-versed, versatile people who can't count on any one thing for long because nothing ever lasts," says twenty-seven-year-old Vinx DeJonParrette of Kansas City, Kansas. Vinx, who now lives in Los Angeles, works out clients in their homes as a private body trainer. He is an unabashedly driven man who has worked as a salesman, musician, restaurant helper, and even qualified for the 1980 U.S. Olympic team. "The elite of this generation can recognize opportunities and adapt to them and *make* an opportunity," he says.

Staying versatile also enables entrepreneurs to tap many different dimensions of their talents in a single work lifetime.

5. A gambler's mentality. Kate Kelley and John Shobe credit the success of their small publishing venture to a gambler's mentality, which enabled them to take a good idea and go for broke. "We developed a kind of tunnel vision," Kate says, "refusing to acknowledge the risk we were taking."

The couple understood that without risk, there can be no reward. The singular generation regards as courageous individuals who are risk-takers, who gamble on their instincts, confident that they will win—if not this time, the next.

6. Flexibility. Patti Miller Fulk is a founding partner of Cross Stitch Collection, a rapidly growing small business in Mount Airy, North Carolina. One of the great advantages of being in business for yourself is being able to accommodate to new situations. When Patti got pregnant, she and her partner agreed that she could bring the baby in to work with her; to that end, they're making space for the newborn in a small back room within eyeshot of the main counter.

In 1982, Patti and her partner, both of whom were laid off from their teaching jobs, opened the shop, which sells fixings for embroidery, needlepoint, stenciling and cross-stitching, and offers monthly classes. The business doubled in 1983, and each partner took home $10,000. In 1984, it doubled again. It is a homespun business, with racks of colorful hanging threads and patterns all around. The partners believe the baby will add, not detract, from that effect.

Likewise, fellow Mount Airy businessman Wesley Brown, twenty-eight, and his twenty-three-year-old wife Sonya own and operate Brown's Nautilus Gym out of the basement of the YMCA in downtown Mount Airy. A sign saying No Pain, No Gain done in needlepoint hangs on the inner office wall, where Sonya works as office manager, bookkeeper and general cheerleader, while keeping an eye on the couple's two young daughters. "We can't stand being separated," says Sonya.

Entrepreneurs Wes and Sonya Brown and Patti Miller Fulk have found ways of integrating their family duties into their work situations. They can be in business for themselves and not surrender their preschoolers to day care.

7. Power and autonomy. Entrepreneurs do not have to follow nonsensical directions or take orders from a boss whom they do not respect. They make their own decisions and abide by the consequences.

"Both of us like to be in control," says Kate Kelley. "Both of us are independent, and it's very hard if a boss tells us what to do."

"The people I keep running into in the world are incompetent," seconds her husband, John Shobe.

For Nelson Friedman, the Los Angeles gourmet food merchant, the best part of being in business for himself is autonomy: "Being able to decide, 'This is what I'm going to do; this needs change'; being able to make decisions and not have to get approval." Earlier in his career, Nelson worked in market research, and he found it frustrating to write a report, "hand it to your boss and maybe never see it again. Somebody else makes the decision on it. What I like to do is make the decision and see what happens. If it does work, I do more of it. If it doesn't work, I know right away."

Indeed, the desire to be self-directed runs through the entire generation. One of Claire Haberman's objectives in her job as traffic manager at Ferragamo Shoes' Manhattan office is to develop a "personal sense of power where somebody comes to me and says, 'What should we do?'" Claire would rather give direction than take it. "I'm not particularly good at following orders, dealing with authority."

THE DOWNSIDE OF ENTREPRENEURSHIP

A good many entrepreneurial ventures fail due to poor conception, poor execution or lack of follow-through. The financial risks can be great and the rewards paltry. For every big success, there are a thousand ventures that just half-succeed. Some would-be entrepreneurs discover that they are not self-motivated, that they need external stimulation to get them moving. Others find that the cash-flow problems and uncertainties associated with starting and maintaining a new business are more than they can handle.

And the mystique of the entrepreneur can sometimes work against you.

"My friends envy me," says Nelson Friedman, "especially the ones who are in a corporation. They always keep dreaming about being entrepreneurs. But it's too easy getting that check every week; the corporation is like a big tit. They don't want to take the risk of losing it." With a few individuals, this envy has formed an insurmountable barrier to close friendship.

When an entrepreneur works out of his home, he has additional strikes against him.

"People see you as doing nothing," says John Shobe, "because you're not controlled by these nine-to-five rigid work hours. They always act like, 'What do you do with your time? All your spare time?' "

"They say things like, 'What do you *do?*' " says Kate Kelley. "And we say, 'We have this book.' And they say, 'Yeah, but what do you *do?*' "

"I can sympathize somewhat with that, because I didn't understand before how much was involved in it," says John, who puts in more than forty hours a week marketing the book.

One neighbor in particular began to get on the couple's nerves. He would drop by on his day off when they were working and make references to how he would run their business if he had it, implying that he could make it more successful.

"He was saying a lot of demeaning things about the book," says

Kate. "I know it's not a great opus or anything, but he would say, 'Basically, this is just a catalog.' "

For a full year, John and Kate worked out of a third bedroom in their rented home in Austin, marketing and updating the second edition. The book was selling and they were making money, but the business never graduated beyond a hand-to-mouth operation. After they put out the second edition, Kate took a job as a writers' events coordinator for the city of Austin.

ON THE FRINGE

The entrepreneurial spirit of the singular generation fosters inadequacies in many of us and pushes a few of us to the fringe. Some members of the singular generation are paralyzed by a career anxiety from which there appears to be no escape. They cannot decide what they should do with their lives, so they wallow in unemployment. Or they flit from job to job, the Peter Pans of the professional world. Before long, no one takes them seriously, and they lose self-respect.

Paula Weinman is a twenty-six-year-old Los Angeles woman who has been searching for some time. Money has never been a problem for her, but self-esteem has been a relentless one. Her parents' generosity keeps her in designer clothing, dinners out and a security apartment in the fashionable Marina del Rey section of L.A. But Paula is not content to live off Daddy. The singular message has penetrated her psyche, and she will not be happy until she has A Career.

The Indianapolis native came to Hollywood right after college, looking for fame and fortune. After a series of low-level secretarial-type jobs in "the Industry," she decided to shoot for the top, to go after the job she "deserves." To that end, she hooked up with a motivational group called Impact.

Impact is a Los Angeles organization based on the marriage of est principles and a kind of work worship. It is tailored to creative individuals who act, write, compose and direct; the overwhelming

majority want to break into Hollywood and most can afford to
pay a hefty three-figure monthly fee.

The first I knew of Paula Weinman was the day I received a
phone call from her. An acquaintance of mine had given her my
name. Paula called to enlist my "support" in her goal: She wanted
to get a staff writing job at a major newspaper, and she wanted
to achieve this by five P.M. Friday.

My first impulse was to move her off the line as quickly as
possible. Even the most accomplished out-of-work professional
could not expect to impose such a deadline on potential employers, much less someone who was the novice that she must be.

A second impulse, however, prevailed, and I kept listening.

Paula said that she was a member of Impact; calling me had
been one of her "goals" that day. Impact, she explained, lets you
have a relationship with your career that you've never had before.

Impact had helped her take "the stand" that "I am the perfect
film and theater critic," she explained. In the last several years,
she'd published several by-lined articles in a Los Angeles give-
away tabloid called *The Good Times.*

Not that Friday, but several months later, Paula called again
with the news that she had indeed gotten a staff writing job at *The
Hollywood Reporter.* She was ecstatic and admitted to being a
virtual celebrity at Impact. "They gave me a standing ovation
when I broke the news."

I couldn't help but be impressed and made a date to visit the
group with her.

The group meets every morning at 6 A.M. in Hollywood.
Though Hollywood is only half an hour from my apartment,
Paula wanted to come for me at 5 A.M. because Impact fines
members $10 on the spot for tardiness. While waiting, I was jolted
by the blare of a car horn. A Toyota was stopped smack in the
middle of the nearest intersection. It was Paula, holding her hand
on the horn. Smiling, she waved me in.

"I hope we didn't wake too many people," I said pointedly.
Paula didn't reply. She was all decked out in a black suit, a silk
blouse and a long strand of pearls. She looked in the mirror and
adjusted her pearls.

As we melded into the group outside the church where Impact met, Paula was still coasting on her triumph. Members smiled and offered congratulations; a middle-aged man whose name tag read "CB" showered Paula with hugs and kisses. CB's "miracle," Paula whispered to me, was that he'd been a chauffeur and suddenly came to own his own record company.

Inside, people were feeding on the kind of manic, early-hours energy of those who feel intensely superior to the rest of the sleeping world. They exchanged compliments as they peeled open their Velcro-close appointment books to jot down last-minute goals for the day. The church filled to capacity, with maybe three hundred adults in expensive, tailored clothing. It looked like any Sunday church service except for the distinct absence of children and old people and the paucity of couples.

A young woman in a purple silk blouse and red skirt darted forward and took the stage. On an enormous green board behind her, in chalk, the Impact philosophy was written in bold relief.

TO CAUSE A SHIFT IN YOUR DAILY OPERATING BASE
FROM: BEING COMMITTED TO HAVING TO HANDLE PROBLEMS THAT ARE STOPS TO WHAT'S POSSIBLE NOW IN YOUR CAREER
TO: PASSIONATELY BRINGING FORTH THE POSSIBILITY OF WHAT IS NOT PRESENTLY POSSIBLE IN THE INDUSTRY.

"Good morning," the woman said to a round of applause, to which she vigorously contributed. She introduced herself as Jean.

After the welcome came the "hug session." Everyone jumped into action, bodies pressing against each other, heads bopping from shoulder to shoulder.

A man hugged me, introduced himself as a screenwriter and asked what I did. "I'm a writer," I told him. He was wearing a baseball cap to which a button was fastened that read: "Not Bad for a White Boy."

"This is the place to do it," he said and moved on.

After the hug session, guests were introduced. Then came "miracles" time for members to stand and relate their latest profes-

The Entrepreneurial Spirit*41*

sional victories. (Theoretically you can use the time to relate your defeats, too, but no one did.) After each revelation, there was a hearty round of applause.

We guests were ushered into a basement room, just like in church before the sermon when the kids file out for Sunday school.

Jean led the session downstairs. Impact is all about your career, she told us once we were settled in chairs. If you're on the verge of changing careers or want to produce better results in your present career, Impact is for you. She submitted herself as evidence. At one time she had been operating at 60 percent capacity, knowing full well that if she ever went 100 percent, she was sure to succeed. At that time, she resolved to, "if you'll excuse the expression, shit or get off the pot." She began to view her career as a game; she'd go to job interviews asking for double her salary, and she'd get it.

The audience was composed mostly of actors and other creative types. There was Pat, a middle-aged corporate wife who wanted to be a writer. And there was Ellie, who was "transitioning" from being a therapist to a photojournalist. And there was Michael, an actor who was perennially out of work.

At Impact, Jean told us, people either produce the results they're capable of, or they find out why they're not. "You better be careful of what your goals are, because most likely you'll achieve them."

"So are you going to join?" Paula asked afterward, clearly expecting me to say yes. We stopped at a nearby coffee shop, where she ate breakfast every morning. She dipped her spoon into her cup of decaf and summoned the waitress to send it back ("too muddy"). She ordered up oatmeal, "extra hot."

"Impact has transformed me," explained Paula. "I used to be at the mercy of other people. It was always *their fault* if I didn't have a wonderful job, if *they* didn't see what a wonderful person I am. Now I have one hundred percent responsibility for my own life."

As an example of how effective the Impact system is, Paula offered the fact that she'd made it a goal one day to pick up some Tupperware she'd ordered. Approaching the end of the day without achieving that particular goal, she called the woman at 11 P.M. and drove over and picked up the merchandise at midnight.

"Impact is about making promises to yourself and keeping them," she said proudly.

In the ladies room, Paula extracted a toothbrush and paste from her bag. "There's something else I'd like you to know," she said, reaching into her mouth and removing a false front tooth. Devilishly, she grinned at herself in the mirror. The tooth, she confided, had been knocked out when her car was hit by a train in Indiana.

This was her deepest, darkest secret, since she intended to become a "nationally syndicated" TV film critic before reaching the age of thirty.

Several weeks later, I called her only to learn that she'd been fired from her job for "political reasons."

Paula has a desperation about her that is haunting. She is obsessed with the idea of her brilliant career, but unable to launch it. A career seems to her a romantic possibility, and at some fundamental level, she can think in no more practical terms about how successful careers are made than to view them as "miracles." Plagued by insecurity and a medley of personal disorders, she depends on programs like Impact to motivate her, because she can find no motivation from within.

Like the rest of the singular generation, she was born of insecurity; but unlike the entrepreneurs or the entrepreneurials, she has been unable to forge an identity through work. When she thinks of herself in terms of her work identity, there is almost nothing there. Whatever work she can find seems beneath her—nowhere close to the glorious image of herself she holds inside. And the lessons a group like Impact teaches only perpetuate a vicious cycle of quick triumph and subsequent failure. It teaches a me-oriented world view, when Paula needs to bring herself up by the bootstraps.

The clapping and group support build in Paula the expectation that her every move should be applauded, when many of them in fact should not. It is good to keep the promises you make to yourself, but you have to know which ones are essential and which ones are not. Impact, of course, is not the problem. It is a kind of placebo for a disease from which Paula is suffering. Paula's malady lies in setting herself such high goals and in so isolating herself that she's in danger of detaching from reality.

BEYOND WORK

The pursuit and establishment of a career has assumed an almost religious character in the singular generation—a route to salvation and a necessary ingredient for personal fulfillment. Indeed, there seem to be no lengths to which we will not go to show our enterprise, devotion and commitment to our careers.

The entrepreneurial spirit at the heart of the singular generation is one of our most positive dimensions. We aspire to be self-sufficient at a time of declining economic power, and in so doing, resist the currents of downward mobility. We bring a new sense of energy and imagination to the workplace at a time when America can use some new blood. We blaze new, off-the-beaten-track trails, since the main arteries are clogged. We confer the powers of our creativity on our professional lives.

Members of the singular generation are fighters who have decided to wage the big battle in the arena of work. We are bringing new muscle to the old American work ethic. We are taking control of our lives at a time when the world seems to be flying every which way.

Entrepreneurs are our heroes because we believe they are the only ones who are living fully—creating their own reality rather than fitting into a preexisting one—in a world that offers us precious few chances for freedom. Through their work, entrepreneurs are expressing something pure from within, and we like to believe that they are not affected by the world's vicissitudes.

Yet our total immersion in the world of work, our never-ending need to prove that we can support ourselves, and our elevation of the entrepreneur to the stature of hero betray our colossal insecurity. The singular generation has a chip on its shoulder. Like the children of the Depression, who grew up feeling tremendous reverence for a job—paid employment—we singulars have the sense that the rug will be pulled out from under us even as we stand on it. We don't assume the economy will get better, or that once we find a job we'll keep it, or that we will necessarily move up the ladder once we find a rung on it. In fact, at some primary level, we believe things will get worse.

We singulars labor under the illusion that hard work will buy us security, and in a sense, we have a point. Money will buy us safer cars, burglar-alarm systems and high-interest bonds. In many ways, our workaholism is a realistic adaptation to changing marketplace conditions. But it will not provide us protection from fickle marital partners, a frenzied economy and an unstable world.

As we draw more and more into the shells of our work realities, extending the blinders around us, as we become obsessive in creating perfection within, work has assumed too large a role in our lives. While many of us have grown self-sufficient through work, our generation has no strength in unity. With our noses stuck to the grindstone, we completely lose sight of larger and more pressing issues—most notably, whether the planet will survive. As we spin round and round in our narrow circles of self-absorption, making no engagement, no connection, no collective interaction, we avoid confronting the danger that could kill us.

At some point, we must look outside our narrow work worlds for greater security. Because even when we succeed at work, ultimately—in our darkest private moments—we feel no security. Not until our generation finds the strength from within to confront greater dangers can we achieve genuine peace. Perhaps our work ethic will provide us a model of single-mindedness and hard work that will help us fight bigger battles.

CHAPTER 3

The Marriage Merger

THE PARTNERSHIP IDEAL

The model for marriage in the singular generation comes from the world of work, and it is the business partnership. In an ideal singular marriage, both partners pull their own weight, contributing as much to the collective pot as they take out of it. Spouses divide domestic duties and other responsibilities in an equitable manner, based on the understanding that both partners have pressing professional demands and individual needs.

The partnership ideal governs our approach to marriage, the structure and texture of our lives once we are married and even the rationale behind the dissolution of a marriage. Unlike some generations before us, who regarded marriage as a harmonious state in which two souls became one, singulars approach marriage as we would start a new business: We believe that we are taking a calculated risk when we tie the knot, and, at the very best, we anticipate a series of differences to negotiate over the course of a matrimonial lifetime. Depending on our success, a given marriage could turn into a firmly established institution or a fly-by-night operation.

Singulars look for marriage partners who are stimulating, whose interests coincide with our own and who can help us along in our careers. Among singulars, the notion that the man should have a financial and chronological edge over the woman has all but vanished. In singular marriages, it is not uncommon for the wife to be older than the husband, to make more money and to carry more authority on the job and at home. Singular women, like men of yore, feel we must be able to stand on our own two feet—to be self-supporting and psychically sound—before we enter marriage.

"Two people should be a hundred percent each when they enter matrimony," says twenty-nine-year-old Debra Nakatomi. To that end, we generally wait until we are older to take the step, deliberating for longer periods than ever before.

Once we are married, we continue to be self-supporting and emotionally self-sufficient. Like business partners, the new marital partners of the singular generation incorporate organizing procedures from the world of work into our personal lives. We are increasingly likely to draw up prenuptial contracts before we wed and to maintain separate finances afterward. We make "deals" with each other over the most ordinary matters: who takes out the garbage and what our reward is for preparing the taxes. We bring to our private discussions the negotiating skills used to strike business deals and the nonalienating ground rules endorsed by communications experts. We seek mutual self-interest through compromise.

GROWTH WITHIN MARRIAGE

Singulars strive to put our own imprints on marriages. Marriage no longer gives us our identities; rather, we bring our identities into a marriage and "grow" them there. In the past, a marriage was supposed to join couples in fixed roles for life. From the singular perspective, a "good" partner is one whose personal growth continues in marriage and whose work outside the home stimulates that growth. Singulars believe that shared happiness invariably derives from a wellspring of personal satisfaction.

By the same token, having children is less attractive to singulars than it was to our parents' generation because we no longer believe that children will or should fulfill us or provide security in our old age. We are less likely to view children as reflections and extensions of ourselves and more likely to see them as their own persons (even when they're still young), with their own particular needs and desires.

Because our identities are not wrapped up in marriage, singulars do not "lose" ourselves if we have to call it quits; indeed, divorce is not as devastating for singulars as it was for previous generations—especially for women, who in the past were largely defined by their marriages.

"One of the things that pulled me out of the divorce is that I didn't only have home and baby; I was working," says twenty-three-year-old Meredith White, an enlisted woman in the U.S. Navy who's stationed at Port Wyneme, California. "I think it would have been harder for me if I was a housewife."

Because growth is built into the singular-marriage equation, so, too, is the possibility of growth away from a partner.

"I think one of the things that's important in a marriage is allowing for growth and change," says twenty-seven-year-old Los Angeles writer Dana Dollard, who was married in 1983. "And one can never anticipate what that growth and change will involve. There's a potential in any relationship that things will change to the degree that you no longer share that commitment. That's just a realistic view. I would love to be able to believe there's a hundred-percent chance we'll be married forever. But I just think you have to take it day by day."

Our characteristic "presentism"—in which we don't consider the future because we can't see that far in advance—colors our marriages. Although we would like to believe in everlasting marriage and that our personal sacrifices will be duly appreciated over the marital long haul, our primary instincts and fundamental insecurity instruct us to pursue our own careers wherever they lead us. A career—not a marriage—we believe, provides the ultimate security.

Once we become convinced that a marriage, like a business that's consistently losing money, exhibits no possibility for recovery or future growth, we shut it down. Indeed, singulars believe that we owe it to ourselves and our partners to call off a dysfunctional marriage because it will hinder our personal and professional development. The marriage-at-any-price premise of just a few short decades ago has all but vanished; these days, even Dear Abby advocates divorce.

DUAL-CAREER MARRIAGE

The partnership model has sprung up in an era in which marriage is no longer an essential organizing principle of our lives. Singulars marry in lesser numbers than did generations who came before us, and we almost reflexively postpone matrimony. Those singulars who do wed in our twenties strive to make the institution work for us and to shape it to our particular needs. We do not let marriage derail us from our career tracks.

Nate Oubre and Linda Seiffert-Oubre, twenty-four and twenty-five respectively, are first- and second-year students respectively at the Harvard Business School. They have established a marriage that serves their professional goals, not vice versa. The desire to optimize their careers and cash flow takes precedence over such values as togetherness and uninterrupted intimacy. The summer between Linda's first and second year of "B school," Linda accepted a job in Washington, D.C. Nate was employed as a research assistant for a Boston consulting company, a lucrative position he did not want to relinquish until classes started in the fall. So for the summer, husband and wife lived apart, seeing each other every other weekend.

As the Oubres look ahead, their chief consideration is planning strategic moves best suited to the "dual-career couple." "You have to analyze each situation as it comes up rather than making trade-offs ahead of time," says Linda.

Tempting as top job possibilities might be for this black couple, who feel a special sense of mission to make it in white corporate

America, they have resolved never to allow theirs to become a two-household marriage. In fact, six months is the ceiling they've set on separations. "We would not live in separate cities for anything other than a temporary period," says Linda, "no matter how good the jobs were; we would take second choices rather than live full-time in different cities."

Their time together is valuable not only on a personal but on a professional level. In a business world in which it's hard to know whom to trust, Nate and Linda lean on each other for professional nurturing. "There's no better sounding board than Linda," Nate says proudly. Nate, who grew up in the Los Angeles ghetto of Watts and parlayed his athletic abilities into educational opportunities, looks to Linda, a child of the middle class, for polish and advice, while Linda taps into Nate's raw energy and ambition. "We're ambitious in different ways," says Nate, who believes that they each bring something distinct and special into the marriage.

To the Oubres, the crowning glory of their marital partnership would be to form a business partnership. "In the future, we intend to work together on a long-term project," he says. "We're looking for a product to manufacture."

COMMUTER MARRIAGE

Most singular married couples, like the Oubres, draw the line at setting up permanent separate households. But the singular partnership ethic makes the phenomenon of bicoastal, bistate, bicity— or even bicountry—marriages understandable. While the exceptional people in society—politicians, movie stars and the fabulously wealthy—have long lived apart from their spouses for a variety of reasons, only in the singular generation has it become not uncommon for upwardly mobile professionals to do so.

Lila Henly and her husband Gordon Phillips have established residences in two different cities in their quest for what Lila calls "meaningful employment." One of them would have to make a major professional sacrifice if they had not struck this arrangement. Lila, twenty-nine, is a second-year student in UCLA's

School of Management in Los Angeles, while Gordon, also twenty-nine, lives in Phoenix, Arizona, where he works for a private hospital firm.

As a highly paid corporate officer, Gordon is able to support two households, to cover Lila's out-of-state tuition and to pay regular commuting costs. When they were discussing which graduate business school Lila should attend, the couple decided that the business program at Arizona State in Phoenix was just not good enough to find a permanent home on her résumé.

"I was concerned about the long-term effects of going to Arizona State," she says. "Gordon agreed with me." Implicit in their decision to establish separate residences is the feeling that Lila should have every professional advantage, that her career, though not as advanced as his, is just as important. What's more, should the marriage break up, it would be even more crucial that Lila attended a top-rate school—for her future and for his conscience.

Lila and Gordon pay a high price for maintaining their lifestyle. There are the thrice-monthly commutes to spend weekends together, and the three-figure phone bills. Lila keeps separate books on her Los Angeles household, and Gordon turns over to her just under 10 percent of his net income each month. Car money, tuition, school expenses and commuting costs take out another sizable chunk.

Commuting is nothing new to the couple who conducted a "two-year negotiation" from separate cities while trying to establish a relationship. They met in 1979 while they were working together on a public health project and married five years later.

"We look at our marriage as a business," says Lila. The language of mergers, acquisitions, development and growth has slipped into their everyday idiom, and they make business studies when evaluating decisions from the complex to the mundane. The question of having children, for instance, "is something we've negotiated. We put a moratorium on it for six years.

"When we review career opportunities, we try to accommodate each person's needs." Recently Gordon was offered a job in Bangor, Maine. Lila's response was to question what his accepting the job would mean to them professionally. "How can the two of us benefit from this move with respect to the relationship? What kind of growth potential does the other person have in the move? It's almost like we run net present value analyses on these decisions."

The bottom line is that for the moment, their careers are best served by living apart. "Regardless of how well you know someone," says Gordon, "when you're trying to think something through, you're distracted by the presence of someone else. We find that by being separated, we're able to accomplish—at least by most objective measures—inordinate, even incredible quantities of work."

Like the Oubres, Lila and Gordon talk about someday going into business together. They envision opening a consulting business. "We try to find our own competencies and complement the other one," Lila says. Like a conglomerate company, the couple "try to keep abreast of what the other is doing, so we can diversify our portfolio."

What, if anything, is the downside of the present arrangement?

"The requirement to regularly explain it to others," Gordon shoots back in what is doubtless a seasoned response. "It's difficult to explain that you live in Phoenix and your wife lives in Los Angeles."

"It takes a lot of energy to keep it going," admits Lila. "You have a tendency to put off dealing with your problems in favor of a pleasant weekend together." She pauses for a moment to think. "There's a loneliness issue sometimes. I've come to depend on Gordon in a certain way."

EMOTIONAL SELF-SUFFICIENCY

A corollary to our need to establish financial and professional independence is our desire to be emotionally self-sufficient within marriage. Singulars believe that the health of a marriage is dependent on being able to tend to oneself emotionally and the ability to be a free agent socially.

Juli Boyington, a Seattle-area secretary, says that emotional self-reliance is one of the hallmarks of her marriage. "We depend on each other for extraordinary circumstances. But we need to depend on ourselves for the smaller things.

"I don't need to come home and tell him my girlfriend was talking about me behind my back, even though that may be troubling to me," she explains. Her husband Bruce, a twenty-eight-year-old bad-debt collections manager, is "open-minded" and "always ready to listen," but Juli prefers not to burden him with problems she can resolve herself. "He doesn't need me to unload on him; he doesn't need anything that would detract from his positive outlook." Not only is Juli's emotional self-sufficiency good for Bruce, but it is good for her, too, she believes. "It makes me stronger, better able to put problems in perspective and not blow them up out of proportion."

Holly Jennings, a public relations writer for a Winston-Salem, North Carolina, bank, says that a major difference between her marriage and her parents' is that she and her husband feel free to socialize independently.

"I remember my mother complaining that my father was not good at partying," Holly says. "She felt that how good the husband was at dealing with social situations was the key ingredient. I've never felt that way. I've never felt that I am limited by Jeff, that I can't go out and make my own friends, that I can't be the one to initiate our own circle of friends or bring more friends into it."

Singulars do not think that having a spouse should hinder us from moving freely in the world. We go to movies, plays, concerts, sporting events and parties alone or with friends who share interests that spouses do not; we may even vacation separately. Married singulars have cast off the compulsion to do everything in twos.

PURSUING ONE'S OWN PATH

Giving your partner the rope to pursue paths that may be of no interest (or even repugnant) to you is considered a sign of strength among singulars. If an individual has a strong impulse, we believe, he or she should explore it and his or her partner should abet the exploration, whether it be social, professional, personal or even sexual. To impede a partner's growth can only damage the relationship. What matters is that the partners negotiate the boundaries of the "exploration" in advance and agree to terms.

Twenty-four-year-old Boston-area "exotic dancer" Annette Jones married Mark Filerman in May of '83 after they agreed to modify a number of the conventions of marriage, the first being fidelity. One of the stipulations she made was that she be allowed to be with others sexually. The others being women. But she says kiddingly that there are strings attached, in that Mark likes the sessions to take place in their bedroom so he can watch—and sometimes participate.

So far, it seems to be working out. "I love him a lot more now than when I decided to marry him," she says.

A more typical case is that of Juli and Bruce Boyington. When they first married, Bruce was studying the Chinese language and applied for a year-long teaching position in mainland China.

"At that time, I thought that if he were to get that position and it wouldn't allow me to go, I wanted him to go, because of the experience it would give him. Because of the cost involved in traveling, I doubt I would have seen him for a year." Although they weren't put to the test in that instance, Juli says that today they would readily extend each other the same privilege.

THE DEMISE OF THE HOUSEWIFE

The housewife has become a period piece to members of the singular generation. She is a curiosity who's been roundly rejected by singulars of both sexes—females do not aspire to be one and males do not want to marry one.

Economically it's no longer feasible for most young wives to stay at home. Today it takes two incomes to come close to achieving the real income level provided by one breadwinner just two decades ago.

But just as crucial as money is the fact that singulars no longer believe that staying at home is good for a woman—or for a man, for that matter. The idea of living in a secondary, even sub-servient, position to someone else defies almost everything we singulars believe in.

Two-career bliss was the object of Tommy Edwards's marital dreams. Before the wedding, the Los Angeles attorney envisioned the lovely home they could purchase on two incomes, the trips they could afford together. But when Sylvia Olsen-Edwards, his insurance-professional wife of six months, suddenly got pregnant and announced her intention of quitting work to stay home and raise the baby, Tommy felt short-changed. "I didn't want to marry a housewife," he complains bitterly to his friends.

Sylvia got her way and, for the time being, is staying home with the baby. "How can you force a woman to go back to work when she says nothing is more important than taking care of her baby?" he asks. When you pit Sylvia's need to be a traditional wife and mother (unexpressed before they wed) against Tommy's desire to have a high-powered career-woman wife, it's clear that their di-vergent life plans may endanger the marriage.

Even those young eighties males who embrace "traditional" values can become jittery when faced with supporting a wife.

Months before the wedding, Paul Marcus put Donna, his fian-cée, on warning. He told her she shouldn't view matrimony as a lifetime meal ticket. "The fact that it's on paper doesn't mean much," says the hulking Harvard football player. "Paper can be ripped up." A big booster of marriage—perhaps its foremost pro-ponent in the Harvard class of '84—Paul proposed to Donna dur-ing her senior year in high school, and they announced their en-gagement his sophomore year in college. With the help of his jeweler father, Paul secured for her a carat-and-a-half diamond engagement ring.

But of late, Paul has backed away from the traditional marriage he always assumed he'd have. Though originally he wanted Donna to be a full-time homemaker, Paul recently asked her to continue working as a $275-a-week medical assistant, at least until his futon bed business gets off the ground.

While Paul's vision of his wife's future—home at the range—places him squarely in the nonsingular, conservative camp, his worst fear seems to be that Donna will take for granted, and advantage of, his breadwinning role. In his case, a trace of the singular message has penetrated: Both man and wife could suffer if one person carries all the weight.

Singular men who are conflicted about which type of woman they'd like to marry invariably come back to the career woman.

After a painful breakup with a fellow video-game designer, whom Rob Fulop characterized as a "junior Miss Mary Cunningham type," the northern Californian consciously sought out "a homemaker type." Millie was a word processor, "a simple person who wasn't going anywhere per se." Her attitude was: "I'm not going to have a career; I would just really rather have a husband and, basically, I'm working now because I'm single now."

The problem with Millie is that Rob got bored—in a hurry. "I don't need to be intellectual all the time; I don't need to be into high planes of thought. I do need to have someone understand what I'm talking about." When they split up, Rob went back to dating career women.

"I can't imagine supporting some princess of leisure," says Rob, who volunteers that he is looking for a mate. "I don't think it's that great a deal to support somebody."

SUPPORTIVE HUSBANDS

Singular husbands can be just as insistent about enforcing new-age rules as their fathers were about resisting them. One of these unwritten rules is to "support" your wife's career, even at some cost to your own.

Peter Rivers, a $38,000-a-year Palo Alto attorney, recently turned down a $50,000-a-year position in Washington, D.C., largely because accepting it would have meant yanking his wife from a good staff writing position at the local newspaper. "I don't feel comfortable screwing up a woman's career," says Peter, twenty-seven, referring to his thirty-one-year-old wife, journalist Nicole James. "I do feel that women in general, for a long time, have given up a lot of careers to be with their husbands. I just don't feel comfortable asking that of her."

Although singulars like Peter and Nicole try to evaluate each prospect when it comes up, they are nonetheless conscious of the inferior role women have held historically in marriage and in the workplace. And though they generally try to look beyond the politics of feminism when making professional decisions, often they can't help but factor it in.

Indeed, singular husbands like Tommy and Peter want their wives to be full partners, not bit players in a marriage. To that end, they are willing to make sacrifices.

OLDER/STRONGER WIVES

Some singular men, consciously or unconsciously, seek women who are already established, who do not need to be helped along. Such men look for strong marital partners who are grounded professionally, financially and psychically. One of the healthier aspects of singular marriages is that men today can and do pursue wives whom they admire, respect and can even learn from— women who may be more "advanced" than they are. Unlike generations of men before them, singular males do not prefer women who are somehow "less" than they are: less educated, less accomplished, less secure or just younger.

"Back in my parents' time, you just kind of expected that your husband would be three to four years older than you, and if he wasn't, then you'd feel real uncomfortable," says Holly Jennings.

Holly Allen married Jeff Jennings in 1983. Holly, who is three years Jeff's senior, was already well established in her job and able to support the couple while Jeff finished medical school. Jeff also looked to Holly to provide direction in their marriage, and he readily embraced her Quaker ideas about simple living.

"I don't think of him as being younger," says the twenty-eight-year-old Holly. Only occasionally does their age difference surface, and then over minor matters. "He really enjoys receiving gifts and things. And I tend to resist handouts. I think of enjoying gifts in terms of being a little immature."

Young wives today do not have to repress or conceal their innate strengths. Sheila Coombs Gutman of Islesboro, Maine, volunteers that in her marriage, "I'm the planner, the architect of the relationship, and Robert's much more passive."

For instance, Sheila has decided that their one-and-a-half-year-old daughter Leah should travel while growing up. Sheila, who was deprived of wide exposure when growing up on an island, wants her daughter to have greater opportunities. To that end, she is already drawing up financial plans.

A BACK-AND-FORTH EXCHANGE

In an ideal partnership marriage, a balance of power exists such that the upper hand at any given moment could be held by either party. To effect such a balance, singulars often employ time-tested principles.

Juli and Bruce Boyington use conflict-resolution techniques to solve problems. When they're bickering or tension is in the air, they sit down and try to put into writing what is on their minds. "We put the two lists together and I find out how he perceives the problem and he finds out how I perceive the problem." There are no rights or wrongs in this negotiation, but only feelings—the need to accommodate diverging feelings. Instead of looking to the other for vindication or approval, they each determine what is bothering them and agree upon ways of altering their own behavior.

THE DECLINING ROLE OF MARRIAGE

At the center of these changes in marital heart and habit is the fact that for the first time in modern history, marriage is an option, not an obligation for the young. It is no longer a rite of passage on the road to maturity, especially in your twenties. It is no longer routinely recommended by our parents; indeed, parents of the eighties generation often urge us to remain single for as long as possible.

Young adults in the eighties can "settle down" without first getting married. To be unmarried no longer means you're biding your time till you find the right mate and embark upon your "real life." Today you can have a satisfying and even stable sex life outside of marriage, and you can even have and raise children as a single parent. If you do not marry today, no one assumes you are hideously unattractive, homosexual or essentially "a loser." Rather, you could be highly selective, intensely romantic or simply too work-driven to have time for marriage. Today making a hasty marriage is considered irresponsible, not romantic or "the right thing to do." Since even the best-constructed marriages routinely fail, a marriage built on sand castles would seem doomed from the start.

Singulars do not believe that marriage is an inherently superior state of being. Indeed, some small number of us believe that it is an inherently inferior mode. According to a December 1982 report in the New York *Times,* based on research at the University of Michigan, "Though most young Americans believe that they will marry, they no longer regard the married state as significantly better than being single." At the same time, much of the stigma against divorce has dissipated.

For Sheila and Robert Gutman, marriage was never a burning issue. "We felt we were married anyway as soon as we met," says Sheila matter-of-factly. They went through with the official civil ceremony to avoid the hassles, to save on taxes, to legitimize their bond for the sake of the baby Sheila was carrying. But they both say that marriage was not something that figured in their imagination.

At the University of Texas at Austin, Dean Robert King of the College of Liberal Arts says that young college coeds no longer marry right after graduation. "The smart college women of the fifties got educated to get married," he says. Their counterparts of the sixties "got married and went to graduate school; those of the seventies went to law school, and delayed marriage." The smart college women of the eighties are "not getting married, that's apparent. Nothing is obvious anymore."

Three members of the University of Texas's elite Kappa Delta Theta sorority were engaged in a recent discussion about their life goals. When one, a sophomore, ventured the opinion that "any woman in the United States wants to marry a wealthy man," her two sisters jumped on her.

"Women today can't go through college just hoping to meet a husband," said Julie Bauer, a junior from Seguin, Texas. "I mean, things don't work that way."

Amy Williams, a junior from Galveston, put in that she doesn't "like to plan on" marriage. "You don't like to depend on that happening. For instance, I'd love to teach kids, but I wouldn't like the income if I didn't get married. So that's the main reason I've shot for higher goals."

As the importance of marriage has declined, the single status has grown not only acceptable but desirable to many. Some singulars see being single as the complete, even ideal, state. A small number of militant singles refuse to marry out of principle, because, they believe, it violates their singularity.

The partnership model has contributed to the growing acceptability of a number of other life-style options. These include unmarried partnerships, either heterosexual or homosexual; nonsexual alliances and even serial monogamy.

The vast majority of young adults no longer disapprove of premarital sex. The experts predict that the trend toward greater freedom and experimentation in sexual relationships among adolescents and adults will continue and expand in the coming years, especially if safeguards against sexually transmitted diseases are developed. Marriage is simply no longer the automatic second step to having an affair, even a serious or an intensely passionate one.

As a result, some singulars push marriage to the side corners of our psyches, assigning it a secondary place in our personal blueprints.

"I intend to keep my career independent of my social needs," says New Yorker Claire Haberman. "And I consider marriage a social need."

"It was a good experience," says one singular of her one-and-a-half-year marriage that ended in divorce. "It was another one of those experiences in my life that I'm glad I had but also glad to be out of."

But whether we've sworn off marriage or have the ideal marital partnership going, whether we're newly divorced or just planning to wed, most singulars relish the new freedom available to us in the marital arena.

"One of the healthier things about growing up in this era is that people are allowed to take more time to search for a mate," says John Carlson of Seattle, a self-avowed young conservative and Washington State Republican Party activist. At the advanced age of twenty-five, John is already an "oddity" in his family—everyone else was married by this age.

THE TENDENCY TO POSTPONE

Marriage is no longer a life calling for young women; neither is it a lifelong financial responsibility for young men. For both sexes, it is secondary to the pursuit and establishment of a career. Indeed, there is the growing suspicion among singulars that early marriage signifies a less-than-total commitment to your career. The age at which we feel we are "too young" to wed is steadily creeping upward.

"I feel that those people who have married or remarried now will not achieve the same heights, the same professional level, as those who prefer to marry at a later age," says Mike Walter, a single attorney from Bellevue, Washington. "I think that's an absolute."

While the benefits of pooling financial and emotional resources in marriage, of finding security and establishing some semblance of order and permanence, are attractive to members of the singular generation, our characteristic insecurity reminds us of the enormous potential for marital failure. So we delay.

The tendency to delay is already showing up on the demographic tables. We are getting married at an older age and remaining single in larger numbers than before. In two short decades, the median age of first marriage has jumped dramatically for both sexes. In 1960, the average age of first marriage for women was 20.3; in 1983, it was 22.8. For men, it rose from 22.8 in 1960 to 25.4 in 1983. And it continues to go up.

"It's not so much a matter of wanting marriage and children, but how long I want to postpone it," explains Marta Taylor, a twenty-eight-year-old resident in internal medicine at a New York hospital.

Since her college graduation, Marta has devoted the lion's share of her time and energy to graduate schooling—first, earning a master's degree in public health, and subsequently, her medical training. Though she's spent an enormous effort analyzing the ins and outs of her future over the years, into this Tomorrowland, men have never fit very clearly.

Marta says she sees marriage in her future, but she tempers that projection with a string of qualifiers. "I sort of think that in ten years, I'll probably be married," she says. "To tell you the truth, it would not surprise me if I were (a) not married and (b) had no children."

HIGHER STANDARDS

Higher marital standards and expectations have also contributed to a widescale postponement of marriage in my generation. Singulars soundly reject many previously acceptable motivations for matrimony, such as security, marrying to have children or to please the family, and romantic whim. Since you don't *need* marriage to find or experience these things, you should not tie the knot without better cause, like a solid marital partnership.

Marta shuns the rationale for her own parents' still-standing marriage. Theirs was a "bloodless" bond, she says, which came about because "they wanted to have children; more so than the strength of their own relationship, that was the primary, motivating force. I don't think I would enter into a relationship to have children. I wouldn't get married just because I was tired of being alone; I would really want to love the person."

Even love or a strong sexual bond is not enough to justify marriage in the minds of many singulars.

April Garrett, a twenty-eight-year-old schoolteacher whose two-year marriage ended when she was twenty-three, says, "We had great sex, phenomenal sex," but an inability to communicate killed the marriage. "We had a very sexual relationship, which is probably why we got married. I grew up with him as a woman. But he wasn't someone I would have chosen as a best friend."

The failed and failing marriages all around us give singulars further pause.

John Carlson, the very picture of the Pepsi generation decked out in his Washington Huskies T-shirt, Levis and Top-Siders, is harshly judgmental about the cavalier attitude many individuals bring to marriage. "It is wrong for anyone who thinks that the benefits you get in a marriage, a partnership, somehow come with no cost in return," says John, a staunch believer in wedlock.

"It's important to regard marriage as a very serious thing. When I finally decide to get married, I'm going to have to devote a lot of time to the woman I love. I'm also going to have to think about family commitments and setting down roots."

Now twenty-five, John has set himself the goal of getting married by age thirty. His rather earnest point of view in large part springs from the rocky emotional climate in which he grew up. His mother, an executive secretary, and his dad, a retired policeman, called it quits in 1965. Their divorce, John says, was "one of life's knocks."

John's ambivalence toward marriage is paradigmatic of the singular generation. He believes that marriage is good in the abstract, but he is in no rush to enter into it. Thus, he has extended himself a lengthy lease on the life of his bachelorhood, but, in earnest, singular fashion, has set himself a daunting deadline at the end of the road.

Singulars like John exhibit an uncompromising attitude toward marriage—setting high and often unrealistic standards for ourselves, perhaps unconsciously erecting barriers to marriage.

"I'm very particular," says Paula Weinman. "I don't date anyone who's not Jewish. I don't have the time if there's not the potential there." Not only must he be Jewish, but he should be well on his way professionally. "He doesn't have to be president of a company, but he has to exhibit those qualities of hard work and ambition."

"You keep thinking there's that little brown-haired girl out there," says twenty-six-year-old Dan Dolan, a native of Nashville, Tennessee. "It makes it hard to settle for anyone with less than perfect looks, great personality. Maybe it has to do with falling in love with TV stars when you're growing up."

A never-ending dose of high standards has created in our generation commitmentphobes of two basic varieties: those who at some fundamental level refuse to accept the new partnership reality (preferring to romanticize the past), and those who have embraced the single singular life-style and do not believe that a marital bond can add anything.

Those in the former category view marriage as a fairy-tale fantasy they'd like to experience someday, when the right person comes along. They tend to see marriage as a fantasy rather than a workaday reality. They do not accept the partnership ethic and instead believe that some prince in shining armor or beauty queen out there will one day appear and transform their lives.

The latter group of commitmentphobes can see no great benefit in bonding; they prefer to make their own decisions and operate at their own pace, and they do not relish compromising their freedom.

Because our standards are high and we refuse to compromise, we find ourselves single for longer periods than ever before; some of us will never wed.

EARNING THE RIGHT TO MARRY

Many singulars believe that the best way to ensure marital bliss (or to find a marriage partner in the first place) is to establish ourselves in a position of strength on the job.

Marla Mankowitz is an options buyer for one of the big-nine

brokerage houses on Wall Street. She makes no bones about her desire for wealth and a wealthy husband. That's why she went to Cornell University to study medicine, and when she couldn't hack it, she took to Wall Street like a fish to water.

Although Marla would like to find "that nice man," she's not pining away nights at the phone, waiting for him to call. In fact, she has decided that her best life strategy is to become "the catch" herself—the kind of woman her dream man would want.

So Marla set out to get rich. "I remember my mother saying, 'Rich men like rich girls.' " Already well on her way, Marla made about $100,000 in 1985. However, "I have more faith in making a million than in finding a nice man [to marry]."

Although Marla's stated goal is to make herself into a good catch, she is also proving to herself that she can support herself in the style she prefers—fur coats, expensive vacations abroad and unlimited nights on the town. Marla is busy *earning* the right to marry. It is not so much a matter of fattening her bank account as proving that she can provide for herself, that she is professionally competent.

Mike Walter's sentiments are strikingly similar. Mike intends to retain his bachelor status until he is at least thirty and a good deal further on his professional way. To this end, he puts more effort into pursuing business contacts than dates and potential mates. In fact, Mike's favorite friend is a "top executive" at Boeing in his early fifties, to whom Mike "hand-delivered" the invitation to his law school graduation. In the end, Mike's marital delay plan will pay off, he believes, because he'll command the kind of respect, salary—and woman—that now he can only dream of.

SKEPTICISM TOWARD EARLY MARRIAGE

Mike and Marla display a certain skepticism about early marriage that runs through the entire generation and is sometimes reinforced by society at large. Among singulars, early marriage is seen as a kind of early death, a sabotaging of one's chance to develop a singular identity in the outside world. This skepticism is articulated by literate writers, but it also crops up in the most unlikely places—in heart-to-heart talks with our mothers and even among the staffers at *Bride's* magazine in New York, who on a bimonthly basis produce lavish, high-gloss paeans to weddings.

Maria McBride Mellinger, a twenty-five-year-old assistant editor who selects models and supervises photo shoots, believes that many of her co-workers, most of whom are single, find her marriage "a little weird." As a result, Maria—married six years to a man who is now a physician—believes she is taken less seriously by some of her peers. Some staffers, she believes, tend to categorize her as "a housewife." It's not anything they say outright, but rather something that comes across more subtly.

"They think, 'You are working on a career right now, but are you really serious about it?' Unfortunately, marriage has some of those connotations; it's something you relate to as what your mother did."

In the case of Janice Lynch, a twenty-one-year-old senior at Guilford College in Greensboro, North Carolina, the pressure not to marry comes from her mother. When Janice's boyfriend of three years dropped out of school to return to his native Bahamas, Janice's mother, a late-blooming artist, was less than sympathetic.

"She said, 'You never thought you'd marry him. Try to get on with your life,'" Janice recalls. "It really annoyed me. In her eyes, I have so many options, how on earth could I be upset that this man was leaving?"

Janice, who hails from Laurel, Maryland, says that people in her age group are "between a rock and a hard place," feeling an excess of pressure to achieve on a professional level, often to the exclusion of their personal needs.

"If you said, 'Yeah, Mom, I was going to marry him,' all hell would break loose. So you end up almost feeling guilty for having felt any emotion at all other than, 'I've got to get on with my own life.'"

DISSOLVING A MARRIAGE

Because we invest less of ourselves and our identities in a marriage than before, singulars are capable of treating divorce casually. Some of us carry over some aspect of the bond into our new lives. Whether we remain friends, lovers or partners in parenting with ex-spouses, we try to retrieve whatever remains of a partnership gone bankrupt. In many cases, marriages don't work because they weren't full partnerships, but that doesn't preclude us from maintaining more fragmentary relationships.

While still a college student, Lani Lindsey of Springfield, Missouri, followed her husband from Seattle when he took a job at the local university as an art teacher. However, she began to realize that her entire identity was that of "faculty wife"—a role she did not care for. "I wasn't going anywhere, so I got out," she says of her two-and-a-half-year marriage. "We're still friends though," she adds.

April Garrett's divorce from husband Fred proved to be an expeditious affair, at least in one sense. The schoolteacher divorced her husband of two years after she learned of his infidelity. The couple had married right after she graduated from Brown University, because they were "madly and passionately in love." April moved to Columbus, Ohio, where Fred was enrolled in medical school. Very quickly April saw that the marriage was a mistake. Not only was the native New Yorker used to the big-city pace, but she realized a great sexual relationship could not prop up a nonexistent marital partnership.

By December of that year, April went home for a month, setting the pattern for a series of stormy separations and reconciliations. Finally Fred managed a transfer to San Francisco, and they moved there together, determined to make a fresh start. When April found out that Fred had been unfaithful (not once but with a "roster of nurses and secretaries"), she went to a do-it-yourself divorce center and filled out the papers.

"I paid $114 and filled all the papers out. That night when Fred came home, I told him we were getting a divorce. I said, 'Sign here.' He was shocked, but at this point, he just did what he was told. So I left; I moved back to L.A. A month later, I went back up there to get all my stuff. I'd gained twenty pounds and broken out in hives. I was devastated and missed him very much. He'd already started seeing someone else."

The strange twist of their relationship was that even after the divorce, they continued to sleep together. Though their postmarital trysts have ended, the divorcés are still in contact. "To this day, when I'm down and out, I still think of him. I'll call him up and we'll talk."

THE ONGOING PROCESS

Marriage was long considered an ultimate step, a settled end rather than an unsettled means. No longer. The singular generation believes that marriage should provide a kind of growth-oriented open-endedness within the negotiated boundaries of a relationship. With marriage, as with life, singulars believe that you strike your own deal, negotiate your own contract. We no longer accept prefabricated roles.

A singular marriage is an ongoing process and a never-ending struggle, not a storybook ending. It is a partnership in which individual goals are placed at a premium and both people's feelings are given their due. It is a partnership based on the premise of equality, of freedom of movement within marriage, of professional satisfaction, of being voluntary. In the absence of these qualities, we believe that a marriage will neither flourish nor continue.

The true marital partners of the eighties are pioneers, forging a better path. The worn, fixed-role marriages of the past simply did not prove equal to the demands of contemporary life. Singulars can only hope that the new partnership model for marriage will be more successful.

While holding out high hopes for our marriages, we singulars maintain a reservoir of skepticism about their long-term viability. As a result, we renegotiate our marriages, sometimes holding public reaffirmation ceremonies. We divorce or separate if things do not go as we think they should. Some of us see marriage as a temporary arrangement that suits us best at present. Even those of us who believe our marriages will last forever cannot banish from our imaginations unfortunate scenarios.

Unlike the young radicals who came before us, today's young adults do not protest against marriage: We simply do not embrace it—or not nearly so rapidly. Marriage is no longer at the center of our mythology. We have become cautious. We approach marriage self-consciously.

Among singulars, there is a profound yearning for the closeness, intimacy and security that wedlock promises. But our realistic bent prevents us from believing that marriage will give us all the answers. With subdued beginnings, we often manage to build our marriages into partnerships of love and create happy homes together. If we do not, we believe we can lead rich full lives as singles.

CHAPTER 4

The Sexes:
A New Integrity

THE FRONTIER OF FRIENDSHIP

In the singular generation, a new integrity between the sexes has
begun to rise out of the ashes of the age of romance. Singulars are
championing a way of relating that is more humane but less intense than was the romantic ideal that came before; it is based on
the simple principle of friendship. This is not to say that men and
women, boys and girls, have sworn off sex—not by any means.
Rather, we have broadened the definition of friendship to include
sex, and along the way have modified and begun to embrace an
emerging, new sexual etiquette.

Singulars do not have affairs, we have "sexual friendships." We
do not fall in love, we build relationships. We do not date, we
"see" each other (trying very hard to see each other clearly for
who we really are). Singular lovers are not mysterious strangers;
we are supportive, intimate friends. Just as partnership has become the model for a singular marriage, we hold "best friendship"
as the ideal for an exclusive sexual relationship.

In both sexual and platonic male-female friendships, singulars
have begun to apply the ground rules of friendship—reciprocity,

honesty, openness and availability—while rejecting the worn rules, roles and games that once tightly governed—and restricted —behavior between the sexes. Singulars see each other's individuality first, their gender second. At the same time, we believe that the best way to become a good friend is to build a strong relationship with yourself.

Sexual friendship is based on the idea of equality between the sexes and the feeling that neither sex stands to gain (or lose) more than the other from sexual intimacy or commitment—that both are equally vulnerable to pain and heartbreak. Sexual friendship can only work when both partners act responsibly, willingly and without coercion in all aspects of their relationship, and if a balance of power exists within the bond. This emerging friendship ideal resounds in conversations with singulars throughout the country.

"He's my best friend," says waitress-cum-artist Lani Lindsey of Springfield, Missouri, about her live-in boyfriend, an electrician. "I'm really attracted to him as a lover. I like being with him a lot."

In many cases, singulars view a strong friendship as the single most important component of a stable bond.

"When people look at what's going to make a relationship last, they know it's friendship," says Lisa Phillips, a twenty-six-year-old Los Angeles student. "You can date anyone you want, or sleep with anyone you want. It's not 'making it' anymore that's important. Friendship is the next frontier."

Recently Lisa advised a female friend who was distressed about her difficulties in meeting eligible men to stop "interviewing" them for the husband position. "I said, 'Pattie, you've got to look at a man as a person first, a friend second and a boyfriend or mate third,'" says Lisa. "'If you don't look at him as a person, you won't be able to see his qualities, what kind of person he is. Being friends with him is the most important part of having a relationship.'"

DANIEL AND JULIE

Daniel Shaw and Julie Day are best friends. They are also lovers and twenty-one-year-old fellow Harvard University students who plan to spend the rest of their lives together. Among young, ambitious adults in the eighties, Daniel and Julie are unusual in having made such a serious commitment to a lover so early in life. Nevertheless, their relationship is prototypical of the new, emerging breed of singular sexual friendships.

Daniel and Julie met during the summer of 1984, when Julie was attending Harvard's summer school program and Daniel, a rising junior, had a summer job at an electronics shop. Soulmates at first sight, they stayed up into the wee hours of the night they first met—talking.

"We sat up talking from about ten that night till eight the next morning," says Daniel.

"We talked about anything and everything," says Julie.

"I went to work and came back, and we stayed up all the next night talking," adds Daniel. "I moved in the third day after I met her, at her request. We decided it was perfect—there was absolutely no hesitation."

"We didn't make love till the third time we slept together," Julie says, "because we didn't want to rush." Sex "wasn't important," she says. "It wasn't what we were interested in each other for."

"It's not a relationship even remotely close to being based on sex," Daniel concurs, "because that's not the only thing we can do together. We can do everything else together. I guess that's the case with every strong relationship." Even though sex, he says, "really didn't feel like a necessary part of the relationship," it "was awfully nice, too."

Come fall, when Julie returned to the University of California at Berkeley, where she was then enrolled, the couple diligently maintained their cross-country romance. Daniel called Julie almost every night after 11 P.M. his time (the rates were in his favor), and they would talk for five or ten minutes. Like the best friends they were rapidly becoming, they wrote frequently, discussing family and friends and brainstorming about course work and future job prospects. Not long into the fall quarter, Julie broke the news to Daniel, over the phone, that she was filing an application to transfer to Harvard.

"He was quiet for a minute," Julie remembers. "I said, 'You're quiet.' He said, 'I can't believe this; I'm really, really happy.' For us, silence tends to precede great joy."

Julie was accepted by the Harvard Admissions Committee and she enrolled in the fall of '85.

But just because the two were deeply in love and had been separated for a full year, when Julie moved to Cambridge, they did not become an inseparable item. Rather, they decided it was important for them both to establish and maintain separate identities. To that end, Daniel decided to finish out his senior year living in Eliot House with his three suitemates, and Julie rented an apartment for one on Trowbridge Place.

"We have tried to keep our individual lives intact," she says. "We're going to have to build separate lives [at Harvard] anyway. I'm going to be there a year longer than he is." (Julie forfeited a year in credits by accepting a place in Harvard's class of 1987.) "We haven't thrown everything away," she says, "to run into each other's arms."

As choreographers of their own relationship, Julie and Daniel know intuitively that it is best to pace their moves and to let their friendship unfold at its own rate. Being "in love" does not mean they have to spend every minute together. It does not dictate the terms for singulars, or tell us how to behave. As in the workplace, where singulars strike our own deals, in the arena of love we set our own terms. Daniel and Julie's decisions are guided by their observance of the friendship ideal and a kind of integrity in which reason, trust and sensitivity prevail over an "I can't take my eyes off of you" possessive—and jealous—kind of passion. To Daniel and Julie, there is nothing appealing about emotional dependency.

Singulars are cautious in our approach to love—and sex—because we are aware of the pain and emotional anguish a relationship can wreak on ourselves and our lovers when it does not fulfill its promise. And so we nurture relationships, trying to build them bit by bit into satisfying wholeness. In some cases, this means going slowly with sexual intimacy; in other cases, it means making gradual and deliberate commitments to our intimate friends. Still other singulars hold potential lovers at arm's length and concentrate upon our personal development, preferring not to reach out until we feel ourselves to be whole.

Whatever the emotional reasons for our caution about love and commitment, for most singulars, it also has a pragmatic component: Business before pleasure has become a kind of credo. While in the past, many young adults felt that you put your emotional shop in order before setting out into the world to seek your fortune, singulars think just the opposite.

CROSS-SEXUAL FRIENDSHIP

The singular generation is pioneering friendship between the sexes. In our parents' youth, conventional wisdom had it that a man and a woman could not be friends. They could be spouses, fiancés, even lovers; they could be brother and sister, mother and son, father and daughter, employer and employee. They could relate to each other only in fixed or prescribed relationships, if the boundaries of their bonds were clearly defined in advance. Romantic, even sexual, relationships were okay if they were exclusive and provided the couple were taking steps to make it permanent.

Cross-sexual friendship, though, was another matter. If you attempted to be "just friends" with a member of what a generation ago was called the opposite sex, you were flirting with temptation and danger—you were probably having an affair. As late as the fifties and sixties, men and women were often shut off from, and sometimes scared of, each other.

As a result of this estrangement between men and women, the conditions under which they did mingle took on a strained and artificial quality. A woman usually did not talk with a man in a straight and sincere manner; she was oblique, she flirted, she maybe even lied; she covered up her strength with a patina of weakness. He was not honest, either; he was boastful, even domi-neering; he banished his vulnerability. Quite rightly, the game of love was likened to the game of war. Honesty and camaraderie existed in the boys' locker room and the girls' powder room, not in places where the sexes met—in the movie theater, on the dance floor, in the bedroom. The sexes were enemies who struck occa-sional truces. But theirs was a lopsided alliance, and they defined everything in opposition to one another. If she wore pink, he wore blue; if she made cakes, he made cocktails; if he was hot for sex, she was supposed to hold out on him.

Some of this changed, of course, during the sixties and seven-ties, when the women's movement held up the examining lens to relations between the sexes. But in many cases, feminists began to mime men, trying to beat them at their own game, and men raised their dukes in response. In the process, the diametrical order of male-female relations gave over to a malevolent competitiveness in which love and friendship were often lost between the sexes.

Singulars are cut of another, newer cloth. We grew up with feminism and with a medley of sex-role models: traditional mar-ried couples, transitional couples, single-parent families and con-firmed singles. We came to understand that any number of options are just that: options. And along the way, we decided that the only way to evaluate and relate to each other was in a gentle and straightforward manner, through friendship.

Somewhere along the way, the ice that had long isolated the sexes from each other began to melt. We concluded that one should no more disallow a friendship on the basis of sex, marital status or even sexual preference than one should discriminate against someone on the basis of race, color or creed. Our new, expanded, cross-sexual friendship pool now can include such one-time outcasts as ex-lovers, ex-spouses and ex–in-laws.

"I've always gotten along better with guys than girls," says Geri Gaye Childress, a twenty-year-old female student at Surry Community College in Dobson, North Carolina. Geri's best friend in high school was a boy named Adam. Every day after school, the two would go down and shoot pool together, "just like two guys going out." Adam even helped Geri land the boy she had her eye on, by slipping her name into conversation with him.

"[Adam] found out that the guy liked me, but the only reason he never asked me out was that he didn't have a car. He didn't think I'd be interested if I had to pick him up in my car, but I was."

Though Rhonda Gainer has a close circle of female friends, male friends give her a lift that she feels girlfriends can't provide.

"Whenever I have a friendship with a male I like," says the New York advertising executive, "it helps my disposition two hundred percent. I don't need to have sex to have rosy cheeks, I just need to know that someone likes me and I like him."

This camaraderie between men and women is possible, in large degree, because the stakes between the sexes have *fallen.* Since male-female relationships among singulars take a backseat to careers, there is less pressure on us to join our lives in marriage or coupledom and, therefore, greater opportunity for friendship. Because both female and male singulars subscribe to the work ethic, we identify with each other's professional aspirations across gender lines in a way that our parents' generation usually couldn't. We can be confidants, colleagues, fellow networkers; so why not friends?

SEXUAL RESTRAINT

Where the sixties generation was obsessed by sex but easygoing about work, the singular generation is intense about work but more cautious, even diffident, about sex.

"I've learned to take relationships slow, and as they come," says twenty-five-year-old Brad Sevy of Encino, California. "If you jump into them real quick, they usually have quick endings. If you let a friendship build into a love relationship, it's always more rewarding because you generally know each other. The caring and feelings are more genuine than in a spontaneous-lust type situation."

In the sixties, sex was the very cornerstone of youth culture, the first in the holy trinity of sex and drugs and rock music. With the singular generation, sexuality has been demystified; we believe that sex, like a good friendship, gets better with time. We do not idealize carnal passion or what Erica Jong called the zipless fuck. To singulars, premarital sex is not a sin; neither is it a newly gained pleasure and privilege, to be indulged in at every opportunity. Indeed, we feel less urgency about engaging in sexual activity because we have come to accept its rightful place in our lives. A 1984 *Time* magazine cover story proclaiming the end of the sexual revolution argued that it has suffered the slow death of widespread acceptance: "The sexual revolution has not been rebuffed, merely absorbed into the culture. America is more relaxed and open about sex, but also blessedly a bit tired of the subject."

Because the revolution is over, singulars no longer feel compelled to make love for political reasons—to show our parents, our friends or society that we *can* do as we please; singulars feel no need to pose as sexual libertines. Relieved of the intense and relentless pressure to engage in flagrant sexuality, singulars are able to exercise a greater freedom of sexual choice than any generation before us. Including the right to say no.

Christopher Austill, a twenty-six-year-old Cambridge, Massachusetts, child-care worker, recently tried an extremist "experiment in loving" to try to "unlearn" some of the destructive sexual patterns by which he believes he's been conditioned. Because sex for him had become estranged from feeling, and because he believed in his gut that men suffer as much, if not more, than women from premature sexual liaisons, Chris and his girlfriend, Leslie, agreed to omit intercourse from their sexual repertoire. For a year, "making love" came to mean kissing and hugging and drawing close. It meant spending the night in the same bed in one or the other's apartment, locked in embrace. During that year they were together, they never once broke their agreement.

Tall, tautly built and boyishly handsome, Chris Austill is no Bible-toting provincial. The honors graduate of Wesleyan University has lived with a woman in the conventional way, and he grew up in New York, a child of liberal, loving parents.

"One of the things I was interested in doing was being with her [Leslie] as close as I felt I was," he explains, "and not sort of going through the motions of being closer than I felt I was, or trying to be something, or trying to please when I didn't feel that."

A jagged middle part bisects Chris's head of limp blond hair. With his faded, loose-hanging cords and blue-and-green plaid flannel shirt, Chris has the look and manner of a sixties angry young man who is destined to join the ruling class.

"How it turns out for me, and I think it's true for most men, is that we don't know shit about being close yet. We've been so isolated and cut off from human beings all of our lives that if you try to go back and be as close with people as you feel, [you find out] that it's a lot further away than you would ever expect.

"Sex has been so genitalized—especially the penis, [which] is such a symbol of sexuality. I tell you, I'm a lot more than my penis. There's lots more parts of my body that feel good than that, but I haven't ever been trained to think that way. I have to learn on my own. . . . Women have not been told that I have a whole body. Everyone thinks, 'He's got to come and then he'll be happy and kaboom, that's it.' "

THE END OF PICKUP SEX

To singulars, one-night stands and pickup quickies seem pointless, desperate, even perilous—not thrilling adventures. The wrong sexual partner, after all, could infect us with AIDS, the Black Plague of the 1980s. Or we could contract herpes or some other sexually transmitted disease this way. For some singulars, the desire to get to know someone well, to gain his or her trust as a friend before becoming sexually intimate, springs from pure self-interest.

After contracting herpes from a sexual encounter with a man she'd known only slightly (and who had neglected to tell her he was infected), Alice Monks of Worcester, Massachusetts, predicted, "Casual sex is going to be dead before long; it already is with me." Alice has let the herpes infection serve as a warning of how easily it could have been much worse. "Casual sex is like taking your life in your hands," she says. "Anyone could get AIDS."

Others of us have been turned off by the patent phoniness and emotional emptiness found in the pickup scene. About a year ago, Rob Fulop opted out of the "scoring" games some of his friends play on "boys' night out."

"Five men go out together in five different cars to the same bar," he says. The object is "to see which one leaves the quickest, [and which one lands] the most attractive girl. The big thing is how you trick this girl into bed, what you say about yourself— you lie. Anything goes to get this girl home. You say you're a movie director. You can say or do anything, with the assumption that the girl knows what she's doing."

Though Rob has no moral objections to one-night stands, he finds them "totally nothing." On the few occasions that he has indulged, he felt "not degraded but depressed." So now he takes his time getting sexually involved. "The new Rob would rather it [the presex period] would be as long as possible," he says.

SEXUAL RESPONSIBILITY

The new singular sexual code dictates that we act responsibly; that before we plunge into a sexual relationship, we lay our cards on the table. Relevant "cards" would include our interest in commitment (or lack thereof), our current obligations (e.g., the existence of a baby at home or a serious lover living in some other city) and any liabilities (like having herpes).

From the beginning, Dale Counter felt obliged to warn a woman he was sleeping with that they had no future together. The twenty-seven-year-old salesman, a New Jersey native, took up with Mindy, a secretary in his firm, when his relationship with his girlfriend, Jeannie, started to crumble. Mindy was attractive, available and had been "hitting on me for four months," Dale says; her interest was a nice ego boost at a time when his ego could use bolstering.

"She's a nice transition person." But Dale knew the relationship had no long-term potential—they are not intellectual equals and could never form an equitable partnership—so he told her where he stood before they even made love.

"I did all the right things as far as telling her: 'I don't think it's going anywhere,' that I was concerned that I couldn't give her the attention that she expected and deserved. I told her I had this on-again, off-again thing with Jeannie. She said, 'Don't worry; it's my decision.' "

Despite his honesty, Dale still experiences pangs of guilt over the likelihood that Mindy will suffer from rejection when their fling ends. "Even though she says she'll handle that, I know she probably hopes at the back of her mind the relationship will go somewhere. I don't like hurting people. And the dynamics of the situation are that it's very easy for people to get hurt."

On balance, Dale derives as much shame as pleasure from the relationship, because he can't help thinking that it is based on raging hormones rather than genuine friendship. "I don't know if it was a nonsexual relationship whether I would see her as much," he admits sheepishly, as if confessing a dark secret.

So Dale goes the extra mile, trying to be friend and professional ally to Mindy, but feeling more like a superior than an equal. "She had a job change in my company. We spoke for an hour and a half before she went in for the interview. I helped her pump up her confidence, and she got a real raise. The fact that I'm concerned about her career knocked her out."

But it seems likely that after their relationship expires, should another "Mindy" present herself to Dale, he might well nix the proposition. Singulars are likely to feel that self-serving sex, in which one party has different expectations than the other and can get burned, is not worth the price. A generation ago, Dale might have been able to relieve himself of the guilt by telling himself that Mindy was "asking for it" by breaking the rules and engaging in a sexual relationship without commitment; in those days, a good girl was supposed to say no. Among singulars, however, such rules have little hold over us and, therefore, the responsibility for hurting a friend falls on us.

To avoid the messiness of a breakup and inflicting pain on another, singulars prefer finding a friend who is at the same place that we are emotionally—whether that means seeking a purely physical relationship without strings or working together toward a long-term commitment.

RELATIONSHIP MAINTENANCE

Like a singular marital partnership, a sexual friendship is organized around principles from the world of work. We negotiate the perimeters of our bond, the stages of intimacy, the level of commitment, with both "partners in friendship" sharing in the sexual and emotional risk taking required to make a relationship go. Singulars do not believe that it happens magically, on its own. We try to extend the same courtesies to lovers as we do to platonic friends. We tend to gauge sexual friendships against the standards we set for same-sex friendships, as the following guidelines indicate:

1. Reciprocity. Both partners should initiate occasions and outings, sexual move-making and the exchange of confidences, trading off the role of aggressor. Right from the start, a friendship should show a back-and-forth exchange.

When twenty-four-year-old Hollywood screenwriter Ed Solomon meets a woman in whom he is interested, he generally writes down his phone number and hands it to her. " 'Give me a call sometime if you feel like it,' " he will say. "I don't like to put pressure on someone by asking for her phone number," he explains. His method paves the way for the reciprocity that Ed values in a relationship; while he makes the first move, she must make the second one, or else they're going nowhere in a hurry.

If a woman makes the initial approach, more power to her. "I like assertive women," says Dale Counter, speaking for most singulars. Dale met Jeannie in a Phone Mart line his second day in town, and she handed him her business card. Still, singulars tend to back off when assertiveness bulldozes over the principle of reciprocity. Coming on strong—like playing hard to get and acting coy—has no place in the singular friendship code.

Once a friendship is established, two friends should share the day-in and day-out servicing that the bond requires. College admissions counselor Amy Harris lives some distance from her boyfriend, and if she makes the "two-hour, round-trip schlep" over to his place one night and then back the next morning, she expects him to reciprocate the next time.

"In contrast to my mother, who goes where my father goes, I don't have the time or energy to follow him around," says the twenty-five-year-old Amy, whose demanding job leaves her precious little time for her personal life. "I need to feel reassured that he'll do the same for me, that I'm not doing all the work."

Not only does the reciprocal system set a relationship on an even keel right from the start, but it comes in handy if and when a sexual friendship ends. Since the maintenance of the relationship is shared by both parties and inordinate sacrifices are made by neither, no one is likely to feel taken advantage of or bitter when it's over.

2. *Self-sufficiency.* To singulars, dependency is a deadly curse, one to be avoided at all costs. So we nurture each other's self-sufficiency and strength, just as we do with a platonic friend. We believe that in order for a sexual friendship to work well, both partners must be able to function as autonomous units.

Henry Holcomb, a twenty-five-year-old Los Angeles actor, says that the reason for the breakup with his girlfriend of four years was her clinginess. "I wanted her to get more secure in herself, so that she wouldn't depend on me for security." When she proved unable to break out of the dependency syndrome, he felt he had to break it off. Likewise, the woman of Ed Solomon's dreams would be "wholly self-sufficient and have an eye on herself and what she wants out of life."

Singulars prefer sexual friends who share our own level of self-sufficiency and self-security, who are assertive enough to stand up for their needs without denying the needs of another. Burdening a friend with our problems, or repeatedly leaning too heavily on him or her for emotional, financial or professional support, constitutes a clear violation of this standard; a self-sufficient friend does not cast a friend in the role of a surrogate therapist or parent.

Singulars value individuals who have a solid base of personal security and self-esteem.

3. *Nonpossessiveness.* Going hand in hand with our desire for self-sufficiency is the need to "possess" ourselves and our lives, not to let a sexual friend gain the power of veto over what should remain our own business. Singulars want the freedom to maintain ties with other friends, family members and personal activities. We prefer like-minded, independent friends, and our backs go up if someone starts to get overly demanding.

4. *Self-sexuality.* Increasingly, sex therapists today say that self-sexuality—the ability to give pleasure to oneself—is the basis for one's sexuality.

Dissatisfied with the frequency of his sexual encounters with his girlfriend, twenty-nine-year-old Joe Pope of Seattle sought the aid of a sex counselor. "She told us that we should each learn how to satisfy ourselves sexually, by ourselves, and not to place all the burden on each other," says Joe. "She said I should masturbate myself to orgasm whenever I was horny and my lady friend wasn't in the mood."

The sexual revolution helped loosen the historical sanctions against masturbation. While singulars are unlikely to abandon relations with members of the other sex in favor of "getting off" solo, we are increasingly apt to turn to self-pleasuring to achieve satisfaction when a sexual friend isn't "there" for us. As we delay sexual intimacy to develop full-fledged friendships with each other, and as we put our energies into pursuing a career rather than a mate, self-satisfaction can provide an alternative—if only as a stop-gap measure.

5. *Honesty.* Singulars expect honesty from our sexual friends, just as we do from platonic friends. If you say you're going to call her the next day, you call the next day, or else you violate the sexual friendship ethic. You are as conscientious with your girlfriend or boyfriend as you would be with your closest sibling or a cantankerous boss.

Singulars value an honesty that is truthful but tactful, helpful but cognizant of each other's personal feelings. Although hidden agendas and unconscious expectations cannot be avoided in sexual relationships, we make an honest attempt to air our feelings. If we're doubtful about commitment; if we want to see others; if we're struggling with sexual identity; that's all all right—as long as we express ourselves verbally. Indeed, just about any kind of arrangement or understanding can be negotiated between two sexual friends.

Even men's magazines are starting to sound this message. "Dishonesty with your partner," warns an article on etiquette for the "morning after" in the October '85 *MGF* (Men's Guide to Fashion), "can come back to haunt you."

6. *Openness.* Singulars value individuals who can take a step beyond honesty, who are willing to divulge their inner thoughts and feelings for the joy of growing close and without fear of emotional reprisal.

Amy Harris remembers a gut-wrenching period just after she and her boyfriend had first slept together. John was "real closed," she remembers. "He was real hard to read for three weeks. He would answer questions in an ambivalent way." On top of that, he seemed to draw away. The first time they went out after he clammed up, Amy says, "I confronted him: 'Are you uncomfortable that we've gotten involved? I sense that from you.' I said, 'Are you sure you're not just a tiny bit uncomfortable?' He said, 'Yes.' "

Though John is opening up to Amy little by little, she continues to be vexed when he is emotionally tight—closed—and she has to pry him open. Her ideal man, she says, would be "open and communicative."

7. *Sharing the cost.* Both friends should be willing to share the financial burden of friendship. The high cost of entertainment and the decreased earning power of young adults compared to young people a generation ago contributes to the growing need for financial parity between the sexes.

"I'm completely in favor of everyone paying for themselves," says Henry Holcomb. "As ridiculous as that seems—'I owe you

75 cents'—keeping tabs makes it all square out right." While Henry finds it "too touchy" to try to collect a friend's share if she does not offer to pay, he will always note her chintziness in the back of his mind.

Even in Austin, Texas, where "gallantry is still very much in style: pulling out chairs for girls, standing up at a table when women stand up, opening doors," says Vance Rose, this gallantry does not necessarily extend into the financial realm. "I don't insist on paying every tab," he says.

A male carrying a disproportionate share of the financial burden could exact a hidden cost from the relationship in the long run. Only in retrospect was Jonathan Rourke able to put his finger on the problem he had with a girl he was seeing off and on: She was "too cheap," he says. "She was saving to go to England. She had five or six boyfriends supporting her, paying for the things of life—dinner out, the little articles." In the end, Jonathan came to feel that he was more a "lunch ticket" than a friend to her, and that's when he bailed out.

Singular males feel that a woman's refusal to accept her fair share of the cost of entertainment indicates a stinginess not only of pocketbook but of spirit. It indicates that the woman does not subscribe to the sexual friendship ideal but is a throwback to the "a man pays, a woman lays" epoch.

8. Compatibility. Singulars value sexual friends with whom we share interests and are compatible; fast fleeting are the days when sexual partners placed a premium on exotic and mysterious lovers.

"I want a Jewish man," says Los Angeles schoolteacher April Garrett. "It has nothing to do with the practice of religion. I don't believe in religion anytime, anywhere. But culture very much affects people. Jews tend to be emotive, hot-blooded, political. We have a certain way of functioning. . . . I understand Jews, and they understand me better."

By the same token, April wants someone who shares her background, education and breeding. "You don't want someone from another class. You want someone you can have similar type friends with," she says.

Singulars prefer supportive companions who share our professional interests and levels of aspiration, individuals with whom we feel comfortable and who are excited by and understand those things that are meaningful to us. We want a best friend and a partner, not a stranger.

9. Confidentiality. Singulars expect sexual friends to hold secrets and confidences the way we would with same-sex friends. Bragging to a third party about a sexual "conquest" or exposing the vulnerabilities of a new lover, for instance, violates the integrity of the sexual friendship.

10. A positive approach. Even if a sexual friendship is only temporary (a summer romance or weekend tryst), singulars seek to swaddle our flings in good, positive feelings. This way we can carry away from the friendship happy memories, while leaving the door open for the friendship to continue.

11. Realistic expectations. Singulars seek friends who are realistic in their expectations of each other and of a relationship. Little frightens us as much as someone who asks too much of a friendship too quickly—such as commitment or marriage. That person's neediness would suggest an imbalance of power in the relationship and, therefore, would not bode well for the future.

"When you let go of expectations is when things work," says one singular. If you want to make something work, you have to forget about your "ideal" man or woman, he adds.

Indeed, singulars do not necessarily *expect* a sexual relationship to go anywhere at all. "You're with somebody as long as you want to be with them," says Henry Holcomb. "I don't expect anything to be permanent; I don't know anyone who does."

Even when a relationship takes off, our expectations remain modest; unlike previous generations, we do not expect all our personal problems to disappear overnight just because we've found a sexual partner. Neither do we expect a sexual friend to meet all our many needs.

Like its platonic analog, sexual friendship is a voluntary bond, based on hefty doses of mutual interest, respect and support. In sexual friendship, you don't lock your partner into position but rather give him or her room to breathe and expand, even if (painful as it might be) that means moving away from you.

Singulars recognize that friendship exists in the here and the now and that it often has a natural course to run, which is affected by proximity, circumstances and expectations. A friendship can grow, and we can help it along by extending to each other our finest selves and the same considerations and privileges that close friends have always offered each other. When we observe the guidelines of decency, even if the sexual part of the friendship burns out, singulars believe that a friendship can remain.

THE DEATH OF ROMANCE

The singular generation grew up with the plague of divorce, the weakening of marriage and during the death throes of the romantic idea and ideal that long defined relations between the sexes. Singulars came of age in an era of pain, confusion and sometimes outright warfare between the sexes, and we came to understand that love and sexual passion are not only fleeting but that they can backfire. We grew up when the sexes were recharting themselves in relation to each other and when almost every image of masculinity and femininity, new and old, was called on the carpet.

Ours is a generation of aromantics, jaded about matters of the heart—often before gaining firsthand experience. As early as childhood, singulars overdosed on sex both from personal observation and media saturation. While our parents' generation was busy breaking the conventions of the morality that had long lent a kind of comforting order to society, we singulars were left in the murk of uncertainty, without a distinct system with which to come to terms.

So singulars found our identities as pragmatic, nose-to-the-grindstone realists. To us, the trappings of romance—the candlelit dinners and the "you are the only one for me" and "I couldn't live without you" routines—strike a false note; they seem corny and false. If such lines are uttered, singulars know them to be untrue. We know that one *could* live without the other, and that he or she probably *will*. Sometimes we like to play along with romance, but we are conscious all the time of what we are doing and so hold out at least part of ourselves in a reserve of self-protecting skepticism.

Indeed, romance and sexual friendship seem almost entirely unrelated. *Romance* is a scripted and tightly staged play with just two roles, Male and Female, while *Sexual Friendship* is a free-form improvisation with as many parts as players. *Romance* seems almost Elizabethan by today's standards, with the same lines of dialogue uttered time and again by posed, posturing players; by contrast, *Sexual Friendship* offers few directions save those basic principles of movement that would apply to all of human nature.

Romance, as it was once known, could no longer thrive in an environment in which the sexes were not systematically separated, in which the differences between the sexes did not surpass the similarities. Romance could not live devoid of the mystery and intrigue of otherness.

In today's singular world, the sexes are increasingly interchangeable, and gender has come to border on the irrelevant. For singulars, there are not even many "firsts" left for women and men to achieve. Females can drive trucks, and males can raise babies. Females can lift weights, and males can bake apple pies. Females can sleep around, and males can stay true.

Romance has collapsed in the singular era, but no tears need be shed. Just as we retired the Model T once its usefulness was past and technology had moved beyond it, singulars have retired the conventions of romance and replaced them with a more workable model of cross-sexual connection.

THE EXPANDED IMPORTANCE OF
SAME-SEX FRIENDSHIP

There is a heightened interest in old-fashioned, same-sex friendship among singulars. The diminishment of the centrality of marriage, the collapse of romance, the transience of sexual relationships and the erosion of the stigma against homosexuality have all contributed to this trend.

The male "buddy" bond has long been celebrated in literature, lore and cinema, but in the past, the boys weren't supposed to get *too* close. They could hunt together, but they were never supposed to *live* together—not for long, anyway. Likewise, female friendship, although intense, was always subordinated to the "higher" bond of male-female relations. A generation ago, your girlfriend understood that any plans you made with her were subject to cancellation if a male were to call.

No longer. Same-sex friendship has quickly gained prominence in the emotional pantheon of the singular generation. On the pedestal once reserved for romantic sexual love, many of us have now placed idealized friendship. Singulars tend to see friendship as a kind of precious resource. And we develop emotional dependencies on our closest friends that are nothing short of familial.

"I will be married and have kids," says one single graduate student, "but I talk about forever with my friends."

Krysia Lindan, a twenty-nine-year-old resident in internal medicine at Stanford University Hospital, recently financed a month-long trip to Burma for her best friend and roommate, Diane Szumowski. Although Diane plans to pay Krysia back on an installment basis when she finds steady employment, Krysia says she doesn't care if she ever sees the money again. "She's like a sister, really. I wish I were wealthy enough to buy all my sisters trips everywhere."

Singulars like Krysia often seek the sanctuary of same-sex friendship when they're unable to trust members of the other sex and make the leap of faith to sexual friendship.

Krysia has found female friendship to be her salvation during the trying years of medical school. "My female friendships have been very intense and involved," she says, "but at the same time, they haven't been demanding. They are what I fall back on when the going gets really rough; they are who I can be myself with. . . . When I get involved with men, I have to temper my desires somehow. I have to be other than what I am—much less ambitious or much less successful."

Homosexuals probably provide the most striking model of intimate closeness among same-sex relationships in the singular generation. "I can sleep with my friends on any night of the week, different ones," says Denise Andrews of Seattle. "I'm not talking about having sex with someone, I'm talking about sleeping with them in the same bed, snuggling close. You [nongays] generally would not sleep with a friend of yours."

While most singulars stop short of engaging in homosexual relationships with our closest friends, same-sex friendships among singulars can become so intense as to hermetically seal outsiders out. For us, sexual intercourse may not necessarily be the highest form of intimacy.

Ed Solomon's friendship with Chris, his writing partner, verges on the incestuous. "Our relationship is almost marital in a sense," Ed says. The partners spend ten hours a day together, churning out comedy screenplays for a variety of producers from the office they share in Burbank. They play tennis together, socialize together on weekends, and last summer, they took their vacation together: white-water rafting in Idaho.

"Part of the reason I don't have a real fulfilling relationship with a woman is because of Chris," says Ed. "Our career is so fulfilling. We just laugh all the time. We talk about everything in our personal life. There's no pride there."

Ed will even go so far as to say, "I probably love him. I haven't been as open with anyone else."

Among the topics the friends discuss is homosexuality.

"Our secretary is incredibly gay," says Ed. "We joke about Andrew seducing us, and Chris and me deciding we're in love." But the men don't think they are inclined that way. Homosexuality is "something you think about" and "joke about" rather than experiment with, says Ed. "It's never the kind of thing that's given me an erection."

Ed's closeness with his business partner fulfills his needs for emotional intimacy without draining precious energy from his writing career, which is just now taking off. "This is the most important time for me in terms of my career."

Ed's decision to steer clear of females is in large part work-related. Past experience has shown that girlfriends invariably cut into his prime creative time. "Every [sexual] relationship I've had has been real unproductive to my career, which is really where my passion is right now," he says. "When I'm in love, I can't think about my work, I just think about the woman."

So for the present, Ed's emotional circle is filled by his friendship with Chris as well as by several other sets of friends, including platonic female friends and one ex-girlfriend. "I have friends from three groups: my friends from growing up—I see most of them still; friends from college; and friends since I've graduated."

Ed prides himself on the care he takes maintaining these ties. "I'm a very generous kind of person, especially to friends. I'll take time for them if they need it, give them things if they need it." He invests so much of himself in his friends that occasionally he feels that he neglects himself. "I would like more time for sitting, relaxing, reading, walking around . . . rejuvenat(ing)."

The theme of intense same-sex friendship has captivated the attention of the newest generation of writers. Elizabeth Benedict's novel *Slow Dancing* dissects the relationship of two women who are "in love" but not making love. "The only person I've ever really been in love with is a woman," Lexie, the protagonist, tells a male reporter with whom she develops a friendship.

For singulars, same-sex friendship has helped fill the emotional gaps left as dating, romance and marriage wane.

CREEPING ISOLATIONISM

Each burst of fresh young blood into larger society comes with its invigorating new ideas as well as its danger spots; the singular generation's sexual friendship ideal is no exception. Our desire for self-sufficiency is good, but not when pushed to its outer limits, where it can become a deadly form of personal isolationism, an emotional anorexia. Paring to size the once larger-than-life notion of romantic love is a positive development, forcing many of us— especially the females—out of dreamland to take charge of our lives, but the danger is that we can reduce love to insignificant dimensions.

A creeping isolationism is the giant downside of the singular generation, and indeed many of us have already fallen under its shadow. Either out of mistrust of love, intercourse, members of the other sex or even members of our own sex, some singulars have recoiled altogether from sexuality, intimacy and in some cases even friendship, whittling our emotional needs to nothingness in the process. Others of us have pulled back from romantic love but not from sexual thrills, partaking in what we call "platonic sex," that is, the engaging of genitals but not of emotions; still others of us have become numb inside, having lost the ability to want, to touch, to feel.

By his own admission, Dale Counter sometimes struggles with emotional isolation. About five months after Dale started seeing Jeannie, she asked him why he was unable to acknowledge that their relationship had meaning; after all, they spent all their free time together and enjoyed an intense and pleasurable sexual relationship. Jeannie convinced Dale to see her therapist with her to confront the problem together.

Dale admits that he was then afflicted with "the barriers a person who's lived alone has set up." In short, he'd become "self-sustaining. I could keep to myself. When you get too good at that, it's hard to let other people in." Although Jeannie did manage to shake him out of his self-protective coating, they have since broken up, and more scar tissue has formed. After each breakup—and there have been several—Dale recedes deeper into his shell; he worries that someday he may never come out again. "It's a fear of mine," Dale admits, "being alone and not letting people in."

Some of us do not let others in. John Carlson, a conservative Catholic from Seattle, indulges in an occasional fling but says that he's never really made a deep connection with a woman. "I've never had a really serious relationship. I define that as being together with someone to the point where you think about marriage. I mean *think* about marriage. . . . My experience has been that oftentimes she takes it as much more of a serious thing than I do, even though there was no previous exchange of words to suggest the seriousness."

SEXUAL DISENGAGEMENT

Some singulars do *not* make sexual contact. "I haven't had sex in a year and couldn't care less," says Paula Weinman.

"I was celibate for five years in my early twenties," says twenty-nine-year-old Bostonian Katie Eastment. "I'd be interested to know how unusual it is, frankly speaking, because it wasn't a difficult sort of thing for me."

Some singulars are not only celibate but estranged and disengaged from our ability to feel. *Ahedonia,* or the inability to experience sexual or any other kind of pleasure, has reared its ugly head in the singular generation.

In the seventies, sex therapists were inundated with clients complaining of "performance anxiety" (i.e., impotence, inability to hold an erection, inability to achieve orgasm); clients of that decade were anxious about pleasing and impressing their sexual partners. The problem of the eighties, however, is "inhibited sexual desire," a lagging—or altogether lacking—interest in sex.

Many of those who have withdrawn from sex and intimacy and from holding out the hope of ever winning a partner have not yet embraced the sexual friendship ideal. They may be more in touch with outmoded and, therefore, inherently disappointing notions of masculinity and femininity; or they may be stuck on the fallout from the war between the sexes, pouring their energies into sexual power struggles; or they may be overly perplexed by the tensions and ambiguities that inevitably occur in a transitional period such as our own, as the age of romance gives over to the era of sexual friendship.

Toby Bauer, a free-lance writer, has done her share of sexual experimentation, but as of yet, has not been able to sort through her experience to arrive at any satisfying *modus operandi.*

"I did all the kinds of things you're supposed to do," she says. "Get wild; get two guys; get some girls in there; be real free; go out with several at the same time; don't have any commitments; do have some commitments; be friends and lovers; be lovers and not friends. None of it ever seems to make any sense to me. I wish it were simpler."

Toby's confusion catapulted her into a withdrawal from men. At present, she sees men only rarely, and though she receives a constant stream of masculine attention, she says she has had sex with a man only twice in the past year. ("Now it's like, I probably know how to do it better to myself than some guy will," she says.) She has a small circle of close female friends, one important ex-boyfriend who pops into her life regularly from out of town and an assortment of ambitions that occupy her time.

In her darkest moments, Toby feels that she's totally eliminated her need not only for men but for deep connections with other people. As a young teenager, she suffered from anorexia nervosa, the eating disorder that afflicts mostly young girls, in which victims go on starvation diets, sometimes reducing their bodies to near-skeletal shapes. Though Toby recovered from the malady before finishing high school, she sometimes wonders whether she's developed its emotional analog, a kind of anorexia in which she has starved herself away from the need for human nourishment. Once she visited a therapist who confirmed her suspicion. "She said I had developed down to this protective shell, rejecting everyone that came in my way."

A NEW INTEGRITY

Despite the downside, the new integrity between the sexes of the singular generation stands before us as a bold alternative to what came before. Out of the confusion of the past several decades, singulars have uncovered a new way of relating, and we have set for ourselves what we believe are more realistic, humane and sensible standards. We view members of the other sex not as opposites but as similars, not as sex objects but as sexual friends. In so doing, we can put behind us the anger, angst and disappointment between the sexes that haunted young adults during the years of our maturation.

Daniel and Julie are the couple of the eighties, two young

adults who have withdrawn—not from love, not from sex, but from the lofty, panacean promises that romance, monogamous love and marriage once offered. Like singulars throughout America, Daniel and Julie have embraced a new, true partnership of the heart and spirit.

The emergence of friendship as the operating principle for a variety of relationships from the commonplace to the most intensely passionate, from the platonic to the sexual, from relations with members of our own sex to relations with members of the other sex, coincides with the growth of singularity. It is the reflexive habit of allowing ourselves to grant others their individuality —their singularity—in all its particulars.

CHAPTER 5

The Body

THE AEROBICS FIX

One morning just over a year ago, Robert Jacobs's girlfriend challenged him to join her in her regular Saturday aerobics class. Naturally athletic, Robert assumed the class would be a pushover. But three minutes into the twenty-minute running segment of the advanced class, the Los Angeles man was on the floor, humiliated by his inability to keep up.

Robert took his poor showing not as a defeat but as a challenge to embark on a quest for true fitness; the first step of the journey was making what he now views as his most important (and just about his only) lifelong commitment—to aerobics.

"For the first time in my life since I learned how to play tennis when I was twelve years old—for the first time as an adult—I had that feeling that I'm going to conquer this," says the tall, striking twenty-six-year-old who is given to boyish enthusiasms. "I realized, 'Wow, this is a workout. This is way beyond running. This is what fitness is all about!' "

Aerobics is now a way of life for Robert. He pumps $200 a month into his two-class-a-day habit. His aerobics fix is his top priority and comes before wine, women and softball.

"I love the smell of my sweat," he says. "I don't go around

licking myself, but it comes out clean, pure, if you drink enough water. What goes in comes out."

Robert lovingly tends his exercise wardrobe the way new parents care for their baby's layette. Every day, before setting out for work, he inspects his black canvas duffel bag: two pairs of padded socks, a pair of gym shorts, sweat pants and shirt for the colder months, two fresh T-shirts (one for each class), soap, shampoo and facial astringent. Three plastic juice bottles filled with spring water are tucked into the pocket of the bag. The interior of his '81 Volkswagen Rabbit has virtually become a clubhouse locker. A drying towel is draped over the passenger seat; nylon swim trunks hug the headrest on the driver's side; fresh T-shirts are stashed in the back.

Robert's zeal has not gone unnoticed by his friends. He once made copies of a *Shape* magazine article in defense of aerobics and passed them out to his buddies. "Aerobics is a *sport!*" the headline proclaimed.

"Aerobics is for girls," his macho friends retorted.

The "boys"—a group of old high school pals—get together on weekends for softball, beer and bowling; at the end of a hard day of play, they treat themselves to dinner out. Robert leaves after softball for his 4 P.M. aerobics class and catches up with them later, as they're wrapping up dinner. He shows up in his black sweat suit, sits down and orders a glass of water. "That's all I want," he explains.

INHABITING YOUR BODY

Obsessive though it may seem, Robert's devotion to fitness reflects one of the central preoccupations of the singular generation: the body.

Singulars are body fanatics. We like to feel the burn of our muscles during exercise, to feel our hearts pumping blood and our bodies lapping up food and drink. Good health is no longer good enough; singulars believe you should love living in your body.

To really come alive, our new ethic holds that you should *seize* and inhabit your body. Mary Lou Retton excites us more than Brooke Shields does, because the 1984 Olympics gymnastics gold medalist feels so good she could almost jump out of her body.

We are a generation for whom, from an aesthetic standpoint, the importance of the body is quietly surpassing that of the face. Body beauty is something you achieve, something through which you express yourself; whereas facial beauty is something you're just born with.

Indeed, the body is to the singular generation what the head was to the hippies and flower children of two decades ago. *Somadelics,* or the revelation of the self through the body, has a grip on the imagination of our time just as *psychedelics,* or the revelation of the self through the mind, did twenty years earlier, according to T George Harris, editor-in-chief of *American Health* magazine.

Exercise is to the eighties what recreational drug use was to the sixties and seventies. It is our means of escape—and more. Back then, tokers, acidheads and drug users saw deep meaning in their avocation. Getting stoned and dropping acid were not only fun but also a statement of who they were and what they stood for; drugs were "mind-expanding", and mind travel or "tripping"—to the end of exploring the outer reaches of the psyche—was an existential pursuit.

Working out is the route to higher ground for singulars; it is our way of expanding and, in some cases, liberating our consciousness. Through fitness and regular exercise, we seek the peace of mind and soundness of spirit that come from having a body that's firm, toned and sinewy.

Our body obsession is at least in part a reaction to the insecurity of our age. By developing strong bodies, singulars build self-esteem. We fantasize that we can have exclusive dominion over our bodies, that we can make them into little fortresses—compact and streamlined on the outside and pure, strong wellsprings of energy on the inside—that can be detached from the economic and emotional vicissitudes of the world at large.

In a broader sense, we enlist our bodies in combatting feelings of powerlessness, discontent, discord and downward mobility. My generation has lost the certainty of upward mobility, of security in marriage, of the inevitability of having children or of finding happiness when we do; many of us have lost confidence in a better tomorrow. Though the world may be going to hell, we're determined to draw the line at our own bodies.

TAPPING INTO THE BODY'S POWER

Singulars are harnessing the human energy and creativity stored in the one natural resource each of us has at our disposal—our bodies—and we are doing so with more consistency than any recent generation.

The proper physical servicing of the body in the weight room, on the track or in the swimming pool is considered a necessary tool for freedom by singulars, a way of unlocking one's true potential and rhythm, like being entrepreneurial.

Singulars on the cutting edge view our newly tapped connection to our bodies with great reverence. We believe that emotional nuances can be expressed through the body, once it's properly wired and tuned.

"What I'm aspiring to do in dance is have a little ball of energy in my body and in my personality that I can bring out organically through my fingertips, in every direction," says Liz Brody, a twenty-nine-year-old Los Angeles dancer and publicist. "I want an emotional impulse integrated with a physical impulse."

The strength of the body's grip on the human spirit was borne out one day when Liz worked through a minor but irritating cramp in her neck, using a new massage technique she'd learned from a fellow dance student. "Learning how to work your body is the essence of personal freedom," she says. "The cramp was siphoning energy away from me, and when I was able to release it, I felt great."

An exerciser at a Los Angeles fitness center recently stepped out of an advanced aerobics class to take a water break.

"In the last few weeks," he said, taking a seat on the bench next to a classmate, "I've felt something I've never felt before. In the middle of the running, I feel complete relaxation." He brought his hand to his shoulder and neck, touching the rough spots beneath the gray sweat shirt. His voice was intimate, confessional. "No tension anywhere in my body," he said, as if he were achieving some kind of corporal nirvana.

It is not uncommon for those of us who take up aerobics, running or any other sport in order to make ourselves more attractive to potential sexual partners, to lose interest in the original goal in the process, becoming absorbed in a dialectic with our own flesh and blood, becoming excited by the power we are tapping into.

"Originally I thought this would make me much more attractive to women, real sexy," says Michael Albright, a twenty-eight-year-old Los Angeles advertising copywriter who signed on with aerobics in the aftermath of a breakup with his girlfriend. "But after three weeks, I realized it isn't about that at all."

What it is about is testing your mettle, building self-confidence. When Michael started, he issued himself a challenge: "If I can develop my body, I can do anything," he recalls thinking. "It's not just the way you look—though that matters—but it's your whole life, the way you deal with pain. You learn to understand that pain makes you stronger. When you *don't* stop, it makes you stronger."

By his own admission, Michael has always been a "head person," a guy whose favorite hobbies were playing piano and shooting the breeze with his friends. When confronted with problems, he was always able to dodge them, doing verbal dances around them; he made a habit of evading responsibility and pain. "In therapy, you can talk your way through things. With aerobics, you either do it or you don't."

Even those of us who do not work out regularly believe that our true identity can be distorted and disturbed when it is caged inside an unexercised body. During an especially stressful period in her professional life, New York advertising executive Rhonda Gainer lost control one night and started shouting at three of her closest friends. "It just wasn't like me," she observed later, tracing her outburst to an abstinence from exercise for a prolonged period.

THE WORKOUT AS WORK

Like just about everything meaningful in our lives (sexual friendship, partnership marriage, rewarding careers), singulars must work for our pleasures. Exercise is a disciplined and active form of recreation. A regular, even rigid, exercise regimen is no longer a rarefied pastime for the occasional sports nut but rather an integral part of a singular's routine.

The centrality of work in the lives of the singular generation has contributed to the fitness ethic. Because we work so hard during the day, we need a release after hours, one that can be counted on. We have come to see that drinking heavily does little good the morning after or in the long term; the same goes for taking drugs and indulging in wanton sex. So singulars turn to personalized fitness programs tailor-made to our interests and/or body goals.

Taking an active part in building and keeping one's body in tip-top operating condition has become an achiever's mark, a must-do of the singular generation. It is a kind of social stratifier that separates the elites from the underachievers.

"Almost everyone I know makes a determined effort to work out," says a twenty-eight-year-old New York City entrepreneur who plans to open a fitness center for choreographed exercise on the Upper West Side.

"There are one or two exceptions in our age group," her partner chimes in, "and I think it's strange."

In the women's locker room of a health club in West Hollywood, California, two young women were overheard discussing an affair of the heart. It seems that the boyfriend of one woman had just about everything—wealth, looks, a great job.

"The only thing about him," the woman groused, "is he will not work out. He flat out refuses."

Her confidante was all heart: "So you're going to have to let him go."

"Do I have a choice?" the complainant said, as if knowing full well that she doesn't.

Among singulars, taking control of your body through exercise symbolizes taking charge of your life. Having a firm, toned body indicates to others high self-esteem and high self-discipline; it shows that at some level, we are our own boss.

What's more, singulars find regular workouts vital to the quality of our real-life jobs. They help us relax and provide a kind of personal comfort zone; they contribute to the winning, upbeat persona that singulars so admire.

"Exercise affects you in a lot of ways; it makes you stronger, more self-confident, helps you succeed," says Wes Brown, owner of Brown's Nautilus Gym in Mount Airy, North Carolina.

Working out at a health club can help us build our professional network. We find that the joint work of building our biceps or the camaraderie of a round of racquetball more effectively forges personal friendships than strict business situations are capable of doing.

Staying fit parallels the steps most of us take to perform well at work. Just as we enter a profession suited to our talents, we can select an exercise program that is right for our particular needs— a routine that works out the buttocks and builds up the calf muscles or one that's strong on aerobics or agility. Our routine is something that we can do alone or in concert with others. When we throw ourselves into it, we make distinct and marked improvements against the starting point of our ability, and the results tend to correlate to the effort invested and the commitment made. Singulars *like* to work—and that includes working out—and we feel most at home there.

PREFERRED EXERCISE: GOING IT ALONE

For my generation, the preferred forms of exercise are "singular" —self-paced rather than competitive, activities that can be done alone and are not tied to the weather, the arbitrary scheduling of courts or the whims of a partner. We see ourselves as our own main competitor; we prefer to take on our personal best efforts rather than compete with an opponent.

Among singulars, exercise programs ranging from dance to trampoline aerobics to such hybrids as Jazzercize and Texercize (the former combining jazz steps with aerobics and the latter marrying country-western dance steps and aerobics) to gymnastics and running are more attractive than the old competitive standbys like racquetball, squash and tennis. The home gym is emerging as a singular favorite because we can work out at our own pace, on our own schedules and under our own roofs. In fact, sporting goods analysts say that home gyms are the latest status symbol— the gourmet kitchen of the eighties.

PLOTTING OUR PROGRESS

Singulars are unabashedly enthralled with the statistical accountings of our bodies' ability to achieve and endure—especially when these reports give any intimations of immortality. Weighing in every morning and sometimes recording that figure on a graph is a common practice, as is taking our own blood pressure and charting its path against the major movements in our lives. It seems that we would measure and chart everything that has a bearing on our health and fitness, if only we could.

Robert Jacobs recently took a fitness exam at a place called Body Dynamics, which operates out of a mobile home in Los Angeles. The test determined that Robert's vital lung capacity was 6.25 liters, or 138 percent above the normal of 4.56 liters, and that his body fat content was 10 percent, against the average American's 25 percent. Robert tosses out these facts and figures by rote, these all-important numbers having stuck in his memory.

"When you get on a scale and weigh yourself, that number is not very helpful if you want to improve the look of your body," explains Robert. The stated goals of the test center, he says, are not for you to lose weight but to lose fat.

High-Tech Fitness, a West Hollywood, California, shop specializing in state-of-the-art home gym equipment, is filled with lightweight rowing machines, the young man's barbells of the eighties, and with exercise cycles that pedal noiselessly, unlike the clankers of a generation ago. The Rolls-Royce of stationary bikes is the Dynavit Aerobitronic 30, a West German–made machine that issues a second-by-second progress report. You punch in your age, weight and sex to the computer on the handlebars, attach your index finger to a clothespinlike electronic pulse meter and start pedaling. Once you start to exercise, the computer issues an ever-changing stream of biofeedback information: heartbeat, miles per hour, oxygen absorption. And at the end of your "ride," it gives an accounting of total calories burned and cardiovascular fitness points earned.

The cost: $3,500.

"How much is your heart worth?" quips Patrick Netter, the shop's owner and author of a high-tech fitness book. "With a computerized machine, you know exactly what you're doing and if you're doing what you should be."

Sporting goods retailers are excited about the sales prospects for high-tech workout gear; most agree that this is the most rapidly growing sector of the market. Puma sells a $200 running shoe, equipped with a microprocessor that tells you how many calories you burn on a given run; you can buy a digital device to strap to your wrist that calculates how fast your heart is beating during a workout.

There is no limit to what singulars want to know about the performance and innermost workings of our bodies.

THE REGIMEN

Singulars follow exercise regimens with devotion, marking the hours of our workouts on our mental (or actual) calendars with Do Not Disturb signs. We discipline ourselves at the dinner table, heaping our plates with salads, fresh fruits and vegetables and low-calorie frozen dinners. We turn away rich foods and prohibited beverages and sometimes other pleasures of the wee hours—all for the lords of exercise discipline.

"I tend to drink on weekends only, and never alone," says Liz Brody, who dances twenty-five hours every week. So rigid is her self-discipline that Liz will refuse a champagne toast if it's given on the wrong day of the week. After all, a sip could lead to a glass. And "with only one or two glasses," she says, "I know I can't perform in top physical shape all the next day." Even coffee, once considered rather innocuous, has found its way onto her hit list. "I used to be able to drink any amount of coffee in a day. Now I drink only one or two cups."

Spending so many hours in dance class has heightened her sensitivity to food, drugs and alcohol—"pet vices" Liz once indulged in on a regular basis. Today her priorities have changed. "I'm concentrating intensely on my body right now."

Just as we enjoy plotting our progress, singulars relish putting together a fitness regimen. We use individual, step-by-step programs prescribed by exercise physiologists and written out on eight-by-eleven-inch cards, and beauty consultants' evaluations, tailor-made to each skin type and coloring. Innovative health-care programs likewise employ the checklist approach to determine and monitor one's health composite. Singulars believe that no one regimen is right for everyone, that each of us needs an individualized program.

MUSCLED BEAUTY

These days, the language of beauty comes from the language of the body. Beauty is strength, agility, grace; it encompasses musculature, trimness and tautness. The mechanics of beauty spring not from pleasing the beholder but from observing the tenets of athletics: Singulars believe that through exercise, we can actually alter our proportions, sculpt our bodies, make ourselves beautiful.

When Robin Lakoff and Raquel L. Scherr, co-authors of a recent book on the politics of beauty, questioned Berkeley undergraduates about their looks, they were surprised to find that "the overwhelming majority answered that they were beautiful or at least okay." This kind of confidence comes from only one source:

the feeling shared by singulars that you can earn your beauty marks.

"I've always been obsessed with my body," says Liz Brody, "with trying to make it perfect. I want to achieve an aesthetic line in my body and not allow fat in certain areas." When Liz relaxes with close friends, she invariably sits on the floor, working an arm, a leg or a foot, extending it in and out, in and out; it seems as natural and ordinary as watching your grandfather puffing on his pipe.

The most dramatic change in self-concept among singulars has taken place among females. A firm, toned body has replaced the anemic, underweight look of the sixties and seventies as the feminine ideal. Today *Vogue* magazine calls for fashion models who appear to work out regularly; the successful models of the eighties are taller, bustier, heavier and more muscular than were the Twiggys and Jean Shrimptons of twenty years ago.

"We are catering to women as much as men in every way possible," comments Wes Brown, the gym owner. "I think women have as much—if not more—to gain than men do. Working out with weights makes a man more of a man and a woman more of a woman."

Toned but not muscle-bound is the going look for women today, according to Wes, though he believes that before long, his female customers will go all the way and enter the body-building circuit in force. "We've got some women who, if they had the courage to compete, would be ready in no time."

Not only muscle definition but also strength is becoming increasingly important for singular women. "For women, strength is the new key element for the future," says twenty-seven-year-old Denise Austin, a Washington, D.C.–based exercise physiologist and national spokeswoman for Reebok aerobic shoes. "Men have always been strong and thought of weight equipment as part of their life," says Denise, who jumps rope at least a half-hour a day when she's on the road. She predicts that women will begin relying more and more on hand and ankle weights in their aerobic workouts.

Though the major change in body look is occurring in women, men, too, are undergoing a revolution in self-concept. They care a great deal about the look of their bodies. Indeed, in my generation, males can be (and often are) as vain about their lines and contours as are females. In part because sex has been demystified and the female body along with it, males have begun to think more about their own aesthetic. In seeking to achieve the right body look, singular males think that neither too bulky nor too wiry will do.

"There are a couple of things I want to change," says the six-foot-two-inch-tall, 174-pound Robert Jacobs. "My chest is too big. I have a short torso, which makes it hard to do a lot of extension work. I don't have good hip turnout." And though Robert is doing exercises in an attempt to remedy these perceived flaws, he adds philosophically, "You learn to work with what you have."

SELF HEALTH CARE

A key component of our body consciousness is that singulars are assuming primary responsibility for taking care of our own health. The singular generation came of age with preventive medicine, with an outpouring of information on health and nutrition and an increased awareness of the human spirit as the hidden ingredient in good health. The adoption of stress- and anger-management techniques; of high-fiber, low-cholesterol diets; salubrious eating habits and regular exercise are the carved-in-stone imperatives with which we grew up. At an early age, we learned about alcohol-, tobacco- and substance-abuse control programs. Being "good" or being "bad" to your body—and, therefore, to yourself—is straightforward stuff in the eighties.

Visits to the doctor and hospital are becoming less frequent (and sometimes prohibitively costly), and young adults are more concerned than ever about beating their bodies to the punch, that is, establishing good health practices before we are forced into it. "Wellness" is our health goal, and it cuts a sharp contrast to the prevailing attitude of our parents' day.

In the fifties and sixties, many Americans regarded their bodies as they did an automobile. You'd drive it till it went kaput, then take it to a doctor to have it fixed. Today the attitude is decidedly participatory. When we're paying a physician or another health practitioner for his or her time, we fire off questions so that next time we'll know for ourselves. We question the professional's judgment and are more likely to ask for a second opinion. We recognize the limitations of conventional medicine, the importance of such intangibles as a good belly laugh, and the fact that the doctor not only is not God but, in fact, is less important than the "patient" in the overall equation.

Many singulars have become obsessed by our own health; like sports buffs, we expand and groom our health-trivia repertoire; when we're among friends, we exchange medical tidbits and dispense advice. Self-test kits that diagnose everything from pregnancy to blood-sugar levels are selling like hotcakes.

Awareness, however, sometimes gives over into a kind of self-consciousness about ordinary daily life.

"When you see a plate of meat in front of you," remarks Eric Horvitz, a twenty-six-year-old Stanford University medical student, "you don't think how tasty this will be, you see a picture of your arteries. By now, people have heard so many media stories about how your arterial system will be clogged, that you have a second of angst and trembling when you look down at the meat."

Every time Eric enters the pharmaceutical section of a drugstore in Menlo Park, he sticks his arm into the blood-pressure machine to take a free reading. His readings have ranged from 110/52 to 131/63. When he gets lower scores, he feels good for a couple of days, and with the higher ones, just the reverse. For the most part, though, Eric feels "well endowed with health."

Liz Brody has not been sick in five years—nothing more than a sniffle every now and then that will pass with a good night's sleep, or a headache that will disappear in the course of a dance class. Her clean bill of health is something of which she is quietly proud. When her friends take ill, she'll commiserate, saying she's heard there's a bug going around. But it is really only lip-service sympathy.

"I never get sick," she admits. Her eternal wellness underscores the difference between her and her friends; their ill health reinforces her own life plan.

Liz attributes her wellness to her 363-day-a-year exercise routine, her strict vegetarian diet and her overall sense of exuberance about living in her body. "I wake up in the morning and feel power coursing through my body," she declares. "I wake up and I feel powerful."

WE ARE WHAT WE WEAR

When Jeannine Stein landed a job as assistant to the fashion editor of the Los Angeles *Herald Examiner* in the fall of '81, the UCLA senior had virtually no interest in or appreciation of clothing. Her wardrobe ranged from blue jeans to polyester tops to Top-Siders.

Before long, though, the brave new world of fashion opened up to Jeannine, and she threw herself into it. By the time she moved to the Houston *Post* as a staff writer in fashion, an expression she heard had stuck to her ribs: Don't go through your life never having worn the clothes of your age. She decided to take it to heart—and have her hair dyed purple.

"I thought, 'What the hell!' " says Jeannine, now twenty-six and society reporter for the Los Angeles *Times.* "My hairdresser loved it; I was a guinea pig. He couldn't do this on anyone else." Unfortunately, the editor-in-chief of the paper didn't share her hairdresser's enthusiasm.

"That was a rebellion against the conservatism of the town," she says, looking back.

Recently Jeannine visited her old stomping grounds, a library at UCLA where she'd shelved books during her freshman year. She spotted some of her former co-workers, still there, still wheeling the book carts, still dressed in the same baggy blue jeans and with the same long, stringy hair that she'd worn during her college years. It was a sad moment of heightened insight, a kind of time warp. As if for the first time, Jeannine realized the immense power that fashion has for saying things about people that they might not say about themselves.

"Those people had not changed," she says. "In *eight* years. If I looked the same now as I did in school, something would be definitely wrong. I would be saying, 'I'm not accepting the fact that I'm maturing, accepting more responsibility and trying to fit in with the people I work with, most of whom are older.' "

Jeannine has since restored her hair color to its natural brown, adding only a few minor blond streaks. For now, her fashion interest centers on thrift-shop-scavenged earrings, à la Cyndi Lauper; currently she owns about sixty eccentric pairs.

But Jeannine put her finger on it. In the eighties, fashion is a reflection of personal growth. It is about embracing the future, not resisting it. It is about choosing life instead of stagnation. In the sixties and the seventies, young adults used their "rags"—as they often were—to convey a different message—that they were not defined by what they put on their backs, that it was what was inside that counted.

Singulars, too, make a statement with what we wear while calling attention to one of our proudest possessions—our bodies. Children in the seventies, the singular generation grew up fashion-deprived. Blue jeans defined that decade; they were the standard dress for everything from parties to school. In becoming clothes conscious, we express a long pent-up interest in fashion, its nuances and variety.

Our reversion to fashion is no exercise in materialistic one-upsmanship. Into an otherwise deadly serious world, singulars use fashion to add joy, fun, color and even flightiness. Throwing vast amounts of money after the latest fashion is not the point. It is about expressing our individuality, our singularity, in what we wear.

A "LOOK" OF ONE'S OWN

Some argue that young adults in the eighties are not fashion leaders but followers, who merely pilfer from other decades. These critics charge that our generation has not created its unique look, in part because of our fashion illiteracy, and in part because of our weakened financial position to do the experimentation and buying that create new looks. However, the singular generation's greatest contribution to eighties fashion may well be an attitude—that being fashionable means discovering and developing our own individual look.

Indeed, experts seem to agree that the fashion leaders of today are those who can create their own look, who know themselves well enough to know what works, whose dress reflects their personalities. People who dress head-to-toe in designer clothing are considered fashion victims today.

"There's nothing worse than to see someone all Bill Blass," says Mary Rourke, a fashion writer for the Los Angeles *Times*. "Those women are held beneath contempt."

The singular ideal in fashion is to develop one's own sense of style. We are bold with accessorizing, confident enough to try the offbeat and different. A collector might wear a dozen watches on her arm, as bracelets. An artist might sculpt herself some jewelry. An athlete's wardrobe might consist entirely of activewear, including a sequin-studded sweat suit for formal wear.

"You can walk into a room and ten people can be well dressed, and wearing ten different things: from preppy, sophisticated clothing, to leather, to glorified sweat outfits," says one fashion-industry professional when asked to define the eighties. "All of them are acceptable."

Anything goes, if you feel good in it and can pull it off. Mary Rourke was recently given an early-sixties celery-green ribbed-knit pantsuit with an "absurdly wide" collar and bell-bottom pants. "It's so outrageous that it works," she says.

The one look that no longer works—even for poets and artists —is the hobo look, the scruffy street stuff. Annamarie Collins, a twenty-eight-year-old playwright from Seattle, has spiffed up her sartorial act. "I create my own look," she says, "and I stay away from styles."

Annamarie (or A.M., as she's known professionally) will typically wear a comfortable tailored cotton T-shirt, perhaps with a V neck, slacks and sneakers without socks. To make her look distinctive, she adds oddball accessories, like a pair of tacky yellow patio-party sunglasses with sparkles on the side. Annamarie found this particular gem for $1 at a local thrift shop and had them fitted with prescription lenses. For rehearsals or watching plays and movies, she found and fixed vintage forties "old-lady-type" frames.

Annamarie has visited Hollywood several times, most recently to meet with TV executives who expressed interest in turning one of her plays into a television sit-com. For business meetings, A.M. believes that "it's good to look sort of eccentric, but work at looking nice. That says something about your work." Annamarie, who is short and always considered herself homely, recently added some blond streaks to her brown hair and began using mascara, base, blusher and lipstick regularly. Her self-image has improved, along with her effectiveness in the business world.

Even for women in the professions, individual flair seems to be the going look for singulars. Whereas the "pioneer" professional women of the seventies often wore the dress-for-success uniform —a stiff navy blue business suit, white shirt and dark pumps— singular women are loosening those rigid strictures. Today's young businesswomen, especially those with confidence and verve, are expressing more softness, subtlety, variety and femininity. The neutered business-suit look of the seventies is fast becoming a period piece.

A recent model for this changing of the fashion guard came from the '84 presidential campaign, when Democratic vice presidential candidate Geraldine Ferraro was not afraid to wear bright or light colors, dresses—even red pumps and pretty jewelry. Instead of dressing like a man, she dressed like a woman—herself.

In the future, singulars can expect continued variety and greater individuality in fashion. We're Europeanizing, streamlining our wardrobes just as we are our homes: We are likely to buy fewer, better, more expensive items, clothes that are seasonless and can be worn for a long time.

The designer, like the physician, is no longer our dictator. He has been dead in that sense for over a decade. His funeral came in the early seventies, when singulars were still underage, and women said no to the "midi look," setting off a fashion revolt that is still raging.

THE STYLISH MAN

Singulars may well be the most clothes-conscious generation in recent history, in large part because our sartorial passion is shared by both sexes. Indeed, singular males are quietly waging a revolution with regard to fashion. For the first time in recent history, heterosexual men are enjoying fashion en masse, reveling in the novelty of a newfound pleasure. They are discovering the joys of fine fabric, of shopping for themselves and of self-expression through clothing. The more they work on their bodies in the gym, the more interested they become in showing them off.

Sam Orlando, a twenty-two-year-old student at Guilford College, is a confirmed clotheshorse. "If I had nothing else in the world, what I would like is good threads. The appearance you give to other people is important." One summer Sam worked at a department store near his New Jersey home and took ample advantage of the employee discount.

"If I saw something that I liked, I'd kind of rationalize buying it by saying, 'Hell, I'm never going to get this at this price otherwise. I'm buying this for a third of what it would cost other people.' " Clothing is the one material "luxury" in which the politically liberal young man indulges himself.

Experts foresee a growth in sales of clothing for men throughout the decade. And industry analysts predict growth in cosmetic sales throughout this decade and into the nineties, largely because of the influx of a new category of consumers: men. "Men's skincare products, which have never caught on before, are now a fast-growing business," reports *Forbes* magazine.

Fashion experts predict that men will soon start to experiment with evening fashions, including such "new" fabrics as brocades, jacquards and damasks. These looks may be introduced in small doses, such as a colorful evening vest or a textured floral tie.

A SECOND SKIN

In conjunction with our newfound reverence for our bodies, singulars are growing increasingly particular about what we will (and will not) wear. We want a second skin that nurtures the precious resource that it protects. Both sexes are calling for more comfort in clothing. We want nonbinding, unobtrusive garments with looser lines; natural, fleecy fabrics such as sweat shirt material and softer, podiatric shoes.

Liz Brody wears the kind of clothes that might make another native New Yorker shudder in distaste. She runs around Los Angeles often wearing little more than leotards; she may throw on a vest, a miniskirt or maybe even jewelry, in a nod to a given occasion. But on the basic item, she refuses to compromise. Clothing, to her, is an intensely personal matter, and occasionally she's butted heads to defend her principles.

While working full-time at a public relations agency, Liz refused to dress in a "more businesslike" manner, as was suggested by her boss. "I'd do almost anything they asked—no lunch break, no personal phone calls—but not that." In the end, her boss continued to gripe, but Liz was so skilled and capable at her job that she could not fire her. Once during lunch break, the boss took Liz shopping for suitable clothes. Liz politely accepted them but put them at the back of her closet, wearing them only occasionally.

Athlete/musician Vinx DeJonParrette, wears sports clothing almost exclusively. It is his professional attire in his job as a private trainer to actors, entertainers and the wealthy. But even at recording or jam sessions, he wears a two-piece suit of black parachute material, red high-top sneakers and perhaps a yellow cycling cap from Italy. His clothes are his second skin, stuff he can sweat in, an extension of his body.

THE PITFALLS OF FITNOMANIA

Fitness fever, when carried too far, can have a deleterious effect on our ability to relate to others; it can lead to emotional isolation. Fitnoholism is already presenting itself as a body/mind infirmity of the singular generation. The craving for an endorphin-induced high, best known as runner's high, can become overwhelming, to the point at which nothing else matters.

"Exercise is a drug," says Liz Brody. "If I don't get exercise, my chemistry is messed up. I can't sleep. I don't feel good." In fact, Liz frets in advance over those two or three days a year when she won't get her kinetic fix. "I have to prepare mentally for Christmas and New Year's," she says, when all the dance studios shut down.

Liz has even developed a coping technique for flying cross country; she will stay up the night before so that she'll sleep on the plane. If she didn't, the confinement of the flight cabin and her inability to move around would drive her batty.

The most fanatical of fitnophiles can worry more about making the right connection with their own bodies than about encroaching disengagement from fellow human beings.

Reporting for *Esquire* magazine on one of Manhattan's fashionable workout centers, the Vertical Club, Gay Talese notes a new indifference between the sexes. The men and women "rarely pause long enough to speak" to each other, he writes. The women, outfitted in form-fitting leotards and "stretched out on the machines and the floor in every sexual position of the 'Kamasutra,' " are playing "their own private game of body solitaire." And when the men in the locker rooms discuss the women out there on the floor, they do so "without affection or strong desire."

Michael Albright turned to exercise to make his body more attractive to females, but found that his interest in women diminished. "You can fall into your body and not *think* anymore," he says. Michael has spotted the problem in himself and is trying to make amends. "I'm trying to draw a balance between work, the emotional, the spiritual and the intellectual."

Eating disorders are a kind of inversion of the singular generation's preoccupation with the body. First anorexia nervosa, in which victims starve themselves, came to the fore in the seventies, and then bulimia nervosa, in which victims regularly vomit their food, followed in its wake.

The bulimia phenomenon, said to be the more common of the two, is especially strong on the nation's campuses today. Unlike anorexia, bulimia can be learned. At UCLA, maintenance workers have installed signs in the dorm rest rooms reading, Please don't induce vomiting—you are ruining our plumbing. And dentists are becoming alarmed by permanent damage to the teeth through the staining effects of hydrochloric acid in vomit, which erodes the enamel on the inner surface of the teeth.

"The key word to bulimia is *control,*" says Jill Carni, an eating-disorders counselor and specialist in Cambridge, Massachusetts. "A woman who feels out of control in her life takes rigid control of food intake. She sees it as control, even though the disease can control you."

Bingeing and purging is not the only form of bulimia; just the most common. Some bulimics binge and then fast, or binge and then put themselves on a mean-spirited diet. Some try to purge by gorging on diuretics and laxatives. A fraction of sufferers, including a disproportionate number of males, eat heavily and purge through excessive exercise. (Men tend to be closet bulimics, as they are more reluctant than women to seek help.)

Some health practitioners believe that the fitness boom has inadvertently triggered a greater incidence of eating disorders. "The media and our culture have pushed the perfect body for so long," says Marjorie Greenhut, co-director of a Santa Monica, California, comprehensive eating-disorder program called ESTEEM (short for Empower Self Through Education & Eating Management). "And the move toward fitness has brought it more to the front."

BODY HEAT

Singulars make commitments to our bodies and therefore to ourselves at a time when making permanent commitments to others is less attractive to us. As we've become less dependent on sexual relationships, we've become more dependent on exercise as a regular means of igniting and enjoying our bodies.

But we must grapple with the narcissism that has been unleashed by our newfound obsession with the body. While recent generations may have underestimated the tremendous powers of the body, the singular generation is in danger of overestimating them, of receding into our shells when the world's problems loom too large.

Our commitment to our bodies is, for the most part, an invigorating development. It enlivens our spirits and promises to prolong our lives. It injects energy, self-confidence and even passion into our other endeavors. We are perhaps the first generation who, when we turn thirty, are likely to sport bodies that can still pass for those of teenagers'.

The fit are out in force in the singular generation. This "discovery" of the body has unleashed a new energy, a new vitality that's spreading to all corners of society. Fitness helps us bridge the gap between body and mind, as science continues documenting their interrelatedness; and while we're at it, we gain greater self-knowledge. The process is what excites us, learning that we can work through the pain of a workout and come out stronger at the other end, seeing and feeling a direct correlation between effort and result. This voyage into our own bodies is a personal and supremely singular saga.

CHAPTER 6

Political Hybrids

POLITICAL FREE AGENTS: AN EMERGING IDENTITY

The singular generation is cutting a new political figure, one that stands in sharp contrast to the liberal, even leftist, politics of youth that have commanded center stage off and on for the past five decades. Without a doubt, young Americans have participated in—even promoted—the rightward political shift of the 1980s. But while we have been conveniently labeled Young Conservatives by the news media and others, in fact, singulars are far more complex. We are a hybrid of traditional opposites: conservative and liberal, right wing and left wing, self-interested and selfless. We are Republican-Democrats, Democratic-Republicans: individualistic independents.

Singulars are political free agents—political consumers, if you will, without strong brand loyalties. When we vote, we believe in choosing the best person for the job without regard to party affiliation, sex, race or religion. We try to make considered decisions about political issues, to see both sides and to travel the middle of the road. We are born-again patriots who grew up at a time when America took some drubbings: from Vietnam, from the presidential impeachment proceedings, from economic and political forces abroad. Cross-bred between two political eras, singulars are attuned to the voices of a solid past and an uncertain future.

"I do not have any political affiliation," says Mike Walter, the twenty-eight-year-old Seattle attorney. "Although I would tend to vote more Republican than Democrat, I vote for the individual."

My generation grew up with the decline of party politics and with the ascent of media-shaped political campaigns. We grew up with the decline of the politics of conscience and the ascent of the politics of special interests. Singulars developed a solid base of skepticism and wariness about politicians and the system but, at the same time, a strong need to believe in our country, to find and feel national strength, to put Richard Nixon's impropriety, Gerald Ford's bumbling and Jimmy Carter's vacillation behind us.

We are at once one of the most liberal generations in American history—with regard to the social agenda—and a reactionary one when it comes to shedding the excesses of our Great Society past. We are the shining embodiment of the sixties, children of that decade who were taught and learned how to love one another right now. We are the most *tolerant* generation in American history, vis-à-vis racial, ethnic and religious minorities. We overwhelmingly favor rights for women, having folded the lessons of feminism into our childhood systems of justice. We are aware of the special needs of the elderly, the disabled, the disadvantaged, and Third Worlders, who have moved into our own backyard. But our methods differ from those of our forebears of the sixties and seventies: We are more subdued, more diplomatic, more modest. We do not endorse radical measures and didactic rhetoric to promote our ideas. Some of us entirely opt out of the political arena.

In general, we are liberal on social matters but conservative on fiscal ones. We do not, for instance, buy the notion of government as the great equalizer. We do not believe in tax-and-spend policies that unfairly burden the middle class. Many of us are skeptical about affirmative action, comparable worth and job-hiring and college-placement quotas for minorities and women. The misapplication of these programs could shunt some well-qualified individuals into the "disadvantaged" position; we do not believe in making white males society's scapegoats. We instinctively understand the complexity of social change and the importance of individual initiative in achieving it.

"Life was simpler in the sixties," Tom Hayden remarked on a

recent "Today Show" special on campus youth. When asked about the apparent lack of political activism on the part of today's students, the sixties youth leader, antiwar protester and current California assemblyman said, "Apathy is a surface condition over a deep anxiety about the future."

Since the drive to achieve on a personal level is the very essence of being singular, our generation's political priorities lie in protecting and enhancing our individual rights. Just as our predecessors twenty years ago railed against the government that was compelling them to go to war, singulars would like to shed any restrictive economic baggage and bureaucratic red tape that inhibit our chances for success in the world of work. If in any way we can reshape America, we would like to get rid of our "debtornation" status, to reduce the foreign trade deficit and the national deficit—all of which threaten us with economic strangulation; we would like to reduce our tax rates and restore the nation's economy to a point at which the incentive to start new businesses and to behave entrepreneurially would be stronger.

SINGULAR INTERESTS

Our emerging political persona in large part derives from our economic position in society. During our economy's rocky transition from a manufacturing base to one centered on information and services, young Americans are bearing a disproportionate share of the nation's economic woes: in employment, in taxation, in the cost of living. From an economic standpoint our youth is not an unblemished gift. Singulars feel we must act now to protect our interests, before our assets are mortgaged out from under us.

Our interests have been encroached upon by a number of parties. The most egregious offender is the federal government, whose enormous deficit will have to be repaid by us and our progeny through the nose, in compounded interest. Currently our government's deficit is $215 billion. According to figures supplied by Americans for Generational Equity (AGE), for every dollar borrowed by the U.S. government today, at current interest rates,

taxpayers will end up repaying almost $24 in interest over the
next thirty years.

"It's just like if you go out with your kid's credit card and you
charge up all the nice things you ever wanted to have, and the bill
doesn't come to you," says Paul Hewitt, president of the Washington, D.C.–based AGE, a public education and research group
concerned with the problems of young Americans. "It goes to
somebody else, later on. Somebody's got to pay it. There's no such
thing as a free lunch."

An enormous share of the federal budget—about a third—goes
to Social Security payments, Medicare payments and other federal
retirement programs. Automatic Social Security cost-of-living in-
creases, or COLAs, were passed by Congress in 1972, as older
Americans gained unprecedented political clout. Though they
were designed to protect the income of the elderly, they've had the
effect of increasing the real income for the growing senior population vis-à-vis the rest of society. The median real income of young
workers has declined since the early seventies as taxes sharply
increased. In 1986, self-employed wage earners will pay a whopping *12.3 percent* of our income, up to $42,000, in Social Security
taxes. For the employed, Social Security payroll taxes are 7.15
percent. (The employer also pays this amount.) These regressive
Social Security taxes hit low-income workers the hardest.

These COLA payments have had the effect of transferring a
sizable share of the wealth from one generation to the next, as
today's workers strongly subsidize the retirement of the elderly.
When today's sixty-five-year-olds were entering the job market
between 1937 and 1949, the maximum annual Social Security tax
was $30 a year, or 1 percent of earnings up to $3,000. In 1956, the
tax for Social Security was 2.25 percent of income up to $4,200, or
a maximum of $94.50; in 1966, workers paid 4.2 percent on a base
income of $6,600 for a maximum tax of $277.20. In 1976, taxpayers paid 5.85 percent of Social Security tax on an earnings base of
$15,300, or a maximum of $895.05 per year. In 1986, 12.3 percent
of our incomes—either directly, or shared with an employer—
goes to pay Social Security taxes, and it's scheduled to continue
increasing.

For evidence of this redistribution of wealth along generational lines, one need only look at the age distribution of poverty. Since the early seventies, the number of elderly living below the poverty line has decreased dramatically, while the number of young adults, teenagers and children living below the poverty line has shot way up. The new disadvantaged of the eighties are the young; the least fortunate among the singular generation are the new "youngerly."

"Today the federal government is playing a version of Robin Hood in a way that is only dimly understood," writes Terry W. Hartle of the American Enterprise Institute in Washington, D.C. "Many programs that benefit the nation's youth are being cut as programs that help older generations are being protected."

While in the past, government has borrowed against the future, assuming that the economy would be better tomorrow than it is today, this assumption is no longer valid. Yet the borrow-and-spend policies, which have been pinned on the liberal Democrats, have risen meteorically under Reagan; this is an ironic development considering that Reagan's credo of fiscal restraint helped him win the presidency. "We're still playing the politics of affluence," explains Hewitt.

While the federal deficit is probably our most daunting problem, it is not our only one. A variety of factors contribute to the short hand of cards dealt the singular generation.

Perhaps the most consistent and disturbing trend we've experienced is that of younger workers losing out to older workers in a variety of ways. During the last decade, the unemployment rate for young adults has remained consistently higher than that of older workers, and no change is expected anytime soon. The "safety net" of unemployment benefits has shriveled to the point that in late 1985, only one in four unemployed persons was receiving them—a record low in the last two decades. Job prospects for new college graduates have been steadily drying up since the mid-seventies, with experts characterizing the outlook throughout this decade as bleak.

We are the last hired and the first fired. Because young workers earn lower wages and depend to a greater extent on earned income than do older Americans, the loss of a job hits us harder. What's more, two-tier wage systems that protect the earnings of workers with seniority at the expense of the newly hired have been catching on nationwide. In a two-tier wage system, new workers are hired at a lower rung of salary and benefits than those who are already aboard, and, in many cases, they can never hope to bridge the gulf.

"We think two-tiered wage systems ought to be outlawed," says Paul Hewitt. "If we adopted a two-tier wage system for women, minorities or other ethnic groups, everyone would be outraged. But when we do it for our 'children,' nobody pays any attention."

Housing, for both rental and purchase, is taking a bigger and bigger bite out of our paychecks. No relief is in sight in the price of homes; in many cases, it's impossible for us to afford the houses in which we grew up.

Some social observers have gone so far as to forecast the demise of the middle class in the United States, with the newest arrivals on the scene—the young—being the least likely to break into the "club."

Today young Americans share the common mission of protecting our economic rights and our future. As the eighties unfold and the nineties approach, young adults are starting to recognize our collective interests. AGE is the first group of its kind, but others are likely to spring up, borrowing their methods from such effective special-interest groups as the American Association of Retired Persons (AARP) and the National Association for the Advancement of Colored People (NAACP).

While the singular generation has taken a great deal of flak for our flight from liberal-era politics, it is not really surprising, once you realize that "liberal-era," "tax-and-spend," "borrow-and-spend" policies—which the Reagan Administration has accelerated rather than slowed—no longer serve our interests; in both the short-term and the long-term, they appear to be defeating them.

THE APPEAL OF THE CONSERVATIVE IMAGE

Kevin Hogan is one of the new singular hybrids. An avowed Republican conservative, Kevin moved to Los Angeles from Pittsburgh two months before the 1984 presidential election and set right to work as a "get-out-the-vote" telephone canvasser for President Reagan's reelection campaign. In Reagan, Kevin found a real-life hero.

"My impressions of the Democratic party were formed through the four years of Carter's presidency," says Kevin, who comes from a family of Democratic steelworkers, "and they were negative ones. So then I see this Ronald Reagan, riding up on his horse, with this big image of 'I'm coming to save the country.' Right away this is something I could go for."

So far, so conservative. But one look at Kevin's personal life shows it is nothing if not liberal new age. While studying drama and voice in a small college in Pittsburgh, Kevin met Pamela Wood, an aspiring dancer and model. She has been the woman in his life for exactly a year now, the live-in lover with whom he moved West. Pamela is three years older than he, and she is black.

The peaceful coexistence of Kevin and Pamela's life-style and their politics is key to the mind-set of this generation of young Americans. Social freedoms for us are a matter of course. The fundamentals of feminism, minority rights and the sexual revolution are so entrenched in our belief systems that they have become nonissues.

"People my age coming up have no experience with the outright prejudice of the earlier generations," Kevin says. Because such practices as interracial dating and sex before marriage are no longer forbidden or even particularly controversial, we have turned our attention to economic advancement and opportunity—not for minorities or ethnic groups, but for ourselves.

Like many young adults, Kevin and Pamela have adopted the mantle of conservatism in large part because they want to be on the winning team. Conservatism has gained luster from its association with wealth and privilege, with success and security at a time when our feelings of weakness and insecurity are gaping. At the same time, the liberal label has become tarnished and altogether unappealing. To us, liberals appear to be trying to suck the last drops of blood from the once-accommodating stone of society. In an unsingular, unselfsufficient manner, liberals are thought to look to government to solve problems and correct injustices that are beyond government's power to control. Liberals seem like individuals who dwell on—even celebrate—their victimhood.

The conservative label appeals to my generation because we do not want to be victims or victimized; because we are terrified about the future and would, therefore, like to keep things as they are. Singulars are preservationists who subject any proposed change in the status quo to sharp questioning. We dress neatly; we wash our cars frequently; we try not to quarrel with our parents; we try not to make a point of ourselves. What's more, conservatism seems like a fresh new look in politics after the relentless liberalism of the sixties and the seventies. But merely wearing the uniform of conservatism and speaking the party line does not a conservative make.

LATENT LIBERALISM

Once you begin to examine the position of singulars on the issues, you find that our conservatism is only skin-deep.

Young adults between the ages of eighteen and thirty are "the most liberal generation in American history on the issues of human rights, the libertarian notions of not wanting to impose one's values on others," says Stephen L. Klineberg, professor of sociology at Rice University in Houston. "There's a support for diversity, freedom of lifestyle and individual choice that's a continuation of a trend that's been going on in American society for two hundred years."

Klineberg draws his opinions from the results of an annual wide-ranging survey of Houstonians, funded by the Houston *Post* and the American Leadership Forum. According to Klineberg, Houston is a bellwether city with a representative mix of the nation's racial minorities and religious and ethnic groups. The city experienced boom growth in the seventies and early eighties and then went bust in 1983, when oil prices collapsed and unemployment rose to the highest level since the Great Depression.

The survey's results reveal a population increasingly identifying itself as conservative, while holding positions on the issues that tell another story. This paradox was especially pronounced among those in the eighteen-to-twenty-nine-year-old age group. Results show that 41 percent of the survey's youngest respondents identified with the "conservative" political label, while just 19 percent placed themselves in the "liberal" camp. (The remaining 40 percent identified themselves as "moderates.") And a greater number of respondents identified themselves as either Republican or leaning in the Republican direction than as Democratic or leaning in the Democratic direction.

But when the survey queried these same respondents on specific issues, support was widespread for traditionally progressive or liberal positions. For instance, 60 percent of those polled say that government is spending "too little" on "improving the conditions of the poor." Sixty-eight percent agree that "protecting the environment is so important that continuing efforts must be made, regardless of cost." Seventy-two percent support "a federal law requiring the registration of all handguns." Seventy-two percent favor "regulations on smoking in public places." Eighty percent favor the United States agreeing to a "nuclear freeze" with the Soviet Union. Eighty-seven percent support "efforts to strengthen women's rights in society." And 89 percent favor the teaching of sex education in the public schools.

These classically "liberal" positions were endorsed by a majority, in some cases an overwhelming majority, of those questioned. Assuming that these young Houstonians are representative of young adults throughout the nation, the results would indicate that my generation is not conservative in the classic sense; indeed, we are liberal in our responses to a variety of matters, from social issues to international politics. When we call ourselves conservative, it is because our style and our sense of self has changed: We believe in supporting America rather than undermining it; we want to be in sync with the mainstream of society rather than stand in opposition to it.

This paradox is most striking when it comes to my generation's apparent endorsement of Ronald Reagan. In 1984, voters from the ages of eighteen to twenty-five gave our nod to the President in numbers slightly greater than that of the general electorate. However, our infatuation with the President has little to do with embracing a rightist social philosophy. Indeed, many of Reagan's staunchest young supporters will have no part of his conservative social agenda.

"I'm pro-ERA, pro-choice regarding abortion," says Gary Grossman, a twenty-year-old from the Chicago suburb of Glencoe, Illinois, who cast his first vote in a presidential election for Reagan in 1984. "I feel there is no reason in the world anyone should be forced to have a child they couldn't afford to raise." Despite Reagan's antiabortion stance, Gary voted to reelect the President because he approves of Reagan's handling of the economy. Gary, who is studying to be a certified public accountant, believes the country's economic well-being is more important than any other single issue.

During the election campaign, even Reagan's election team seemed to concede that many of its youthful supporters might not buy the entire conservative agenda. "Realistically the young people today are going to be a different kind of voter, in the sense that they may not agree on all the social programs of the president," said Ed Rollins, Reagan's '84 campaign director, in an interview in *The Prouder-Stronger Times,* a paid advertising supplement prepared for the nation's major college newspapers. "My estimation is that the young voter [sic] are going to become more and more conservative on fiscal policy and foreign policy, and probably a little more libertarian on the social issues."

A nonpartisan survey indicates that young Americans are increasingly seeing themselves as less liberal, not more conservative. "The American Freshman: National Norms for Fall 1985" report, based on an annual nationwide survey of some 250,000 full-time entering students conducted jointly by UCLA and the American Council of Education, shows that new freshmen have not embraced a conservative political philosophy.

Rather, over a fifteen-year period from 1970 to 1985, the most significant shift in student self-identification has been from the liberal or far left categories to the middle-of-the-road designation. In 1970, 45.4 percent of all students considered themselves moderates, but this number had leaped to *56.7* percent by *1985.* Clearly the moderate, not the conservative, political point of view is on a long-term growth curve.

A DECLINE IN ACTIVISM

Probably the most important political benchmarks do not come from political identifications, which by their generalized nature are almost inherently ambiguous and imprecise. Rather, they come from gauging the level of political activism and feeling among the young.

At many college campuses, political activism is minimal. Many of us are simply too preoccupied about our grade point averages, our college scholarships and loans, our summer internships and job prospects to give time to political causes. For some, it's not that we don't care; it's just that we believe that the best way to further our political interests is to gain a foothold in the world of work. That will put us in a position to contribute financially to causes that we support; it will also help us gain the real-world, workaday expertise needed to succeed in the political realm. Others do not think they can make a difference and therefore opt out.

"The American Freshman" report shows that political activism is down. According to the 1984 report, first-year students are increasingly reluctant to become actively involved in political and social issues. Among 1984 freshmen, only 8.9 percent indicated that they had worked in a political campaign during the previous year, as compared to 14.1 percent in 1970 who participated in a local, state or national political campaign. (The question was dropped in the 1985 questionnaire.)

"If politics continues as usual, youth will be more 'alienated' in the future," says Curtis Gans of the Washington, D.C.–based Committee for the Study of the American Electorate. "I don't like the word 'apathetic,' because I think youth makes choices." Withdrawal, he says, is a conscious choice. An election offering two distinct *positive* alternatives would be the best way to draw young voters back from their flight.

Even among students at the predominantly black Agricultural and Technical University in Greensboro, North Carolina, where in 1960 the Boston Tea Party of the civil rights movement occurred, political activism has slowed to a virtual standstill. On February 1, 1960, four young black students sat in at the nearby Woolworth's lunch counter to protest its dehumanizing whites-only service policy; this act of civil disobedience captured national headlines and helped ignite the movement across America.

Two and a half decades later, the students at A&T dress in designer knit shirts and pressed jeans or slacks and wear their hair close-cropped; many hold part-time jobs to save for after graduation and to pay tuition bills. Their first concerns are in getting good jobs. Few are active in political causes. The only issue abuzz on campus during a recent visit was a protest on behalf of coed visitation rights in the dormitories.

"When Jesse Jackson first said he was going to run for president, it kind of shocked me," says Sam Warren, a black sophomore majoring in business and computer science. Sam supported Jackson's bid for the Democratic presidential nomination in 1984 and estimated that 80 percent of his fellow students at A&T were behind the university's most famous alumnus. However, Sam was not devastated when Jackson lost; in fact, the Democrat from Detroit took it all rather philosophically. "The United States is not ready for a black president yet."

Sam seems to understand that change is a gradual process, and he seems not to resent this. "Blacks were nobody, and it wasn't too long ago that they were nobody. Now we are a struggling group of people. . . . Until we get to the top of our struggle, we're not ready to take on an office like that." Fifteen years from now, Sam says, Jackson would have a better chance of winning. In taking this moderate position, Sam puts distance between himself and black radicals of the past who demanded change *now*. While he does not reject their goals, he views their methods as unrealistic.

Many of the most politically progressive singulars are similarly reluctant to tie their hopes to pie-in-the-sky political campaigns and crusades. Sometimes just joining or participating in a political cause, even if we believe in it, can be too much to ask.

"I'm not involved in any activist organizations on campus at this moment," says twenty-one-year-old Lisa Wedeen, a political science major at University of California at Berkeley specializing in Arab politics. "I don't feel that belonging to the El Salvador Committee does much good. It's a much more complex thing than just belonging; it requires revamping our life-style to save El Salvador."

"I feel a little embarrassed at my lack of enterprise," admits Mia Kissil, a student at Guilford College. Currently the nineteen-year-old is simply too involved in her studies to go out and rally, much less to spend the time needed to develop informed political opinions. "I've got a whole lot of studies I want to do, a lot of work to do to get where I want to go." Her goal: medical school.

Singulars like Lisa and Mia sometimes flagellate themselves for not being the political animals they imagine they should be. However, it's important to remember that we are following in the footsteps of an extraordinary era in youth politics, one in which the level and intensity of activism reached a fever pitch. Two decades ago, politics was poetry for vital young adults; it was also fashionable, meaning that some of its practitioners lacked conviction and depth. Singulars may be circumspect, even cautious about political involvement; we are not often hasty or ill-considered in our judgments.

"Are people forever going to be asking me, 'Why aren't students as radical as in the sixties?' " wonders James Forman, Jr., the nineteen-year-old son of one of that decade's most dynamic black activists: James Sr., the former executive secretary of the Student Nonviolent Coordinating Committee. James Jr., himself now an activist at Brown University, bemoans the fate of living in the shadow of that era. "Let's compare us to students of the 1940s, fifties, seventies," he says. "If you look at those decades, there are as many, if not more, student activists on campus today."

THE POLITICS OF PRAGMATISM

Those singulars who are committed to political activism are arguably more effective than were our predecessors of the sixties and early seventies. We understand that the world is too ungainly to budge much. A streak of political pragmatism runs through my generation, as we increasingly devote ourselves to mainstream rather than radical-fringe politics. Instead of fighting for such abstract goals as brotherly love and universal disarmament, we devote ourselves to single-issue campaigns and local politics, like saving a park, funding a preschool lunch program or lobbying for a particular foreign policy initiative.

We take our cue from the world of work, where you must learn the rules of the game before you can succeed at it. We try to practice the politics of pragmatism rather than the politics of pure passion.

Unlike social activists of two decades ago, Jeb Brugmann, the twenty-six-year-old director of the Cambridge (Mass.) Commission on Nuclear Disarmament and Peace Education, has learned that he must meet those he is trying to influence on their turf— with reason and without bitter, accusatory rhetoric. Though Jeb is basically a T-shirt and baggy blue jeans kind of guy, he wears a suit when meeting with business and community leaders whom he would like to win over. This way he establishes a comfort zone, thus enhancing his chances of persuading them that it's in every businessman's interest to work not only to stop the nuclear buildup but to "build down" our nuclear arsenal.

"I'm serious about getting the job done," he explains. "I'm not interested in blocking any options." Jeb is critical of those who talk a good game about effecting social change but unconsciously undermine their efforts with a defeatist attitude or by making a point of their existential angst. "I have friends who have committed their lives to political change. But they don't have a positive vision of the world without nuclear arms. They are effective organizers, but they are whiny, and people do not relate to them as they could."

Activists like Jeb are result-oriented, singular in our approach to political work. We have cast off—and moved beyond—many of the methods of the sixties and seventies. We are not out to stretch the imaginations of those we meet, to confront their politics or to shake up psyches; we genuinely want to make a difference. Singulars don't go in for exercises in futility or preaching to the converted.

"You can write a petition," says Don Halliburton, who works in sales and marketing for a resort hotel in Baja California and is a strong opponent of nuclear power and weaponry. "You can hold hands around a nuclear power plant, but that doesn't make an impact. Who listens to mass demonstrations? They just opened up Diablo Canyon (a nuclear power plant), for chrissakes. People need their power, their electricity. Big corporations make the decisions."

When working on a political project, the singular style decrees that we be politic, even if that cuts against our grain, even if it means restraining our emotions.

"When some visitors come into the museum, it's real hard not to speak your mind," comments Barbara Lawrence, a spunky twenty-six-year-old museum tour guide on the eight-thousand-acre Suquamish–Port Madison Indian reservation on Seattle's Puget Sound. "It's a big decision for me to make, on an individual basis, when a person asks a political question. 'Okay, do I get on my soapbox now?' I have to bite my tongue. I really have to have the tribe's interest at heart."

Barbara's tongue gets bruised some days when questions and comments from the public are stupid, or worse.

"Strangers come in and say, 'Well, you don't look Indian,' " says Barbara, a vital, personable mother of three who is herself half-Indian. (Her mother is of Norwegian origin.) Though Barbara's commitment to the tribe is her life passion, the genetic pool failed to confer on her the characteristic dark skin and hair. "That one always gets me. I had some guy come in and tell me if I just wore some buckskin and feathers and beads, my comments would be more valid because he'd feel like he was talking to a real Indian."

Instead of telling off people like this, Barbara will move her lecture tour along and try to take such remarks in good humor. The former welfare recipient does not want to let herself become distracted from her main objective: grooming her political polish and reputation so that someday she can become a tribal leader.

"I know that I can represent my peer group on tribal council and that when I finish my education, I'll be somebody that they need." Barbara has been passionate about the Suquamish tribe since junior high school, when she was elected president of the Indian Club. "Politically, I just can't sit back and read about it. I have to be out there."

Among the issues Barbara would like to work on in the future are protecting the indigenous salmon population whose runs have been endangered by non-Indians; improving the medical care and quality of education on the island; encouraging young tribal members to complete high school and to find steady and fulfilling employment.

Media savvy helped John Carlson further his conservative political objectives. The Republican activist from Seattle spent his teen and college years cultivating his journalistic skills. He and a partner interviewed a wide variety of national political figures, including columnist Jack Anderson, Nelson Rockefeller, Jesse Jackson and Ronald Reagan, for a self-published newspaper supplement and later a local television show.

In 1982, John applied his media knowledge to the founding of a conservative newspaper, *The Washington Spectator,* at his alma mater, the University of Washington. "We wanted to prove that a respectable, credible, conservative newspaper can thrive and be accepted by students and even professors on a liberal campus."

The paper, an alternative to the *UW Daily,* was seeded by a $2,200 grant from a private foundation sponsoring conservative campus newspapers nationwide. It has given John and his colleagues a forum for their viewpoints and a chance to develop their right-wing perspective, along the lines of such heroes as William F. Buckley, Jr., Irving Kristol, Norman Podhoretz and Benjamin Stein. "The reason I could probably be described as a conservative," John says, "is that I think when government is involved in solving a problem, it should be involved at the most local level possible. Because that's where government is most sensitive to the public. Bureaucracy just gets on my nerves."

In 1984, John ran for the state assembly in west Seattle's thirty-fourth district and was narrowly defeated. He has now joined the private sector but continues to contribute to the *Spectator* and occasionally the Seattle *Times.* For example, John wrote an article indicting the movie *The Killing Fields* for its purported liberal, anti-American view of the Cambodian revolution.

As one of the organizers of Brown Divest–Free South Africa, Brown University sophomore James Forman, Jr., is similarly result-oriented. James and fellow organizers are concerned with a number of social problems, including third world issues and American involvement in Central America. But they choose to focus on ending apartheid in South Africa, in large part because the timing is right.

"We saw a national divest movement beginning and we wanted to join," James states. "At universities around the country, the pace was quickening; there were protests in front of the South African embassy in Washington, those types of things. We decided that Brown University, long a home of political activism, should be a big mover in this."

Despite a sense of urgency about divestment, the leaders took their time getting organized before jumping into the fray. In the spring of '85, the core group devoted itself to "the groundwork you have to take care of before you get a movement going. We met with the treasurer, had an educational forum." In the summer of '85, the Atlanta native traveled to Chicago to participate in a national student conference on South Africa. They wanted to cover all bases before plunging in.

The group, which consists of forty active members and thousands of supporters on whom to call for demonstrations, has managed to persuade the university to partially divest its portfolio. By fall of 1985, Brown had divested itself of companies doing business in South Africa that had not signed the "solvent principles" drawn up by the group. Now Brown Divest is lobbying the university to drop holdings of *all* companies doing business in South Africa.

James does not inflate the importance of his role in making Brown a "big mover" in the antiapartheid movement; neither does he exaggerate Brown Divest's sphere of influence. "I'm not here to say that we can affect what goes on in the world, but we as students can affect our universities. We're not talking about quantum leaps in logic; we're talking small steps."

Small steps is all that most politically involved singulars strive to take. Ours is not a politics of radicalism and revolution, but of small steps, of delayed gratification.

The character of our political drive has also changed. James is not fueled by righteous anger; things are not that simple anymore. "There are a lot of things I'm angry about," he says, "but I'm not *consumed* with anger. I don't think the best way to change those things is to be angry, with a tear-down-the-city approach. I don't think that's going to work in this decade. We have to challenge the system and work within the power structure."

A mitigation of the injustices against blacks, minorities and women has curbed the anger level of two decades ago. "It's much more difficult to talk about racism today," says James, whose father is black and mother is white. "It's more subtle. There's not legalized segregation in Atlanta like there was when my father and mother were working there. People may be angry at their life, that it's not better, but . . . it's difficult to vent that anger at a particular institution."

The indisputable though qualified success of many of the social crusades of the last twenty years has drawn singulars closer to the center and has ushered in the politics of pragmatism, in which each of us decides and negotiates our own issues. In a sense, the singular generation has "lowered" our political sights to more accessible horizons; in another sense, we have come of age politically, at a younger age.

BORN-AGAIN PATRIOTISM

Young adults have rediscovered patriotism, which goes hand in hand with our attraction to the conservative style, our middle-of-the-road political bent and our pragmatic approach to problem-solving. We put pro-American bumper stickers on our cars, wave and display flags year-round and make Bruce Springsteen's "Born in the U.S.A." our anthem of youth. We purchase American-made products when we can and respond to Madison Avenue advertising campaigns that employ American symbols and motifs to peddle everything from ice cream to designer clothing. Military service has become desirable to many of us, and increasingly competitive. The appeal of patriotism is in part a reaction to the anti-American excesses of the sixties, but it is also a response to some very real changes in the reception, perception and clout of the United States abroad.

Growing up, singulars weathered our country's defeat in Vietnam, the Arab oil embargo, the Iranian hostage crisis, the Beirut massacre and the proliferation of anti-American terrorism worldwide. We have come to see that in the global arena, our country is as likely to lose as to win, that America is no longer a shining beacon of liberty and enlightenment in the eyes of much of the world but is all too often a kind of rich-kid whipping boy. We find such treatment both terrifying and undeserved. The last generation drove home the point that America had betrayed its ideals around the world, in many cases carrying their criticism to an extreme. Singulars, by contrast, seek to defend America, despite its acknowledged flaws.

To singulars, patriotism has become synonymous with free enterprise and, in some cases, protectionism; it has come to stand for feeling good about ourselves. Patriotism is a collective means of bolstering our flagging national—and personal—self-esteem.

Debbie Fleming York, a twenty-nine-year-old sales clerk at an upscale dress shop in Mount Airy, North Carolina, pulls garments from the racks for customers and, as a selling point, exclaims, "Made in the U.S.A.!" When Debbie shops for herself, her husband and her nine-year-old daughter, she favors products manufactured domestically.

Singulars like Debbie think that our country needs all the support it can get. "I have always been a patriotic person," says Debbie, a registered Democrat. "I've always thought, 'Let's help the United States first.'" Debbie's patriotism has been flamed of late by America's woes. "I'm concerned for the very simple reason that I feel our country is in a lot of trouble. Practically everything we wear is made overseas, because the labor is so much cheaper over there. . . . Yesterday on the television, I heard that we have borrowed so much money from other countries, we don't have any money."

Sonja Harvey recently organized a three-week-long retrospective symposium on Vietnam at Wake Forest University in Winston-Salem, North Carolina, where she's a senior. With Vietnam ten years behind us, the twenty-one-year-old from Bowie, Maryland, finds that students have moderated their once-strict interpretation of that conflict. Vietnam used to be a "dirty word," Sonja says. "Now it's got more of a neutral ring to it."

Students in the eighties do not necessarily believe that our country's motives were all bad in that war. The point of the Wake Forest symposium, she says, was to "allow students to make their own decisions on Vietnam. By no means were we trying to say it was right or wrong."

Just as my generation's political identity borrows from two opposing traditions, when singulars come to terms with U.S. history, we examine both sides of an issue, trying to be realistic rather than idealistic, to be fair-minded to ourselves as well as to the other guy.

RONALD REAGAN'S APPEAL

At the University of Maine at Orono on Election Day '84, the students were huddled around television sets in the dorms, awaiting election results. When Ronald Reagan was projected winner of the state's four electoral votes, they let out cheers and celebratory yelps. Throughout the nation, to many young adults like them, Reagan is more than just a figurehead in the White House. He's a real, live hero whose impact transcends his overwhelming success at the polling booths. After all, Lyndon Johnson won a landslide reelection mandate in 1964, as did Richard Nixon in 1972, but neither of them captured the heart of the country, let alone the young. With Reagan, the attraction is intense and, often, intensely personal.

"What I get from Reagan is a feeling of optimism," says Kevin Hogan. "If you continue to say, 'We're going to work,' 'Things are going to be okay,' then I can look for that and apply it to my own life, not just politics. That's how you can personalize the politics of your life."

"Reagan is such a great leader," says John Carlson. "He projects optimism about the future, says nothing about limits to growth, gives off unbridled optimism about the future."

In 1984, the Republicans managed to sell themselves success-fully to the electorate—and to young people in particular—as the party of strength and optimism. They parlayed the 1983–84 re-covery into a political triumph, taking credit for the drops in interest rates and unemployment. And job-driven young adults, uninspired by Walter Mondale and his special-interest coalition politics that no longer seemed to apply, responded in record num-bers to the conservative pitch, with its dangling carrot of upward mobility through free enterprise and entrepreneurship.

Exit polls taken at the voting booths in 1980 show that Reagan commanded just 41 to 44 percent of the eighteen-to-twenty-five-year-old vote, as against a 51 percent plurality in the general elec-torate; this means that young voters were the *least* likely of any age group to go for Reagan that year. (The hidden factor in the 1980 election was the candidacy of Independent John Anderson, who took 11 percent of the eighteen-to-twenty-nine-year-old vote, as against 8 percent in the general population.)

Just four years later, however, young voters gave one to the Gipper in a percentage that was slightly *higher* than that of the general electorate. In '84, Reagan captured between 59 and 60 percent of the youth vote, as compared to 59 percent of the gen-eral electorate. In just one term in office, Reagan managed to install himself at the head of my generation's rather limited pan-theon of political heroes.

Reagan's presidency of charm and smiles, with his lighthearted, whimsical persona and TelePrompTer intelligence, arrived on the national scene at precisely the right moment in history, at a time when all Americans—but most especially the young—needed someone to lift our sagging spirits. Ronald Reagan has fulfilled the promise of his political tryout; he's played the role of an aloof but omnipresent chairman of the board of America to a tee. He is that someone you can count on, whose shoes are always polished, whose jokes are always corn-pone and kind of predictable; that someone who never seems to lose a sense of amused irony about life.

Jimmy Carter's chief failing was in projecting a dejected attitude, according to Kevin Hogan. "He wasn't saying, 'Guys, come on, let's start,' 'Let's do something to get excited about your future, your kids' future.' "

Carter was too singular to do much for us. He was too much like us, with his doubts and his earnest, hard-driving perfectionism. He wanted to get every detail right and he wanted to think each thing through. He seemed to twist and suffer in the storms. And he took it all too seriously to be quite comfortable with the job.

The need for a strong, steady president who drives away our innermost fears is apparently widespread, especially among a generation with an uncertain sense of security. It seems that when we're not secure ourselves, we simply cannot tolerate unevenness in a president. What's more, we look to President Reagan's life as an example of the vaunted success story, the it-could-happen-to-you American Dream.

What is extraordinary about my generation's Reagan-adulation is that we seem to adore him even though his fiscal policies are undermining our best interests, even though he has not delivered on his campaign promises. We adore him while knowing that he is leading us down the primrose path. So strong is our need to feel successful, to believe in ourselves and the system, that we look the other way in his case.

After the 1984 presidential election, Donna Ray, a black twenty-four-year-old ex-staffer for the campaigns of Jesse Jackson and later Geraldine Ferraro, opined that "Reagan is the white man's Jesse Jackson; he tells them, 'I am somebody.' "

However, there is only one Ronald Reagan. And despite his appeal, the President's coattails have not swept his protégés into office. Reagan has been enormously successful with my generation in perpetuating his own popularity, but he has not been able to convert us to his political vision or even to draw us into the rank and file of the Republican party.

THE RISE OF NEOLIBERALS AND NEOCONSERVATIVES

An old saw goes something like this: If you're not a socialist at twenty, you have no heart; if you're not a conservative at thirty, you have no head. It has long been universal, the perception that the young are the romantics who long to make a better world, but once they get their feet wet in that world, they come to accept it and turn rightward. Even Ronald Reagan followed this pattern, as a New Dealer in his youth and a Goldwater conservative in later years.

In our own way, my generation has defied yet another long-standing social precept: the inevitability of this age-based, liberal-to-conservative odyssey. We are political hybrids for whom simple answers and paradigms do not apply. We borrow from sometimes competing traditions in forming our own individual political personas. We are political eclectics, coalitions of one.

We grew up with piped-in disillusionment about politics and are more wont to idealize the power of hard work, enterprise and friendship than political parties, ideologies and, in most cases, leaders. When we do get involved in politics, we are pragmatists who realize that in order to make a dent and a difference, we must play by the rules.

Following the sixties, as we do, it should come as no surprise that singulars would reject the liberal, progressive mantle and gravitate toward the beacon of conservatism, or that in some cases we would see ourselves as conservative before we've reached the age of consent. Conservatism is the flirtation of my generation, just as communism was that of the thirties generation, following the wildly capitalistic twenties. But singulars make no deep connection with classic conservatism, just as the thirties generation never really abandoned democracy.

Fundamentally, singulars have been steeped in too many brews to pledge our allegiance to any one ideology. For us, so many other social fixtures and inevitabilities have also bitten the dust; there is no conventional wisdom in our politics because there is no convention in the texture or progression of our lives. We have grown up with the decline of romance, of marriage, of parenthood, of traditional religion, of upward mobility, of security in the future.

The 1985 elections started to register a shift in the political winds, away from strict conservatism and toward neoconservative or neoliberal (the two actually being quite close) politics. In Virginia, a Democratic slate was elected to the offices of governor, lieutenant governor and attorney general; the slate consisted of a white male, a black male and a white female. This was the first time since Reconstruction that the voters of traditionally conservative Virginia have elected a black to statewide office, and the first time ever that they've elected a woman. The ticket's success was in part an endorsement of its popular neoliberal predecessor, Democratic Governor Charles Robb, who practiced fiscal conservatism and social progressivism and refused to identify with any particular ideology. Their victory was also a testimony to the eroding importance of party affiliation and the coincidence of racial and gender identity to the voter.

"Strong candidates and policies of broad general appeal therefore cracked color, sex and ideological barriers in a state where all three might once have seemed impassable," wrote Tom Wicker about this election in the New York *Times.* "When Virginia Republicans stuck to their outdated formula of appealing strictly to conservatives, they abandoned the middle—which is to say the political future."

Further evidence of "dealignment" along party and other lines came from the 1985 elections in New Jersey, where Republican Governor Thomas Kean was reelected with a majority of the black vote. His victory disproved the theory that blacks are died-in-the-wool Democrats.

The political challenge of the singular generation is enormous: It is nothing less than preserving America as a great nation, a leader in the world. Right now our success appears to be in doubt, imperiled by our economic woes. But when we follow our political

instincts, wedding political conservatism and liberalism, we may
be able to come up with new answers and a political identity that
could make the "America is back" slogans reverberate with meaning.

CHAPTER 7

Homebodies

THE NESTING IMPULSE

Upon graduating from Stanford Law School, Peter Rivers set right to work—as a general contractor. Not just any contractor, to be sure; Peter retained himself to work on his own future home.

"I was sick of being a tenant, for one thing," says Peter. "Second, I knew I couldn't afford to buy in Palo Alto, and I wanted to own. Third, I didn't feel like going out and practicing law right away."

Unusual though it may seem, Peter's decision to put housing ahead of everything else in life, especially his career, underscores a heartfelt, even urgent, need of the singular generation: the desire to settle down, to find a place to call our own.

Whereas our counterparts of the sixties, for the most part, came from strong, stable homes—or at least from a time of societal stability—the singular generation grew up during an insecure era. Children of the sixties and seventies, we moved from place to place and came of age in anxious times. Our first glimpses of the world were from the electronic hearth, where television issued forth a nonstop barrage of dangers: race riots, antiwar demonstrations, political assassinations and government corruption. We learned that a deadly pesticide called DDT was poisoning the food chain; that violent crime was on a sharp upward spiral; that in all likelihood, a nuclear war or accident would wipe us out before we could reach old age. Our earliest impressions told us that the world was not a very safe place.

Unprecedented numbers of singulars saw our childhood homes split from the war between the sexes and the epidemic of divorce. But even those of us who hail from more stable backgrounds absorbed the seismic tremors of our time. My generation has entered adulthood during a period of downward mobility for Americans. We are conscious that the job market is weaker than before, and that a young, two-paycheck family of the eighties, on the average, earns less income in real dollars than did a young, one-paycheck family of the sixties. As income has declined, the cost of housing has steadily increased; it's harder for a young family of the eighties to buy a home than it was during the three preceding decades. Today a good home for the right price is hard to find; buying a home almost always exacts a major sacrifice.

A confluence of these factors has caused singulars to draw inward, to retreat into our bodies, our jobs, our homes. We are a generation of nesters, homebodies who settle into our private domains with a relish our sixties counterparts reserved for hitting the road. Just as we try to shape our bodies into steel-belted strongholds within which we can suffer no harm, we visualize homes that are similarly self-sufficient: controlled environments in which each of us reigns supreme, in which order prevails, in which the world makes sense.

In the same way that we think our fashion "look" should correspond to our personalities, singulars believe that our homes should reflect our interests, our singularity. So we invest huge sums, often in small spaces, meticulously ordering them in a manner that reflects our selfhood and individuality. Clotheshorses keep extensive, carefully tended closets, and collectors build museums to house their particular passions. We build up our movie collections on videotape and pelt our interiors with home-fragrance bombs that set the mood—a crackling fire, an ocean breeze, the smell of an evergreen Christmas tree. We may willingly trade off financial freedom and flexibility to have a place to call our own, and, if we buy, to build equity.

Because singulars often delay marriage and sometimes omit it altogether from our life plans, we no longer believe that making a home and settling down are synonymous with tying the knot. In fact, we have begun to make homes for ourselves while we're still single, buying property if we can. We create home nests while living in what once would have been considered temporary quarters and conditions: while living alone or with roommates or lovers in "nontraditional" households, or even in our parents' homes. Singles no longer view our homes—or, more fundamentally, our marital status—as way stations en route to some better destination. Females feel free to unleash domestic proclivities outside of marriage, and singular bachelors are embracing domesticity in large numbers and with great relish.

One of the most startling demonstrations of the emergence of this new, singular concept of home can be seen in the growth of one-person households. In 1970, approximately 5.7 of all Americans lived alone, but just ten years later, that proportion jumped to 10.9 percent. The percentage of men living alone grew a full *85.7 percent* from 1970 to 1980. And the percentage of women living singly grew 46.6 percent over that same period.

Peter Rivers was still single when he bought his house. Luckily he had access to enough capital to finance the purchase of the circa-1940s $160,000 home. After closing, Peter spent a year and a half and another $134,000 refurbishing his gem. He did everything from sledgehammering the existing garage to supervising workers as they poured the new earthquake-proof foundation that was required in order to add an upper-level unit to the existing one-story house. Putting over a year's worth of "sweat equity" into the property won Peter the dubious distinction of earning the lowest income in his law school class.

By all measures, however, his decision appears to have paid off. Today the property, including rental units, is valued at well over $350,000. Peter and his new bride, who occupy the brand-new upper unit, enjoy a lovely two-bedroom home, complete with energy-efficient fireplace, plenty of closet space and hardwood parquet floors in the dining and living rooms. The kitchen is the couple's pride and joy, with its twin skylights, jutting greenhouse window, custom oak cabinetry and Spanish tiled floor.

Although Peter's conversion was an ambitious one, some singulars will go even further to establish comfortable and imaginative quarters. In parts of the country, singulars have adopted the mantle of "urban homesteaders" and have found townhouses or run-down homes in the wilderness of the inner city to "reclaim" and bring back to habitability. To them, it is both practical venture and adventure rolled into one.

THE INCREASING DIFFICULTY OF BUYING A HOME

The singular generation has stepped into the housing market at an inauspicious moment, when it is increasingly difficult to buy a first home.

"Up until 1980, homeownership was something that young people entering the work force and forming families could count on, as part of the economic fruits of a free-enterprise society," says Jay Janis, past chairman of the Federal Home Loan Bank Board and former Undersecretary of the Department of Housing and Urban Development. But with skyrocketing housing prices and with home financing opportunities rapidly drying up, young adults are increasingly disappointed and frustrated that their ability to buy is lagging so far behind their desire to purchase.

To make matters worse, for the first time in thirty years, the *overall* homeownership rate has begun to drop. This rate peaked in 1980, when 65.6 percent of the population owned homes, but each year since then, the number has declined.

Young adults under the age of thirty-five still account for the great majority of first-time buyers, although our share of this group has declined sharply in recent years. The median age of a first-time home purchaser—which has been rising rapidly—may soon leave the twenties behind. In 1977, it was 27.8; by 1983, it had climbed to 29.3.

And despite temporary fluctuations, the "homeownership gap" —that is, the difference between the actual price of a home and what buyers can afford to buy—continues to widen. In 1983, it was $16,000. That year the average income of an American family was $24,000. Using a standard formula, that family could afford a house costing $58,000. But the actual median price of a home in 1983 was $74,000. This compares with an affordability gap of just $2,400 in 1977.

A September 1983 report from the U.S. League of Savings Institutions' Homeownership Task Force indicates that this unfavorable climate is not likely to improve anytime soon.

"The very factors that caused the severe real estate and housing recessions of the last few years persist," the report states, "and profound changes in the home-finance delivery system have substantially altered the opportunity for homeownership. . . . These changes include the deregulation of savings institutions and savings rates, prompted by the popularity and rapid growth of unregulated financial entities. Specifically, deregulation has contributed to the shortening of deposit account maturities at financial institutions, which inhibits long-term lending."

Not only has buying the first home become a problem for singulars, but so has buying the second one. In the recent past, when young adults made the leap to residential adulthood, they would save up or scrape together a down payment for a "starter" home. The starter home was just that—the first step on the long upward ladder to the bigger and better abode.

Today the steps on that ladder are shaky. In recent years, the so-called move-up market has become clogged. For many, the old American starter house has become a stayer house, with the biggest growth segment of the relatively flat market in sales to first-time buyers, who often have to scrimp, save and put everything on the line just to get in.

HOMEOWNERSHIP: THE NEW STATUS SYMBOL

As homeownership becomes more elusive, it grows more desirable to singulars, both as a status symbol and for investment purposes. Owning a house, condo, townhouse or even a share in any of these, is now an achievement for young adults, another benchmark of success.

"You can sit there and say, 'This hunk of land, no matter how small, is mine,' " exudes thirty-year-old Noel Bermudez, a first-time homeowner and father of two. "You can put holes in the wall; you can hang up pictures; you can paint it a strange color, and nobody can say you can't." Bermudez, together with his wife, Engie, purchased their three-bedroom ranch-style home in the Los Angeles suburb of Valencia on Memorial Day, 1983, for $112,500. In just one year's time, it appreciated 10 percent.

In junior high school, long before he discovered the wonders of *Architectural Digest* and *Gourmet* magazines, Noel spent six months sketching out his dream home. It was a circular house, complete with heliport, in the rustic mountain resort of Lake Arrowhead, California.

"It was ultramodern in design and fabrication, but had the feel of something Frank Lloyd Wright would design in the sense of being integrated with nature," says Noel, recalling his youthful labor of architectural love. "Right in the middle of the dining room, there would be an indoor waterfall."

Noel is a soft-spoken, light-skinned black man who grew up in New Orleans and Los Angeles. Now a Reagan Republican who works in retailing at the managerial level, Noel has never lost sight of that formative dream of a fantasy existence of his own creation, a confirmation in plaster and stone of his own aspirations.

Though Noel and Engie are proud owners of the standard all-American suburban home with a large private backyard, in their estimation, it falls short of being a genuine *dream* house.

"In my mind, the next home is certainly going to be farther out in the country, on a nice piece of land that is somewhat secluded, with lots of trees and much more open," says Noel. "In this one, we haven't had a chance to decorate yet, to do something that makes it distinctive, that gives it a certain air, a certain style, that is entirely coordinated. We probably won't do that with this house."

When Maureen Fitzgerald, an unemployed attorney from Seattle, was sizing up her future boyfriend, one of the first clues she had to go on was his description of a dream home. At the outdoor barbecue where they met, guests were standing in a circle, playing what Maureen described as a "little head game."

Explains Maureen, now twenty-eight: "You're given a million dollars and you can't give it away; you can't spend it in multiples. What would you do with it? It's pretty funny because you get to see people's values immediately. I said I wanted a house on the ocean, my dream house. And he (Charley) said he wanted a dream house, too, but it was totally different. His was in the mountains someplace."

At least part of the pair's attraction, or commonality, was that each would invest in a dream home—not a yacht or a Jack-in-the-Box franchise or a famous work of art. For Maureen, though, the sad reality is that now, five years after meeting Charley, she is still living in her old bedroom at home, with three younger siblings underfoot.

A LUXURY LAIR

Manhattanite Rhonda Gainer had tired of the student look of her two-room first-floor apartment in a doorman building on Manhattan's exclusive Upper East Side. As an advertising executive, the wicker wall decorations and unstable knotted-pine couch with jumbo throw-pillow "upholstery" no longer seemed appropriate for business or personal entertaining.

In her bedroom, she had lasted five years on a mere mattress. "I was sick of sleeping on the floor and having myself or a man fall off and be bruised," she jokes.

So one day Rhonda went shopping for furniture; she came home having placed an order for a set of black Italian lacquer furniture for her $580-a-month apartment. The tab came to $20,000.

"I got carried away," admits Rhonda. "I didn't plan on spending this kind of money." Rhonda had actually earmarked her savings for a down payment on a condominium or co-op apartment, but once she spotted the luxurious furniture in the showroom, she couldn't resist.

"I saw this bedroom set. It was the first thing I saw and I fell in love with it. And the dining room set and everything else—they were beautiful."

Not all singulars would behave quite so impulsively when it comes to parting with hard-earned dollars. But Rhonda's enormous—some would say foolish—investment in home furnishings offers a window into how important the look of our homes is to many of us.

For Rhonda, the furniture provides the appropriate ambience for the kind of life-style she likes to see herself leading: luxurious, high-style and sexy. What's more, the interior provides a fitting backdrop for another one of her passions—clothing.

A definite sartorial hierarchy exists in Rhonda's digs. Her newest and most expensive pieces—the latest silks and cashmeres and suedes—rate the inner sanctum of the black armoire, with its built-in shelves, drawers and hanging space. A mixture of good summer and good winter things vies for limited space in her built-in bedroom closet; the "yucky winter stuff" hangs in the closet between the bathroom and the bedroom, while yucky and non-yucky summer things share the portable free-standing closet right at the front door. Everywhere but the armoire, her clothes are jammed in, crammed in, jockeying for position. Rhonda frequently has to re-dry-clean them—without a single wearing—just to get the wrinkles pressed out.

"Clothes are my weakness," says Rhonda, while pointing out that dressing right is crucial for maintaining her image at work, where she must look not only good but high-style every day of the week.

Rhonda's wardrobe almost comes to life inside her little lair. Her clothes are tended to, tissued and scrutinized. Every night before going to bed, Rhonda lovingly selects her outfit for the next day, right down to the jewelry and stockings.

FEAST OR FAMINE

While Rhonda puts a great deal of thought into what she wears and how she arranges her home, she pays very little attention to the state of her kitchen. Her refrigerator is barren, except for a couple of low-calorie frozen dinners, a bottle or two of rosé wine and some cheeses, rubbery at the edges. She rarely eats at home, and certainly the concept of having a hot dinner every night eludes her.

Singulars often work such long hours that we don't have time to bother with the ordinary. But when we cook, we cook up a show. Cooking is a revered "found art"; kitchen labors have taken on the aspect of a performance, with appreciative guests as audience. Cooking is not something you do every night; it is reserved for special occasions. If someone invites you over and says, "I'm cooking," you know he or she is probably talking about home-made dishes prepared with fresh and often exotic ingredients.

The in-between stuff—the casseroles and vegetable dishes and scrambled-egg breakfasts—seems too tedious to deal with, so we prefer to go out. Gourmet restaurants and fast-food joints both have their appeal. After all, my generation grew up with McDonald's and Arby's, with fad food and fast food, with health food and ethnic cuisine. Eating out is not a convenience but, to our way of thinking, a necessity, so we do not hesitate to take full advantage.

THE DOMESTIC MALE

Singular-generation men are migrating to the domestic wilderness, with marketers—smelling a new pool of customers—following close behind. After extensive market research on this newly domesticated animal, market researcher Judith Langer concluded that companies selling such basic products as laundry detergents and cooking ingredients needed to add detailed instructional information to their packaging. In a 1984 New York *Times Sunday Magazine* article on the "new man," Barbara Ehrenreich wrote that today's single man no longer eats "canned-hash dinners" and lives on "orange-crate furniture." Today, she said, "They cook; they furnish; they may even decorate. . . . and the magazines that guide their consumption decisions are proliferating and expanding."

"In college, I started reading *Architectural Digest* and *Gourmet,*" says Noel Bermudez. "Those two magazines established a certain style and a certain mind-set for me."

After a short-lived and disappointing first marriage at the age of nineteen, Noel settled into eight years of bachelorhood, in which he discovered "the finer things"—like kitchen wares and home furnishings—by himself. During this period, he transformed himself into something of a gourmet chef; Southern gumbo became his specialty. This coming of age took place in Oklahoma City, where Noel moved for a three-year stint in the Air Force.

After finishing his tour of duty, Noel enrolled in Oklahoma City University and, in 1977, started a part-time catering concern, La Cuisine de Noel. At the time, Noel saw himself as "an odd fish —I wasn't your typical man. I used to love the outdoors and I still do. But even when I camp, I like to camp with a certain style."

THE EURO-LOOK

A new, heightened sense of style is a key not only to this new "soft" man's basic tastes, but to those of the entire generation. Singulars prefer a compact, streamlined, "superpremium" living space to an oversize, ramshackle sprawl, just as we'll invariably opt for a sporty, foreign-made, compact car over a comparably priced American-made mid-size sedan and take a pint of Häagen-Dazs ice cream over a half-gallon of the generic brand.

New housing today is being "downsized" to maximize the cubic inch rather than the square foot—a trend that insiders in the housing and home-furnishing industries term the Europeanization of American homes. Today builders and buyers pay more attention to details like cabinetry, fixtures and wall texture, while paring down total volume. The average size of a newly constructed single-family home today is just 1,300 square feet, down from 1,600 square feet twenty years ago. Some condominiums are as small as 600 square feet, while some rental units have shrunk to a mere 300 square feet. This is a response to both economic realities and the new demographics of the smaller household.

The only buy some singulars can afford these days is in condo complexes, which have been called the Levittowns of the eighties. Developers and real estate consultants marvel at the rapid acceptance of less, often for more. Instead of a full yard, for instance, young buyers today are satisfied with some kind of "terrestrial affiliation," which often amounts to an enclosed, pint-size patch of ground. In California—harbinger of many of the nation's housing trends—many condos are built that give an illusion of privacy but are actually tightly packed, with as many as eighteen units per acre.

We pay dearly for small places, especially in the city, and we like to dress them up with flair and distinction. Home furnishings have undergone a similar transformation toward smaller size but higher quality.

"People don't want a lot of everything," says Richard Stolzman, vice president in charge of the booming home furnishings division at The Broadway, one of the nation's top department stores. "They want better quality. They're looking to buy a better sofa."

If we can afford it, that includes minimalist furnishings and all manner of electronic gadgetry: laser-disc stereos, home computers, entertainment centers and upscale bathroom equipment. Industry experts say that the bedroom has taken the place of the den for our generation, and many of the latest beds reflect this trend; they include built-in cabinets, storage units and even tables that can be pulled out of the headboards.

The public area of today's upscale home cuts a sharp contrast with that of twenty years ago. In the circa-1960s version, "You'd see an old wooden dining table, a server with hutch, six chairs," says Stolzman. "You'd have a seventy-two- to eighty-inch sofa, a love seat, a pair of chairs, an important chair and an ottoman around someplace. There would be a plant table, three lamp tables, a magazine rack. It was very cluttered-looking.

"Now I think what would be in the same space might be an entertainment center, an angled sectional of one sort or another— no couch. A swing-armed floor lamp, and maybe a simple coffee table. In the dining area, you'd have a table and chairs, glass-topped, perhaps white lacquer base, which is much less weighty than wood. You'd still need to seat six people, but your dining room chairs would not be high-backs, they'd be simpler. You'd have one important piece of artwork, not a grouping of pictures."

GOING HOME TO ROOST

The stigma against living at home with one's parents has eroded tremendously for singulars. A downsized earning capacity has edged some singulars out—not only of the real estate market but of the *rental* market. The recession of the early eighties contributed to young adults returning home to the roost after college or after a financial struggle the first few years out. Some young adults move back to their parents' homes in order to save, and others, because they have no choice. Some do it graciously, reveling in the familial intimacy; others do it grudgingly, with an eye toward escape.

A rapprochement between parents and their adult children has contributed to this trend. Because we tend to be goal oriented, pragmatic and conservative, we are less likely to be at odds with our parents than were young adults of a generation ago.

"Today's under-thirty generation is staying home longer than any generation since the first years after World War II," says a 1984 report in the New York *Times*. "Whereas young adults in the 1950s and 1960s tended to establish their own households not long after they reached the age of twenty, it is becoming less unusual for them to live at the parents' home into their late twenties, demographers say."

"The most difficult time was coming back after college," says Janice Orefice, a staffer at *Brides* magazine in New York City, who lives with her parents in Westchester County, a half-hour train ride from midtown Manhattan, where she works. Janice, twenty-six, shares the bedroom in which she grew up with her fifteen-year-old sister and pays her parents $125 each month for the privilege.

Although she has a "terrific home situation," in which her mother does all her laundry, Janice is itching to move out. She finds that her role at home does not jibe with her professional persona. "It's difficult to be a daughter and sister when you are a manager and coordinator."

Though she is now finalizing plans to move out, she has no regrets about having lived at home. By doing so, she was able to "acquire some nice things," including a 1983 Nissan Sentra, which transports a carload of friends to the Jersey shore on summer weekends.

Until recently, when Janice's salary was raised, she wouldn't have been able to find comparable—or even decent—quarters in Westchester, much less "the City." She would have been able to get by, yes, but living at home was not the odious option for Janice that it might have been for her counterparts a generation earlier. Like many singulars, Janice is career-minded and practical about finances. While living with her family, she has been able to keep her priorities in mind and put some of her desires on hold.

Saul Tarcher, twenty-five, would have been able to afford a nice place and even a new car with his high-paying job at an electronics firm in California's Silicon Valley. But living at home meant that he was able to buy a BMW. Without having to wait.

"To me it was worth it," he declares. "Besides, what's the big deal? I'm going to be out on my own soon enough."

Some young adults, sensing a cold, cruel world out there, cling to the nest. Scott Smith, a nineteen-year-old student at San Francisco State, still lives with his folks in Pacifica, California. His boyhood room is cluttered with sports team decals and pennants and stacks of board games from another era. He still sleeps on a bunk bed. Instead of scheming how to get out, Scott's figuring how to extend his stay at home. The best strategy, he's decided, is to stretch out his college years, taking six rather than four years to complete his education.

Clearly singulars are not offended by living with mom and dad. It may not be the best of worlds, but it certainly isn't the worst. Just as we don't feel a need to flaunt premarital sexual relations, singulars likewise don't have to flaunt the demarcation between ourselves and our parents.

"If you have to sponge, you might as well sponge off your parents," says Maureen Fitzgerald, who moved back into her childhood bedroom after an unsuccessful job hunt in the lawyer-glutted Seattle market. Although Maureen finds the situation bleak, she is grateful for the safety net the option has provided her.

"You do have certain advantages, obviously," she says. "You don't have to worry as much about finances." For spending money, Maureen works full-time as a cashier at a local convenience store. "I wouldn't even consider living at home if I weren't in the place that I am in financially."

She is the first to admit that living at home exacts its price.

"In terms of your own autonomy, it's just gross. I feel as though in exchange for having the financial advantages, having my dinners cooked, a place to do my laundry for free, and things like that, I do have to at least consider my parents' feelings when I decide to do something."

The house rules at the Fitzgeralds' are certainly not unreasonable. Because Maureen's bedroom is separated by only a bathroom from her parents' room, she observes their 10:30 P.M. bedtime. If Maureen wants to listen to music, she'll wear a headphone set, and if she won't be home for dinner, she lets them know in advance. She observes the rules but wishes that at this stage in life, she could be setting her own.

"You don't want to tell people you live at home," says Mindy Davidson, a twenty-one-year-old aspiring artist who has lived in her parents' spacious Los Angeles home for a year. "When I first saw this guy, he looked really cute. . . . He asked me where I lived. 'Oh, do you have a roommate?' [he said.] I said to myself, 'This guy is not going to respect me if he knows I'm living with Mommy and Daddy,' which is a whole different thing from having your own place." So Mindy lied and told him she lived alone. The lie came back to haunt her, though, when the two started dating. When she finally confessed, she was surprised at his reaction: "He was totally unfazed."

Living at home compounds Mindy's dual struggle for identity as an artist and an adult. A Columbia University dropout, she cannot comfortably entertain her friends at home, and sometimes she lays in wait for weekends when her parents go away so she can have the place to herself. Though her room is adjacent to the downstairs family room, complete with a fine stereo system, Mindy rarely uses it. Rather than putting on Parliament and her other favorite funk groups, "I'll close my door and put on a tinny fifties AM radio in my room. Listening to static-y, semi-okay music is much better than having the door open."

Parents aren't always eager to receive their adult children for indefinite stays. "It's not a burden so much as a joy when we're alone," comments Stephanie Davidson, Mindy's forty-six-year-old mother, who has two adult children living at home. Her three children, aged twenty-three, twenty-one and eighteen, have been coming in and out of the revolving door for the past year or so, wreaking havoc on Stephanie and her husband's life.

"When they left for six months, I felt like the house was so quiet, I could hear the sound of the refrigerator going off and on. It was so depressing. But by the time I began to appreciate the quiet, they returned."

In her own mind, however, Stephanie has set a one-year time limit to the stay of the two older children; she likens this period to graduate school. "I feel I can help them out because I was lucky enough to have bought the house at the right time."

NONFAMILY HOUSEHOLDS

Many singulars settle into apartment and house shares with lovers, friends or even roommates found in the want ads. The Census Bureau reports that "non-family households" grew 136.4 percent from 1970 to 1980. A "non-family household" is one in which those living together are related neither by marriage nor blood.

When she enrolled in Stanford Medical School in 1980, Krysia Lindan took out a lease for a three-bedroom, two-bathroom luxury condominium at over $700 a month. (It has since been raised to almost $1,000.) Through the years, she's become a kind of mother hen to a revolving den of roommates, many of whom have become close friends. Almost always, her roommates are female, but a heterosexual couple and an occasional male have occupied the one room that tends to turn over frequently.

The place is a new brand of "student pad" in that Krysia considers it to be her home. Well stocked with many comforts, there are almost always fresh flowers on the dining room table and whole coffee beans in the freezer. The kitchen is filled with gourmet gadgets, and Krysia invested in an expensive set of dishes. The New York *Times* and the San Francisco *Chronicle* are delivered every morning. Krysia and her roommates jointly purchased a modern floral couch and a color TV. Once Krysia even rented a piano, but she sent it back when she realized she was not using it enough to justify the expense. As a group, the roommates work out to Jane Fonda's exercise tape in the evenings between 9 or 10, when they have generally wound up their days.

To Krysia, there is simply no other way to live. She was not willing to postpone enjoying a decent life-style until after completing her residency. "I worry sometimes about the expense, but to tell you the truth, I couldn't see living like a student for eight years."

OUR PRIVATE SANCTUARIES

In the late sixties and early seventies, housing was considered by many young adults as yet another bourgeois trapping of life. Hippies and flower children were careless with their quarters. Any hovel, the cheaper the better, would do—as long as it was their own. Drugs, travel and music were priorities, not bone china and custom closets. The hipper you were, the more your place resembled a dive, a crash pad, with perhaps some "interesting" woodwork and old, rusty plumbing.

Today the home has become the fantasy destination of the singular generation. Slapdash, thumbtack decorating is as dated as Earth Shoes. Singulars pore over lush, glittery spreads in home-furnishings magazines; the pages of decorator-designed interiors are the domestic equivalent of the Busby Berkeley fantasy films of the Depression-era thirties. We fantasize about our dream homes while building up our real-life nests, piece by piece.

The singular generation's enormous yearning for a home, for a peaceful place away from the chaos and craziness of the rest of the world, is not surprising. If we cannot change the state of the world, at least we can rearrange our living rooms. At a time when the world out there seems very dangerous, our sanctuaries—our homes—exert a magnetic pull.

CHAPTER 8

Parenting

PARENTING: A LIFE-STYLE OPTION

The question the singular generation faces with regard to children is not how many to have or when to start a family but whether to parent at all. Though many of us long to have children and believe that parenting will add a new dimension to our lives, we take our time about it, responding to internal timetables and professional schedules rather than outside pressure. If we choose not to have children or if we postpone the decision, we are not making the mistake of a lifetime but rather exercising freedom in choosing a life-style. When we become parents, we act consciously and, in some cases, self-consciously; singulars are unlikely to back into parenting.

Having children was an implicit obligation of the last generation. In the late fifties and early sixties, when many singulars were born, most people felt that becoming a parent was the final step on society's prescribed path to adulthood: first marriage, which issued the card-carrying credentials, then bearing and rearing children, which conferred the full privileges of maturity. It was expected that everyone would—or should—want children. And there was a whole set of rules as to how to go about it: You should start in your twenties; you should have at least two; you should by all means be married and stay married—at least until the children graduated from high school. If you showed no interest in children back then, you were thought to be either barren, homosexual, impotent or self-centered—and almost certainly destined for unhappiness in later life.

For singulars, these long-standing precepts no longer hold sway. As with other aspects of our personal lives, in the realm of parenting, singulars enjoy a wide range of options. We can become a parent while single, or we can parent jointly with an ex-spouse, a live-in lover, a live-out lover or even a friend. We can postpone parenting well into our thirties (and sometimes forties); we can adopt. Being gay does not prevent us from parenting as it once did; homosexuals can adopt or bear a child through artificial insemination or a surrogate mother. If we do not have our own children, we can be "partial parents"—stand-ins or godparents to children who are not technically our own but belong to us in spirit.

The most common form of parenting remains the standard male-female couple. But even this equation has changed dramatically in character in just a few decades. Young couples are now partners in parenting. Just as in marriage, where singulars have abandoned the predefined sex-role dichotomy of the past in favor of a more entrepreneurial marital partnership model, in parenting, we no longer buy the traditional gender-based parental roles. Fathers and mothers are thought to be equally competent to provide the nurturing and love needed to raise a healthy child. Indeed, we think that the child will be healthier and happier with the active participation of both parents.

Despite a widening of options, singulars aren't rushing to sign up for parent duty. Our sluggishness is borne out in demographic tables. Our generation tends to have our first babies later in life; we have fewer children, often stopping at one.

More and more of us are opting out of parenting altogether. And we can be up front about wanting no part of children. "I would like to be married," says twenty-three-year-old Southern Baptist missionary Pam Bruns, "but it's not number one on my list. As far as having children, I'm not interested at all." The Springfield, Missouri, native, who is currently posted in South Korea, simply does not see herself "as a family person."

For many of us, the high cost of parenting effectively tables the question, especially in our twenties. As the stakes rise in the world of work, our careers extract greater emotional, financial and time commitments from us. Many of us must choose between buying a home and having a baby, and often the former comes first. Since we marry later, most of us postpone parenting till the question of commitment has been resolved. Singulars tend to live in the present and put an almost religious stock in developing and expressing our potential. We seek to raise our careers, our bodies, our sexual and platonic friendships and our professional networks to high-yield, low-maintenance levels before we begin making the necessary sacrifices of parenting.

HIGH PARENTING POTENTIAL

Singulars have the potential of being among the most effective parents ever. Since we are parents by choice, our offspring are among the most wanted, planned-for children in history. In many cases, we prepare for their arrival years before trying to conceive. Because we have fewer kids, we feel we are able to give more of ourselves and our resources to each of them.

Singulars can make emotionally healthier parents than, say, our own parents, as we do not generally suspend our own personal development "for the sake of the child" or cast ourselves into subservient or predefined roles ("This is how dads are supposed to behave around kids"). Since we tend to be older when we become parents, we know ourselves better and are less apt to see parenting as a substitute for living. In two-parent families, we do a better job because father and mother share the satisfaction and the gruntwork of parenting.

The body of knowledge about early childhood and the special abilities of infants and small children is growing rapidly and has led to beneficial child-rearing techniques. Singulars are less likely to pass restrictive sex roles on to our boys and girls or to apply blanket rules to child rearing. We look for signs of our children's individuality as early as in the crib. We seek to nurture their particular natures before messages of what "should be" cloud their consciousness.

But all is not rosy in the singular nursery. Singulars are capable of conferring on our children our characteristic anxiety, apprehension and insecurity. Some of us enter our babies in the competitive heat early on, adorning them with designer diapers and enrolling them in selective preschools. Some seem dead set on rearing a "superkid," drilling and coaching our children to master cognitive skills at ridiculously early ages, sometimes even in infancy, teaching them languages and gymnastics and computer literacy before most of us, at their ages, were permitted to switch on the family TV set. Our justification is that our offspring need to be prepared for an increasingly competitive and complex world; but to that end, we may be effectively stripping away what sociologist Marie Winn, author of *Children Without Childhood,* calls the vital cocoon of "childhood innocence."

PROUD, PREPARED PARENTS

It would seem that every aspect of Maxwell David Spector's life has been planned. Before they decided to get pregnant (singular couples consider pregnancy a joint venture and so refer to the condition in the plural), Ellen Spector and her husband Greg took a three-week trip to Europe as a kind of last fling with their carefree days of childless, marital bliss. When the two twenty-nine-year-olds returned, they were ready for parenting.

To that end, the Los Angeles couple set a goal of saving enough money for Ellen to take off a year from work. Though they got pregnant right away, they nevertheless managed to put away $10,000 by the time Max was born. They enrolled in a Red Cross class that taught them about car seats and how to give a thorough bath. They took Lamaze classes, which taught them breathing and birthing exercises. And Ellen bought and studied a dozen books on child rearing and child development.

"I memorized passages in the books, I reread them so many times," she says. "It was such a mysterious endeavor I wanted to know as much about it as possible. Greg finally took the books out of the bedroom and put them in the service porch because it was driving him crazy."

Ellen was more prepared in a "textbooky" way for her baby than was her mother. All her mother did to get ready was to buy a copy of Benjamin Spock's *Baby and Child Care,* which she read and then "kept on hand for chidhood diseases," says Ellen. "I doubt that my mother was reading child-development books." Despite this, Ellen suspects her mother was more emotionally prepared for parenting, having known since girlhood that she was destined to become a mother. While she was growing up, Ellen was never certain she would have children.

Because parenting does not come naturally to us—it is a considered, even self-conscious, life decision—many of us prepare for it as if we were required to operate some mysterious piece of machinery, as if we had to pass a parental competency test before we were granted license to conceive.

Long before getting pregnant, Lauren Watson, a twenty-six-year-old mother of one from Utah, says she "took a lot of classes in college on parenting."

After all this careful planning, a certain parental pride almost invariably accompanies the arrival of the newborn. We keep records of our babies, thinking they and we might later find significance in these first vital signs; we record their movements and expressions and accomplishments on videotape, slide film and snapshots. Since Max's birth, Ellen has kept a meticulous diary of his development.

> Aug. 8: I almost forgot to write down one of Max's stunning accomplishments. Last Saturday, after we got home . . . Max was put down on his back on the rug. He started to roll to his side. He threw his leg over the other and tried to get some momentum going. He kind of buried his head in the rug; he persevered. It was all I could do to keep from helping him over. I let him go and, sure enough, he succeeded to roll from his back to his stomach right before our very eyes. It was definitely the first time he had rolled in this direction. All three of

us were really thrilled. We can't keep him on his back anymore, the instant he's put down, he rolls over.

Every several days Ellen records such trivia as the kinds of sounds Max makes, the way he looks and moves. "I'm writing paragraphs where my mother just recorded the day in the baby book."

Like other singulars who elect to have babies in their twenties, Greg and Ellen are *volunteers* in the truest sense of the word. When we decide to parent, we throw ourselves in wholeheartedly. It is a role in life, our life path, and so we try to prepare for it carefully and to follow through with conscientiousness and verve.

PARTNERSHIP PARENTING

Married singulars view child rearing as a central aspect of their partnership. Both husband and wife participate in every aspect of child rearing, from changing diapers to disciplining. We believe that it is best for the child, best for both parents, best all around when both parents are involved. For two-career couples, this arrangement is not only desirable but necessary, as the demands of either job might beckon at any time. But even if the mother stays home with the baby or children, singular fathers pitch in.

Greg Spector generally arrives home from work at 5 P.M., just in time to take over on the Max "detail" as Ellen heads out to teach an evening class in the Los Angeles Unified School System. Greg changes diapers, gives Max his nightly bath and generally goes ga-ga over his four-month-old son. There is nothing Greg cannot do, no drawer of his son's dresser whose contents he is unfamiliar with, no chore too difficult or exacting or insignificant for him to handle. For Greg, hands-on fathering is a privilege, not a burden.

Greg loves everything about being a parent, and he sometimes fantasizes about staying home with Max full-time. Unfortunately he could not take time off from his business reporting career without jeopardizing it. So instead he spends as many of his off hours with his son as he can; occasionally Greg wonders if his bond with Max is as strong as it could be.

"I don't think I have the physical and mental connection with him that Ellen does," he says. "But I don't think my relationship with Max is suffering."

"Sometimes I feel guilty because Max is so delightful during the day," observes Ellen, "and almost like clockwork, when Greg comes in, he is tired and will turn off the smile and turn on the frown."

The couple does not believe that Ellen is any better equipped to parent than is Greg. Greg insists that if he were a schoolteacher, too, he'd be just as likely to stay home with Max.

At least in principle, most singulars agree that it makes little difference who stays home with the kids or who is the primary parent. For us, there seems to be no special magic about a female raising the children, especially after the breast-feeding stage.

"If [the father] worked from the home, then I would not be averse to his staying home and taking care of the child," says New Yorker Janice Orefice, "and vice versa, if I work from the home." Often, who stays home is a moot point, as neither parent can afford the cost to his or her career or the lost income.

In the case of Greg and Ellen, they decided jointly, in true partnership style, that it was desirable for Max to have a full-time parent, at least during his first year. They worked out an arrangement so this could be possible. They drew up a budget and determined that they could swing it with a three-point plan: savings plus Greg's regular income plus Ellen's part-time income.

NEW-AGE DADS

Just as singular women look to men as role models in the world of work, singular men take their cues from women in the domestic domain. While no tidal wave of young males has rushed home to be full-time fathers and househusbands, many, like Greg Spector, at least entertain the idea, often jokingly and sometimes wistfully. This in itself represents a major departure from the behavior and attitudes of the previous generation of men. If young men are inclined to parent at all, they almost invariably create new ground rules so as to avoid the deleterious patterns of their fathers, who were all too often aloof, unapproachable and capable of anesthetizing their emotions. Once singular men decide to become fathers —an agonizing decision for many—they want to do it right.

"To be quite honest, I've made a commitment to myself, if I were to have kids . . . I would have a lot more time [for them]," says twenty-four-year-old Karl Miller, a 1984 graduate of North Carolina's Guilford College. "I would not pursue such a grandiose income" explains Karl, as did his father, a wealthy Baltimore physician who sired six children. "In my family, my father was mostly involved in his work. After a certain part of each of our lives, he did not spend much time with us. When he came home, he was tired; he had to go to bed early."

Just as singulars no longer abide by outmoded rules that govern relations between the sexes, we do not accept restrictive and obsolete terms for fatherhood (or motherhood, for that matter). Singulars often cast up for stringent scrutiny received wisdom about the sanctity of the mother in the parenting equation, akin to the way feminists examined women's roles in society a generation ago.

"The old balance [between the mother and father] was too restrictive for this day and age," writes Jessie Bernard in *The Future of Motherhood.* "It did not make room for the male strengths required of mothers and it did not extend the nurturant virtues to fathers who, at least in archetypal form, must also be protective. The trend of the times is in the direction of seeing the two ideals or principles in both sexes rather than as separately specialized in one or the other, of seeing the polarity in both men and women rather than in only one sex."

Singular dads try not to be weekend or armchair parents whose depth of intimacy extends to offering Suzy the comics section of the newspaper before sinking into it themselves or taking Joey to a baseball game once a month. They invest time in their children; they are tender and caring and place a high premium on developing quality relationships. If their marriages break up, singular fathers often petition for joint custody of the kids, and increasingly for full custody. Despite the pain involved, singular fathers recognize the importance of maintaining an active relationship with their children: for themselves and the children.

Every month or so, twenty-six-year-old Richard Hanes flies to Phoenix to pick up his daughter and bring her to Los Angeles for the weekend. "I love my little girl more than anything in the world," he says about twenty-two-month-old Stephanie, who lives with her mother. Richard calls regularly just to touch base. "She says, 'Hi, Daddy, I love you and miss you.'"

"We have the best time" on those weekends, says Richard, doing simple things like "taking a walk. She's been to Disneyland a couple of times. I sit around and read to her a lot. I enjoy sitting around holding her. We play hide and seek; I teach her how to count, the alphabet."

Although Richard would prefer to have full custody of his daughter, who was born out of wedlock, he has agreed to her mother raising her, provided his visitation rights remain liberal. He tries to put Stephanie's best interests above all else. "She's in good hands, I know that."

A 1985 survey of Houstonians funded by the Houston *Post* and the American Leadership Forum indicates that the great majority of young adults would not object in principle to Richard assuming custody of his daughter. A full 85 percent of the survey's respondents between the ages of eighteen and twenty-nine said that "a single father can raise secure and happy children just as well as a single mother can." The notion that "a child needs its mother" above anyone else is fast growing obsolete.

Despite a desire to forge a new role for themselves as fathers, young men are not without their trouble spots, many of which derive from cultural conditioning, some from biological fact.

As early as pregnancy, prospective fathers can feel alienated from their wives, left out of the process; they have to work harder just to stay involved. "Your wife is bonding internally with a fetus," explains Los Angeles psychologist Jeff Marsh, a leader in the movement for fathering awareness, "and the husband often feels at a loss." Most men go through a number of changes during their wives' pregnancies, "physiological changes like gaining weight. Men get nervous and don't know what to do with their nervousness. They put on five to ten pounds. Almost invariably, men will work harder. They worry: 'Am I going to be a good provider?' Or they will pick up additional hobbies. Not too infrequently, it's an extramarital affair."

Lust alone does not drive men to seek other women, insists Marsh. Rather, it's an overwhelming sense of neediness during a pregnancy and an uncertainty about where to find help. However, with so many young men now involved in preparing for childbirth, which Marsh calls the "first step to active fathering," the situation is rapidly improving.

HEALTHIER MOMS

Since female singulars who do have children are acting more by choice, we are arguably better suited for the job than was the previous generation of mothers. In addition, we usually combine work outside the home with motherhood and increasingly rely on spouses and child-care services, thus making it easier for us to maintain a balance, not to get carried away by maternity.

When we stay home, we are usually there by choice and, increasingly, privilege. Singular homemothers like Ellen Spector believe that we're working for the benefit of the entire family and that we are not drones living off the generosity of our spouses. Therefore, we feel entitled to time off, vacations, discretionary dollars and outside recreation. Staying home is our end of the partnership contract; it does not define the outer limits of our life or potential.

"When I got pregnant, it was assumed that I was going to stay home with the kids, full-time, and Roger was going to finish graduate school [at the University of California at Berkeley]," says twenty-five-year-old Josie Roberts, primary parent of the couple's two toddlers. "But then, when I started staying home all the time, I couldn't stand it. . . . I finally told Roger I had to get out of the house."

Josie's life turned around when she took up jogging and enrolled in a nightly Jazzercise class. She found part-time work, just to get her out of their claustrophobic student apartment. "It took me awhile to get into the routine of being a mother and of finding myself as well—of how to utilize my energy." But the Arizona native never doubted that she had to strike a balance, never doubted her own mettle because she was not content being a full-time mom.

Singular women try to avoid the mistakes of the previous generation of mothers. From the advantage of hindsight, we can see that in many instances, mothers of the fifties and sixties were overly involved in their children's lives, in controlling their movements and appetites, in grafting their children's identities onto their own. Singular mothers try to better draw the line between mother and child, not to live vicariously. In the case of single mothers and mothers of only children, this can be a daunting goal, but one to which we aspire.

"I try to make sure that I don't see his accomplishments as my accomplishments," remarks Maria Linscott, a Chesapeake, Virginia, thirty-year-old single mother of a four-year-old boy. "I'll always love him whatever he does, good or bad. But he has his own self-worth, his own place in the universe and scheme of things. Nothing I am has anything to do with that finally."

Child-care and preschool programs enable singular parents to work outside the home and to preserve our own interests and free time if we do not. Not surprisingly, singulars make greater use of day care for preschool children than any generation before us, and that usage is rapidly growing. In 1982, 48.2 percent of all mothers of preschoolers under the age of five were working outside the home. And this number is growing. This compares with 40.6 percent in 1977. Even with children less than one year old, 41.4 percent of all mothers in 1982 worked outside the home, compared with 31.9 percent five years earlier.

Even those of us who would be logistically able to watch our preschoolers full-time take ample advantage of child care: full-time, part-time or on a relief basis.

Josie and Roger Roberts' children qualify for University of California at Berkeley's state-of-the-art preschooling program. But if they did not, "I would have paid for private child care," asserts Josie. The couple also has the benefit of a baby-sitting co-op in their student-family apartment complex.

Because we see mothering as a choice, not a requirement, of young women today, we tend to enter into it with open arms, with greater self-confidence and a better understanding of how to take care of ourselves and satisfy needs that are separate from those of our children.

WATCHING ANNA GROW

Singular parents appreciate and respond to the inherent individuality of our children. Our child-rearing practices are increasingly tailored to the wee person in our midst rather than to some hypothetical child. When given the choice between following the book and following our instincts, we almost invariably choose the latter.

"I've been raising Martin by how he reacts and how I feel at the time," says Meredith White, a dispersing clerk in the U.S. Navy. Meredith's ten-month-old son is large for his age and has already begun to "speak" his mind; his first order of business was gustatory in nature.

Martin had had his fill of baby food and was ready to take on the harder stuff—scrambled eggs, stuffed mushrooms and the like. "I'd give him the bottle, and he'd look at me like I was insulting him," explains the divorced mother of one.

So Meredith took it up with the experts. "Dr. Spock and my doctor said Martin should be on formula for a year," she says. Undeterred by these admonitions, Meredith continued to petition her physician for his go-ahead in accelerating Martin's diet. "I've finally gotten the okay from the doctor. I kind of wore him down."

"You have to react to your specific child," says Kate Kelley about four-year-old Rosalie. "General theories of child rearing just won't work because children are all so different." In Kate and John's case, their "specific child" is a strong-willed creature, and they've had to adapt to her willfulness. When they get into a dispute with her, they've found that their only recourse is to change the subject.

"We went out the other night with our neighbors, and Rosalie was such a brat," says Kate. "Our neighbors were really horrified. He was saying, 'One of the things my education taught me was that you have to be firm with your child.' I said, 'Being firm doesn't do any good.' And he said, 'Well, you can't be afraid of a confrontation.' I said, 'You can if it goes on for eight hours.' He said, 'Well, you have to win it.' I said, 'There are some that are unwinnable.' "

"You can get her to the point where you could argue back and forth, and she would scream, 'No, no,' " John explains. "All you have to do is just stop for a second and distract her, and then you can mention it to her again, and she'll say, 'I'm really sorry for doing that. . . . I don't know why I was yelling like that.' All of a sudden, she is this totally rational being. But unless you break it —if you kept up the confrontation with her—you could stay there and slug it out; you could do anything you want, but you'll never break it. She has to save face sometimes."

The biggest surprise about parenting for Linda Pillsbury, a first-time mother at age twenty-eight, was in picking up on her child's distinctive personality. "I never was a baby person," says Linda, "but Leah is much more interesting than I thought. She's alert, curious." When they're out in public, Leah is not shy about expressing herself. She's "a little person dictating what to do: fussing or crying. You have to take her seriously as a person," says Linda.

The singular imperative to respond to a child's uniqueness is confirmed by the latest neonatal research and early childhood studies, which indicate that infants and toddlers are emotionally complex and innately individualistic at birth. Pioneering Boston pediatrician T. Berry Brazelton, for instance, introduced the Brazelton Neonatal Behavioral Assessment Scale, which was designed to detect developmental problems in premature infants; a side effect of the test is to offer a window into the baby's future self. A simple rattle-ball-and-flashlight series of tests indicates how the infant responds to jarring interruptions, stress and annoyance, and shows whether he's privately or socially inclined.

Young parents today are advised to establish a trust-inducing system of "justice" with their babies. This means, in effect, extending to babies the courtesies you would to an adult. For instance, a baby's sense of justice is violated if parents sneak out when she's asleep, leaving her to wake up and find a baby-sitter there, says Helen Reid, coordinator of Pre-school and Infant Parenting Service (PIPS), an affiliate of Thalians Mental Health Center, Cedars-Sinai Medical Center, Los Angeles. Better they should wake her to say good-bye. The baby "may cry and it's good," Reid explains; she may "feel anger or sadness," but at least she knows what's going on. Another no-no, according to Reid, is breast-feeding the baby to sleep without first nudging him awake to remind him he's being put down for the night.

Lauren Watson, a single mother by choice from Logan, Utah, tries to follow the philosophy of natural consequences in rearing her four-year-old son. She treats Troy much as she would anyone else. "I don't let him get away with a lot of stuff. If he doesn't do something that he's supposed to do, it doesn't get done. If he complains about dinner—that he doesn't like it—I say, 'That's too bad, that's what's for dinner; if you don't eat it, you don't.' "

Singulars seem to agree that anger is an inappropriate and coercive force, especially when coming from a parent. "I won't yell at him or try to urge it [food] on him," says Lauren.

Singulars prefer to exercise quiet confidence and gentle strength, as is borne out in the way Josie Roberts serves her two daughters an early dinner. Three-year-old Anna, just home from preschool, sits herself at the table, and Josie plunks eighteen-month-old Michelle into her perch on a battered high chair.

Anna requests a tuna fish sandwich, a peeled apple and some cheese. When her order comes, she is dissatisfied. "Mommy, I want mayonnaise with my cucumber," Anna says.

"I don't want you to have mayonnaise with your cucumber," Josie replies evenly.

"Why?" asks Anna.

"Because too much of it's not very good for you," her mother replies.

Josie does not shoot down her daughter's desire for mayo with, "Because I say so"; neither is Josie bothered by her daughter's request. Instead she supplies a straightforward, level-headed argument that Anna can't refute. She addresses the tot's health concerns as she might when speaking to a peer.

The eat-your-peas-or-there's-no-dessert threat has bitten the theoretical dust among singulars. Even babies are believed by some nutritionists to be capable of selecting a healthy, balanced diet for themselves if given the unlikely opportunity to do so. Nutritional experts, convinced that many of today's rampant adult eating disorders trace back to the high chair, recommend the enactment of "self-demand feeding habits," thus ending the use of food as a reward/punishment system for children.

We try to raise our children to be nonclingy and self-sufficient. "Troy knows how to take care of himself," Lauren Watson says proudly. "If I'm not awake, he'll get up and take his own breakfast; he has since he was one and a half."

Singular parents have become increasingly natural and free with our children about sexuality—ours and theirs. Nudity or the hint of sexual activity is not as threatening to us as it was to our parents' generation. Some young parents encourage sexual self-exploration at an early age, while most simply take a nonintervention policy, neither encouraging nor discouraging juvenile masturbation and play-acting.

Bath time is a nightly ritual of pleasure and attention for Rosalie Shobe. After her father bathes her, he carries Rosie in so she can kiss her mother good night. John deposits her on Kate's lap, and Kate unwraps the jumbo towel to check her daughter out.

"Is your vulva dry?" Kate asks.

Rosalie breaks into a peal of laughter and burrows herself into her mother's body. Kate and John's unselfconscious approach and use of anatomically precise words help to convey the message that our bodies are beautiful, a precious and pleasure-giving resource, not something to be ashamed of.

By the same token, singular parents try to avoid inflicting sex-role stereotypes on our children. We encourage our daughters to be athletic, outspoken and confident, and our sons to be gentle, kind and sensitive.

Recommended and favored discipline practices of singular parents place the ball in the child's court, forcing him to be self-policing at as early an age as possible. Josie Roberts's approach is to make discipline "as boring as possible" rather than something a child might derive perverse pleasure from. When Anna acts up, she's sent to her parents' bedroom.

"First we'll warn her," Josie explains. " 'Please don't whine, Anna.' Or, 'Anna, don't knock Michelle down again.' If she doesn't heed, then we put her in our room. She hates it; she hates being made to go sit on our bed. . . . We tell her, 'When you can come out and apologize, come out.' 'When you feel like you can behave yourself, come out.' Sometimes she won't come out for ten minutes, so we know she's still angry."

Corporal punishment, though still used by many parents, is frowned upon by singulars. Settling disputes with brute force violates our principle of natural interaction among individuals.

WHY SINGULARS HESITATE TO HAVE KIDS

Despite our ability to raise a healthy child, many singulars are reluctant to have kids. While we may hope for a spouse to be a lifetime companion, we cannot and do not count on it. Children are different. Children are our own flesh and blood, whom we cannot divorce. And although the number of parents who are single by default or choice continues growing, not all of us are convinced that single parenting is fair to the child—or to ourselves.

Census Bureau reports show that in this country, the median age of mothers at their first child's birth is steadily going up, while the overall birth rate is declining and the average family and household size is steadily going down. In 1960, the median age of all women in the United States at birth of a first child was 21.8; in 1970, it was 22.1. By 1981, it had reached 23.1.

In 1960, the birth rate in the United States was 23.7 per 1,000 people; the average household size then was 3.33; the average family size was 3.67. In 1970, the birth rate was 18.4 per 1,000; the average household size was 3.14; while the average family size was 3.58. By 1980, the birth rate was 15.9 per 1,000; the average household size had fallen to 2.76, while the average family size was 3.29. By 1984, the year ended in March, the birth rate had dropped to 14.6 per 1,000, while the average household size was 2.71 and the average family size 3.24. These demographic trends are clear, and they announce a bold and rapid streamlining of families and households.

The singular generation came of age in the sixties and seventies, when our parents were unfastening their marriages at record speed and trying to find themselves, in spite of the children. Self-reliance became our first and most heartfelt principle. As a result, it is hard for many of us to trust in love—even the love of an unborn child—and it is hard for us to open up, to see the benefit of sharing our "wealth" with anyone else. Having a child represents the ultimate commitment, which is increasingly difficult to extract from a generation of commitmentphobes.

Drew Harwood is a twenty-eight-year-old New England native whose parents divorced when he was two. The Missouri business-man reluctantly married his college sweetheart last year; the standard marry-me-or-we're-through marching orders eased him toward the altar. But the subject of children is simply off limits between him and his wife.

To Drew, a handsome man who seems perpetually ill at ease with himself, the prospect of having kids is overwhelming, perhaps because of its irrevocable nature. "I would like some kind of escape clause," he admits.

Drew has such an outlet from his marriage: divorce. But there would be no escaping a living, breathing human being he might father. "I'm not 100 percent averse to having kids, but damn near it."

Like Drew, many married children of divorced parents are skeptical of their relationships, even if they are going well by all objective measures. "I don't want to make history repeat itself," he says, referring to his parents' divorce. "I would like to wait to see if my feelings [about my wife] remain the same."

Even singulars who did not have to reckon with a broken home while they were growing up often use the same vague, noncommittal language when discussing parenting. "If having a kid is going to interrupt my job, I may not have one," says Claire Haberman, a twenty-three-year-old New Yorker. Careers are uppermost in our minds, and we view children as a hindrance to their growth.

"Children are out of the question for the next five years," says Joanne Fong, a twenty-five-year-old architectural apprentice living in Berkeley, California. "I'm just trying to get my experience now. I want to wait till I get established more, and then, if I can get time off. . . ." At that point, she will start thinking more seriously about starting her own family.

Still others feel that children represent an unacceptable cramp in life-style.

However, even when we identify a maternal tug, eighties women are unlikely to abandon, or even delay, career plans to start a family.

"I used to think kids were alien pestilentials," says Stanford University medical resident Krysia Lindan. "Right now I respond to them much more on a gut level. Every once in a while, I see a baby and think, 'I'd really like to have babies.' It's an instinctual thing." But Krysia estimates that it will be another six years before her career will give her the time to become a mother.

Anxieties about our future further contribute to a generational reluctance to have children. Many socially conscious young adults, who would like nothing better than to bear the next generation of socially conscious children, worry about nuclear annihilation.

"I have a fear of bringing a child into the world when we're not all that sure that the world will go on," worries Holly Jennings of Winston-Salem, North Carolina. "Or that it will go on in the way we've made it for the child's lifetime." The leading concern of Holly and her husband, Jeff, is the "arms-race situation." But for all the couple's misgivings, they intend to summon faith from their Christian backgrounds to see them into parenting. They plan to start their family within the next year, after Jeff has completed his first year as a medical resident in Minneapolis.

Today's economy has thrown yet another monkey wrench into the economics of parenting and prospective parenting. Downward economic mobility; the spiraling costs of housing, education and taxation; plus the fact that it takes two incomes to reach rough parity with a one-paycheck household of a generation ago, make it more expensive to rear children now.

The fact that we increasingly depend on lower-paying, less-reliable employment further contributes to our conservative parenting posture and puts some of us in danger of having our unborn children priced out of the market. We often scrutinize the cost-benefit ratio of having a child long in advance of pregnancy, keeping in mind that we can expect to spend roughly 30 percent of the household budget on him or her in a one-child family. Estimates for the cost of rearing a child, from delivery room to employability, in real dollars, vary from $135,000 to $200,000. For some, one child is all we can afford. For others, kids fall into the luxury category. Some small numbers of us feel that the genetic grab bag represents too great a risk; better to make a calculated investment on some better known quantity.

Claire Haberman says she wouldn't have children unless she was assured that they would enjoy the same standard of living that she did when she was growing up. "I want to at least give them what I've had." At her present salary of $14,000 a year, she has a long way to go to provide any child with trips abroad and a summer country house.

"We think of parenting as being at least several years off, if not five," says twenty-eight-year-old Chris Sands, a Hollywood film industry executive. Chris and his long-time companion want financial stability before starting a family. "Primarily we want to get our careers and finances in place and provide as good a home as possible," says Chris. "In life you get away with a lot more when you're rich, to be crass about it." Having money will put the male couple in "a stronger position to take on the very bold act of being gay parents."

LESS PRESSURE TO PARENT

Further contributing to the declining birth rate is the fact that the pressure to parent is now a shadow of its former self.

Singulars often complain about feeling pressure *not* to have

children. Young women especially can be admonished against falling into the "motherhood trap"; nothing more effectively stunts a
promising career or makes us seem unconcerned about our work,
we are told, than getting pregnant and carrying the fetus to term.
The media version of success in the eighties has it that singulars
should build our careers, build financial security, work out and
dine solely on gourmet cuisine—to the exclusion of anything that
might get in the way. Parenting can fit into the idealized picture,
too, but only if it doesn't undermine these goals. The reality is
that almost inevitably, it does.

A widening definition of the "family" further lessens the importance and centrality of children in contemporary life. The nuclear
family unit of mom, pop and 2.3 kids has been supplanted by the
"reconstituted family," consisting of live-in lovers and nonrelated
singles. Many singulars remain attached to our growing-up families for longer periods than ever before, relentlessly probing for
the roots of our own psyches in family relations, insisting that our
psychic confusion be sorted out before creating a family of our
own. Once-unorthodox family combinations will gain greater acceptance in the eighties and beyond, demographers and social
analysts predict.

Just as the current wisdom maintains that unhappy parents do
themselves a disservice by keeping their troubled marriages together for the sake of the children, adult children are no longer
expected to produce children for the sake of their parents.

When twenty-one-year-old Paul B. Marcus cited "bringing happiness" to his parents and grandparents as the primary reason he
and his fiancée plan to have children soon, he sounded curiously
archaic. "Because my grandparents are getting old, my father isn't
that healthy," he said, "we plan to have children probably within
two years."

PUTTING OFF PARENTING

Twenty years ago, single and married women who were not yet
mothers but who wanted to be started to get antsy in their mid- to

late twenties. Men of that time generally felt a need to settle down by the age of thirty. But singulars bring our postponement tendencies to the childbearing arena.

"I definitely want to have children," says New Yorker Rhonda Gainer. "I don't really think about it; it'll happen when it's ready to happen." At twenty-eight, Rhonda does not hear even a faint ticking of the biological clock. "I'm still a young female," she insists.

"I want to have a little baby girl when I'm about forty," says twenty-nine-year-old Los Angeleno Liz Brody, while sunning herself on Venice Beach. "No husband," she says. According to this scenario, she has all the time in the world—over a decade—to accomplish her goal.

With advances in medical technology and the recent baby boomlet among women in their mid-thirties to early forties, we have no reason to panic while we are still in our twenties; many of us do not even think about parenting until we hit thirty. This tendency to postpone will certainly expand the number of increasingly common "late-life" babies. Other postponers, undoubtedly, will never have children. A 1981 U.S. Census Bureau report on fertility projected that as women currently in their twenties and thirties reach middle age, the proportion of childless Americans over forty could double, increasing to 15 to 20 percent, from today's 10 percent.

Married couples are increasingly choosing sterilization to prevent pregnancy. According to figures from the National Center for Health Statistics, surgical sterilization of both men and women has risen dramatically in recent years. Recent figures show that in 1982, in 8.2 percent of all couples aged twenty to twenty-four, one spouse elected sterilization, while 19.6 percent of those twenty-five to twenty-nine chose sterilization as a means of limiting family size or preventing children altogether. According to the NCHS study, in 1965, 73 percent of all married couples of childbearing age were able to have children; by 1982, just 52.7 percent were able to.

SINGLE MOTHERS: BY CHOICE OR DEFAULT

Those with a strong drive to have children but with no mate in sight sometimes elect to go the parenting route alone. Many more women find themselves cast as single parents through divorce, separation or death. However we get there, the ranks of single parents—90 percent of whom are female—continue to expand. In 1983, just over one in every five babies were born to single mothers, with births to single Anglo teens on the greatest growth spiral.

The stigma against never-married and divorced mothers has diminished substantially over the last two decades. Single mothers report that nary an eyebrow is raised nowadays about their marital status, a change in attitude that is reflected in the contemporary vernacular. The term "bastard," for instance, has an archaic ring to it, as does the notion of an "illegitimate" (vs. a "legitimate") birth. Eighties babies are born to "single mothers" rather than "unwed" or "unmarried" mothers. In fast-track spots like Manhattan, some single moms have become hot items on the social scene because they bucked the careerist tide to have a child and because they can provide a man with a "ready made" family.

However, this enlightened attitude has not carried over to the economic front, where single mothers face a bleak financial picture as the dual trends of "feminization" and "childization" of poverty continue to expand.

Despite a bleak economic forecast, many single women consciously or unconsciously enter into motherhood because they do not want to miss out on this primary life experience. A growing number of singulars have come to view solo parenting as a positive alternative to either remaining childless or casting about for a spouse when procreation, not marital partnership, is uppermost in our minds; it makes no sense to us to enter into a false bond with a member of the other sex just to have children.

It was with precisely this attitude that Lauren Watson deliberately got pregnant at age twenty-two with Doug, a male roommate and good pal who was not her boyfriend. While Lauren did not tell Doug that she intended to get pregnant, she says he was aware at the time they made love that she'd recently gone off the pill.

Lauren had always liked kids and so decided to have one of her own. Her scheme was specific: She wanted a child but did not want to have to deal with a man. Marriage, she says, was not then and is not now "at all an ambition of mine."

Upon announcing her pregnancy, Lauren says she had pressure from all sides to abort, from her wealthy Catholic parents and from her dear friends—pressure from everyone but Doug. Doug even offered to marry her, for the sake of the child.

"He said, 'Come on, let's just do it. You can always divorce me later,' " Lauren recalls. "I just said, 'No, *I* got pregnant; this is my responsibility. I didn't consult you; this is something I'm going to have to deal with myself.' "

Lauren has remained close to Doug—"best friends"—during the almost five years since she got pregnant. Doug subsequently married someone else, fathered two more children and got divorced. When he left his wife, he moved in temporarily with Lauren and Troy. Lauren remembers Troy saying, " 'I know Daddy can't but sometimes I really wish he could live with us.' "

Originally from New Jersey, Lauren migrated to Logan, Utah, to attend Utah State University; she continues to stay in the area so that her son can maintain regular contact with his father. "Troy is crazy about Doug," she says, a feeling that is mutual. Doug pays Lauren $150 a month in voluntary child support and comes to visit Troy every week, taking him for the weekend to ski or home to play. Once it became clear that Doug was exercising his parental rights and observing his parental responsibilities, Lauren added his name to her own on Troy's birth certificate and legally hyphenated the child's last name.

Lauren is convinced that she's raising a healthy, happy, smart, self-sufficient child who will grow into adulthood bearing those same traits. Only occasionally does she worry that Troy might suffer in the long term from her decision to raise him alone. Even then, her doubts are negligible.

"I am concerned a little bit," she admits. But when Lauren

looks around her at the children who were born to women who didn't want them, or to women who didn't love their husbands or boyfriends, her doubts vanish. Troy has it better than those children, Lauren reasons. "At least I can tell him, 'Hey, you were really wanted.' "

Though they are growing in number, single parents by choice represent but a fraction of the single parent population. In most cases, parents become single by default—when a marriage breaks up, or when we find ourselves pregnant outside marriage and decide to carry the fetus to term. In divorce, the mother usually gains custody of the children. Occasionally, and in a growing number of cases, the father does.

Though lone parenting is taxing on the finances and wearing on the emotions, singular single parents feel that it's better for the children to raise them alone, in relative harmony, than in the heated atmosphere of an unhappy home.

Rosanna Gold, a thirty-year-old hairdresser and mother of two from Belmont, California, has gone "from month to month" making ends meet for the last three years since she divorced the husband she married when she was seventeen. The rent for her three-bedroom ranch-style house in the San Francisco suburb is $800 a month, and child-support payments from the kids' father come in only sporadically. She has tried renting out one of the bedrooms to an assortment of roommates, doubling up her eleven-year-old son and eight-year-old daughter, but none of the roommates ever seems to work out. So Rosanna has taken on extra work, teaching hairstyling at a beauty college and doing hair shows at conventions.

For all her struggles, Rosanna believes that her parenting performance has improved since she and her husband split up. "The relationships I have with my kids have probably grown closer since the divorce," says Rosanna. "When I was married, I would scream, 'These kids are driving me nuts!' Let him take care of them. [Now] I never go to sleep angry at them; I never go to sleep with them angry at me. Things have to be talked out."

The kids have also helped to keep her down to earth, causing her to confront (and overcome) her overuse of drugs and tobacco. "Sometimes it's like a reversal with them—who's the parent and who's the child. They say, 'Mom, you swear too much,' or 'You've got to quit smoking.' " Rosanna exudes self-confidence and a certain joie de vivre and seems to have gained inner strength in her struggle to land on her feet, financially and emotionally.

Many single mothers are not so fortunate. However, the emerging idea of the singular generation is that single parenting isn't necessarily tragic or unfortunate; it can be a positive endeavor whose yields are directly proportional to what we put into it. As society casts off the stigma formerly attached to the situation, single parents are gaining legitimacy and respect and getting on with the business of rearing children.

ERODING STIGMA AGAINST THE ONLY CHILD

A generation ago, the "only" child was a pitied personality, defined almost apologetically by his or her solitary status and seemingly destined to be neurotic; parents were thought to do a child a gross injustice by having just one. But just as singulars reject the notion that you have to be married or coupled to find fulfillment in life, we no longer believe a child must have a brother or sister to make the "right" social adjustment. Increasingly, singular parents are stopping at one.

In rethinking the conventional wisdom about only children, some of us believe that only children may be *better* off. Like oldest children, only children receive a greater share of their parents' financial and emotional resources and, therefore, tend to have higher IQs and become more successful in life than second, third or fourth children.

Singulars would prefer to raise one happy, healthy child—a "gourmet baby"—than to strain our resources to try to produce a larger but lesser brood. One child seems to us manageable, while two or more seem to require exponentially greater attention.

Since singulars postpone having a first baby until we are older, and since the cost of parenting continues to expand as our ability to support children weakens, it seems probable that in the future, many more of us will have "single" children.

VOLUNTEER PARENTS

Singulars are the first generation of young Americans who feel that parenting is optional, not obligatory. We grew up with legalized abortion and readily accessible contraception. Long ago, we accepted as fact that we didn't *have* to get married or have children or follow any conventional path to find our way.

Singulars become parents simply because we want to and because the time is right and the circumstances permit. We parent for parenting's sake. No longer is having children tied into our sense of security about the future or into fulfilling society's expectations of us. Indeed, many of us harbor doubts that tomorrow exists, and if it does, we cannot see the future clearly. If we do believe in the future, we no longer think that children are obliged to care for their parents in old age or that they can provide security that the parents cannot provide themselves.

Singulars parent because we love children and want to enjoy them and nurture them in the here and now. When we have children, we surrender a share of our freedom, but we give it up willingly, eager to assume the challenges of the job. We are excited at the prospect and the reality of raising a child—an individual—from birth to fulfill his or her potential. We try to treat our offspring as individuals and to communicate with them as best we can, rather than to cast them as "infants" or "male" or "son of Sarah." Even as babies, they are their own persons.

Where eighties parents may stumble—if we're not careful—is in being too permissive, in instilling in a child an inordinate sense of self-importance, in allowing the ever-diminishing gap between childhood and adulthood to shrink beyond all reasonable proportions.

Despite these pitfalls, singular parents are eminently qualified for the responsibility of parenting. As volunteers, we have the patience and preparation to rear the next generation in an increasingly pressurized global den. Whether or not we acknowledge it, singulars who take on the task of parenting are the hope of the entire generation.

CHAPTER 9

Having Fun

SCHEDULED RELAXATION

Having fun is a self-conscious endeavor to most singulars. We schedule in the good times, just as we make time for career advancement and regular workouts. Fun is no longer spontaneous; its pursuit has become paradoxically purposeful. We have fun in short bursts, on certain nights of the week, certain weeks of the year: hitting a health club, treating ourselves to dinner at the finest restaurant in town, taking in a new vacation spot. Fun does not come naturally to us—if at all—and it is not well integrated into the lives of most singulars.

"What do I do to have fun?" asks New Yorker Tony Gittelson. "I'm drawing a blank."

Though seriousness was the style of the young in the sixties and seventies, the flipped-out element of that epoch actually provided a ready model for having a good time. Fun—that is, amusing oneself to no particular end—was not hard to come by. Youth was one's ticket to the heady, exhilarating merry-go-round of life, and going nowhere was not only okay but desirable. Today you need money to enjoy the popular forms of recreation: to buy high-tech home-entertainment equipment and rent tapes for your VCR, to pay for the expensive vacations and fine meals out. And the decade's pet drug, cocaine, neither comes cheap nor lasts long.

"Fun to me in the end," says one singular, "is how you spend your discretionary dollars."

On the surface, the singular generation appears to be a fun-loving, self-indulgent group. We dress in flashy neon colors, strut our bodies narcissistically; even men wear makeup and get their hair permed. On campus, we pursue the madcap merriments of another era with raccoon coats, frat parties and senior soirees. But somehow, it doesn't work. We're just lip-syncing the lyrics, trying very hard. Cyndi Lauper's hit single "Girls Just Want to Have Fun" is more a yearning than a motto in an era in which the boys and the girls are preoccupied with getting aboard and getting ahead.

On the economic front, singulars must swim against a strong tide of downward economic mobility. At work, we put in long hours to move ahead and sometimes just to keep our jobs; the immediate and cumulative work-related stress can be hard to shake after hours. Between networking, keeping our bodies fit, eating the right foods, organizing our homes and our lives and forging our religious and political identities, our agendas are full. If we're married, we strive to maintain our end of the marital partnership, and if we're parents, we work at nurturing our child's true identity so as not to impose our wills or ways unfairly on him or her. It is not an easy task, being a singular. And having fun can be the most elusive of the many goals to which we aspire.

What's more, many traditional forms of fun-making and frivolity are going by the wayside. Ritualized dating is less prevalent than before, because singulars are more apt to be friends with each other than boyfriend-girlfriend. We drink and smoke less than did our counterparts twenty years ago, and taking drugs is no longer the thing to do.

Sports and recreation are supplanting these waning forms of behavior. But unless we work out with friends at a gym, are members of an athletic squad or have a standing tennis date, these are apt to be solitary pursuits, measured against internal benchmarks and having little to do with interacting with others.

Social recreation for singulars increasingly revolves around food, staged parties and exotic travel. Most of us are not social animals by nature, but that doesn't stop us from playing the part.

When we go out or throw a party, we are capable of pulling out the stops to camp it up and vamp it up.

Sarah Folger strives to maintain a lighthearted spirit by building a toy collection and keeping alive the teenage giggles, pranks and inside jokes with her two best friends from college.

"I'd be miserable if I didn't have that sense of fun," says the twenty-three-year-old L.A. recording company junior executive. She and her friends often meet at a coffee shop and sit there for hours, downing coffee and pancakes and floating absurdist jokes. They joke about the other customers—the way they look and walk and dress—and insult each other in code words no one else can understand.

Beneath the fun lies a deep sea of worry. "Everyone has absolute angst about what we want to do with our lives. There's this unceasing pressure about growing up and deciding what we want to do. We keep telling ourselves we are still in our early twenties."

THE SPIRIT OF DETACHMENT

Not surprisingly, today's leading entertainers reflect the singular state of mind. In popular acts, a spirit of detachment and contrivance has edged out the spontaneity and gut-level passion of two decades ago. Human warmth is decidedly lacking in the cerebral lyrics of the B-52s and the Talking Heads' David Byrne. Madonna is the walking embodiment of the material (even mechanical) girl, with her gaudy jewelry and cluttered outfits that parody overstatement. Michael Jackson has introduced into vocal performance such theatrical high jinks as precision dance, mechanically complex lighting and sound effects, raised to the heights of near-machinelike perfection.

Music video, with its fragmented, sharp-cutting format and story within a song, has revolutionized the way music is enjoyed. Instead of listening, we now *see* music. We can get so involved with the images on screen that we don't have to ponder them, much less communicate with each other. Our postpunk but punk-influenced music contains the brittle, brutal, mechanized sounds and images of hopelessness, despair and disengagement. The themes of popular music have made a dramatic departure from the narrow constrictions of boy-girl love songs, reflecting our larger defection from that tight-knit heterosexual model.

The humor we respond to tends to be laced with extreme irony, drawing heavily on the past and on media representations of life rather than life itself. David Letterman, who is probably the last word in humor for young sophisticates today, "embodies the eighties," according to Robert Burnett of North Caldwell, New Jersey. "He's detached from what's going on on his show," explains the twenty-two-yea.-old aspiring comic. "He's talking to guests and he's slightly condescending. More often than not, he repeats in a funny way what his guests are saying."

On one recent Christmas special, for instance, Letterman brought on as guests Pat Boone along with Letterman's wife, kids and brother. In reality, however, Letterman has no wife and kids. The "family" were hired for the occasion in order to satirize the idea of the Christmas TV special. What Letterman is really doing is commenting on commentators and on the process of commentating, rather than creating a reality of his own.

"This is the time we're in right now," says Robert Burnett. "Everyone is looking at situations instead of being in them. Everyone is making fun of everyone else. Everyone has that aunt who comes over and asks about your summer vacation, and you're there answering her but inside saying 'Oh, Jesus.' Everyone is doing that to each other, even husbands and wives."

The decade's up-and-coming new comics specialize in wacky, surrealistic humor, doing bits that are full of non sequiturs and nonsensical allusions. Pee-Wee Herman, the new age Howdy Doody, uses toys in his act. Poker-faced standup comedian Steven Wright draws laughs with one-liners such as, "I got into the elevator the other day and pressed Arizona." And: "Babies don't get vacations, but I always see them at the beach." These are quick takes that reflect the electronic media's preference for fast action.

Laura Levine, a veteran Los Angeles television sit-com writer, sees a growing nihilism in humor today. "I'm alarmed at what's funny to young audiences in the eighties. It's vicious stuff, where people get hurt. Mr. Bill gets destroyed, mutilated—it's not the least bit amusing." She cites a recent takeoff on Cole Porter's "Birds Do It, Bees Do It" that goes: "Nuns on their knees do it; amputees do it." "There's a hostile edge to that kind of humor."

While not all eighties humor is malevolent, the central strain holds the media reality of the past at arm's length and tinkers with it rather than creating or stating much in itself. For instance, Dan Coffey of the San Francisco–based Duck's Breath Mystery Theatre plays Mr. Science in an ongoing skit called "Ask Mr. Science." Coffey plays a local-TV Einstein, a stiff, white-coated, fifties-style scientist who explains everything in technical terms because, he says deadpan, "I have a master's degree—in science."

Poking fun at the stiffness of the fifties and early sixties is a stock-in-trade of eighties humor. To members of the singular generation, the past makes for funnier fodder than the here and now.

OUR PLEASURE DOMES

In keeping with our private, self-sufficient natures and our home-body predilections, the locus for making merry has shifted inward with the singular generation. Though we still enjoy going out, we no longer *have to* leave our living rooms—or even our bedrooms —to have a good time; though we still have fun with others, togetherness is no longer a requirement for good times.

New technologies have made it possible to enjoy high-quality entertainment in our private pleasure domes. A big night on the town for singulars is apt to take place in front of the television as we stretch out in our sock feet. We clear the decks, unplug the telephone or turn on the answering machine and sit back to watch the film of our choice on our VCR, or to listen to a high-quality concert on our laser-disc player. We no longer have to fight—or join—the crowds to indulge our favorite pastimes. Neither must we wait for a concert tour or a favorite old flick to be played at a revival house or on late-night TV.

No longer at the mercy of network or even cable programming, VCRs enable us to see what we want when we want. We can control our own environments and direct and produce our own entertainment to develop and express our individual tastes and preferences as never before. If we're fans of science fiction, we can rent or own every tape that's made. If our fancy runs to pornographic films, we don't have to frequent X-rated theaters to indulge. If we enjoy public television, we can tape it and save it. We can replay scenes on screen or freeze the action to take a Häagen-Dazs break. We can exercise with Jane Fonda and Arnold Schwarzenegger. And the quality of sound and the clarity of image are so fine that outside theaters have little competitive pull.

Often our electronic equipment and home appliances are our most prized possessions. "I love my computer," confesses twenty-seven-year-old aspiring Los Angeles actor Allen Fine. "I love my speaker phone, my cordless phone, the microwave. My roommate has an IBM PC Jr. I have a Kaypro. Video, definitely. There are two video machines here."

Whenever Lance Guest and his two roommates happen to be home on the same night, the L.A. trio tapes a jam session on their tape deck, hooked up with two microphones. They play rhythm and blues, funky stuff, sometimes adding vocals. Lance's taste runs to the absurd, and recently his roommate Mike picked up a story from the *National Enquirer*, "UFO Aliens Repair Kitchen Appliances," and sang it as lyrics. "Both of us play guitar and we make tapes," explains the twenty-five-year-old actor, who played the lead in the 1984 feature film *The Last Starfighter*. "It's like being in a studio on a small scale."

If singulars like home computer games, we can shoot-'em-up in umpteen different ways, or plant ourselves in the cockpit of a Cessna airplane in true-to-life simulated adventure. We can play the stock market or take the helm of a major corporation. We can be babes in computerland, kids in a candy store.

Singulars have fun in our kitchens, orchestrating a variety of appliances from cappuccino machines to Cuisinarts, to whip up any number of gourmet delectables. We revel in our bathrooms, closets, home gyms and greenhouses. "When I think about how appliances have changed my life in the last several years," says Jill Kearney, a Los Angeles writer who works at home, "it's considerable: between the answering machine, the word processor, and the video recorder. I like them; I've gotten used to them. It would be hard to go back." Though we no longer must depend on others or on outside recreations to keep ourselves amused, in expanding our pleasure domes and indulging ourselves therein, we create a new sphere of dependency—on inanimate objects and mechanical devices.

ZEN AND THE ART OF SOIL-SAMPLE COLLECTING

Hobbies are probably the quintessential form of singular fun, because they are our private passions and pastimes, cultivated and tended alone, at home. In the pursuit of fun, as elsewhere, singulars need to lay claim to one particular area, one special domain: to specialize. If we cannot move as quickly up the corporate ladder as we would like, at least we can be the only person in our office with a collection of antique apple peelers.

Our hobbies can be as quirky and idiosyncratic as we are, and through them, we express our individuality—our distinct, even exotic, inner selves. Some of us may gravitate toward the obscure, others, the traditional. We collect algae, rocks, soil and water; guns, stamps, postcards and Christmas cards; books, magazines, matchbook covers and antique jewelry; marbles, thimbles, globes and gloves. We create museums dedicated to particular performers or celebrities—Elvis, JFK or even Mickey Mouse—and sometimes to ourselves. A spokesperson for Christie's, the New York auction house, says that young collectors are now snapping up such classical collectibles as rare china and old silver.

Like other forms of singular leisure, hobbies are purposeful, resulting in an end product. The inward discipline of a hobby underscores the singular generation's preference for the small picture, for trading in minutiae.

Twenty-six-year-old Lucy Johnson of Boston has half a dozen crystals that decorate the mantelpiece in her bedroom and that she believes have curative powers. For good luck, she tucks one into her handbag before taking an exam. Southwestern Virginia's Ed Bowman stows his gun collection in the spare room of his trailer. Susanna Hoffs, lead singer/guitarist of the all-girl L.A.

rock group The Bangles, has a passion for old postcards, especially hand-colored ones of the Eiffel Tower and the Empire State Building. Someday the twenty-six-year-old, who sang the hit single "Manic Monday," plans to create a free-standing "wall" of postcards from two clear plastic shower curtains, sewn together to hold horizontal tiers of postcards, to be viewed from front and back.

Elements of absurdity, irony, nostalgia—and even personal compulsion—often figure into our collections.

Toys serve as the major motif in the decorating scheme of Sarah Folger's Spanish-style single apartment in West Los Angeles. They are everywhere—displayed on shelves, tacked on walls, marching toward the bathroom, wedged between dishes in the kitchen cupboard.

"What appeals to me about toys is that they're simplistic," says Sarah, picking out a miniature exam-crazed Japanese student and winding him up. The plastic toy writes furiously while rocking up and down on his chair in a frenzied study that has turned his eyes into black spirals. Another windup boy wonder, this one from Hungary, walks in circles, toting an enormous suitcase. "There's nothing else you can get out of it but childlike fun. Nothing you can do but smile and laugh at the absurdity of them."

Krysia Lindan collects dirt samples from remote spots of the world to offer escape from the long, grueling hours in her medical residency. "I began because I have such an interest in traveling, and it seems like I have a little piece of each place that is acultural."

To date, Krysia has collected (or been given) seventeen soil samples from such distant points as Alum Bay and the Isle of Wight in the British Isles, to Mount St. Helens in Washington State. In Burma, she personally gathered dirt from the ruins of a pagoda; some of it was broken-down brick.

Krysia's motley collection, stored in neat glass bowls, zip-lock plastic bags and even in a six-ounce baby bottle, is displayed in her bedroom atop the footlocker that her physician parents brought back from Africa in the forties. It is at least in part a spoof of the scientific model with which she grew up.

"My father said, 'I can't believe you have all this education and science background, and you would get a collection ridiculously simple like dirt,' " she recalls. Compared to Olgierd Lindan's extensive collection of antique medical equipment and quackish devices, gathered mostly from auctions near his stately midwestern home, Krysia's trunk-top collection does seem rather paltry. And yet she finds it strangely satisfying.

"It gives me a little thrill; I can't exactly say why. Sometimes I just come and look at it, or plunge my fingers into the soil." Yet Krysia never intends to become so attached to the collection that it would take on real meaning. Someday, she says, "when I have a massive collection, I plan to mix all the samples up together and make a rock garden."

PLAYING MY SONG

The one area in which singulars are experts, hands down, is our own personal histories. For many of us, our hobbies are ourselves, and we specialize in compiling and collecting tidbits and fragments from our pasts: exams and essays, photographs and favorite clothes to create a personal archive. We make videos, slide shows and films about our pasts; increasingly we employ electronic equipment in cataloging and documenting different periods of our lives.

Allen Fine recently devoted three months of spare time to making a master tape of his family history. Allen, who lives in Los Angeles's San Fernando Valley, took his family's 8-mm films, transferred them onto video and added a sound track. Using editing techniques, he was able to make the family memoirs into an entertaining three-hour show, adding music for effect and intercutting between scenes. To the scenes from when his brother was born, for instance, Allen added the music from *2001*'s "Star Child" sequence. With the shots of Mom undressing Allen for his first bath, he played striptease music. The end product was a video in which he and his family are the stars.

Though Allen's working knowledge of video and his ready access to electronic equipment sets him apart from most of his peers, his fascination with his personal history does not.

Susie Hoffs, likewise, is possessed by her life story, even as it unfolds. She meticulously keeps copies, sometimes in multiples, of the publications in which she and her band have been written up: *Rolling Stone, People, Cream* and *Bam* among them. And she digs deep into the family's photo albums for clues about her early years, signs of her emerging identity.

"There are some pictures of me playing guitar when I was twelve," she says. "I could see I was playing a real chord. I wasn't sitting there holding the guitar." These photographs mean a lot to Susie, and eventually she plans to select one for an album cover. Another invaluable memento is a tape Susie's mother made of the singer performing as a young girl. "She made tapes of songs I wrote when I was a kid. She's had these tapes and saved them. This year, I'm going to get ten copies made."

PURPOSEFUL PURSUITS

For singulars, the pursuit of leisure and recreation has become paradoxically purposeful. When we "relax," we want to accomplish something: to improve our body tone, enhance our appreciation of a symphony or expand the number of concerts we've seen. We are recreational overachievers, and we keep close track of our personal scorecards.

Sports and body-improvement work, we remind ourselves, are necessary for our vitality; whatever fun we might have along the way is almost incidental. We seem to be more motivated by the stick than by the carrot: If we don't get enough exercise, run hard enough, sweat long enough, we have failed. Even the cult of eating and dining out has at its roots the earnest health-food movement of the seventies.

Vacation trends continue moving in a more education- and goal-oriented direction. Club Med, the international vacation village giant, expects to expand its new computer-workshop centers and underwater photography laboratories. Add this to the plethora of sports-related classes and activities at every Club Med, and you can see that the idea of going just to catch the rays seems inexcusably lazy.

"FOODIES"

The preparation of fine food has emerged as one of our leading recreations, even art forms. Singulars approach cooking with reverence and respect, probably because my generation is the first in which regular home-cooked dinners were not necessarily part of the family routine while we were growing up. We admire an at-home chef for her or his skill and versatility, while a top-flight professional has become something of an auteur to whom we pay homage.

"Cooking is a lifetime skill," says twenty-nine-year-old Los Angeles attorney Laura Christa, who enrolled in cooking class at Ma Cuisine, an adjunct to Los Angeles's famed Ma Maison restaurant. "I can cook fine from recipes but I don't feel I know what to do in the kitchen on my own. Last week, the teacher said if something's tasting too salty, add lemon. That's the kind of thing I never knew."

At the evening classes, which cost about $50 per session, participants go through the steps of preparing a multicourse gourmet dinner. One class member remarks that you pay as much for a meal at the restaurant next door, and this way you get to learn how it's done. If dining out is purposeful, learning how to make and then feasting on one's gourmet labors is downright resolute.

Among the elite, dining out today more closely resembles travel than grubbing down; it is an experience in which having been there often counts most of all. "Restaurant madness" is how *New York* magazine describes this rage; the Los Angeles *Times* dubs its adherents "foodies."

"The new restaurant obsession is changing the whole way we live our lives," says Ruth Riechl, restaurant critic for the Los Angeles *Times.* "We're spending all this time in public spaces. If your first impulse when you meet people and like them is not to have them to your house to dinner, which is what I do, but rather to say, 'Let's go to this new hot restaurant,' I find that very strange. People don't even know what the insides of their friends' houses look like."

Restaurant-hopping has replaced bar-hopping as a form of entertainment, with people comparing notes on the latest find. "Have you seen this restaurant?" we ask, as if discussing a movie or a hot new singer. Foodie singulars are unlikely to find a favorite old standby restaurant and eat there every Saturday night; staying up with the times means eating around.

"Keeping up on new restaurants is about my favorite pastime," says twenty-seven-year-old Los Angeles publicist Marijane Levee. "It's more exciting than dancing. Going out to dinner is a major, big event."

Eating out is the perfect complement to a long day at work. It gives everyone a chance to be served. And in its inimitably singular fashion, eating out accommodates the particular preferences of all present. You can drink, get plastered or abstain. You can eat as much or as little as you desire. And if the menu allows, one member of the party can dine on sautéed shrimp and another can sip borscht. If we want to be collective, everyone can order a different dish, so that we can graze the table, sampling a little bit of this, a little of that. What's more, meeting and eating at a restaurant puts everyone on equal footing; no one is host, and everyone is a guest.

Many young adults, of course, cannot afford membership in the cult of haute cuisine. But whether we dine at McDonald's or from Wong's Chinese Take-out, at all income levels, Americans are spending more on eating outside the home. In 1980, Americans allocated nearly twice as much of our food dollar to eating out as we did in 1960.

Not surprisingly, young adults devoted a higher proportion of our food budgets to eating out than did any other age group, according to a National Restaurant Association report. Those under age twenty-five spent 42.8 percent of their total food "pie" on food away from home, while members of the twenty-five-to-thirty-four-year-old age group spent 35.8 percent on eating out. And an April 1984 report in *Foodservice Trends* shows that singles lead the eating-out pack by spending a whopping *"45 percent* of their

total food budget on dining out—substantially above the 32 percent average."

To cater to our grazing tendencies, restaurants are adding a
wide variety of appetizers and mini-entrées to menus. And the
number of small stores, salad bars and food courts, which consist
of clusters of one-item and specialty cuisine offerings, is growing
to meet the demand.

"The evidence is clear," reports the New York *Times*, "that
more people, especially those under thirty-five, are eating smaller
meals more and more frequently throughout the day—mostly on
the run, more often than not alone." The harried, hurried state of
many of our lives suggests that we may be well on the way to
dispensing with the at-home sit-down meal altogether.

THE DECLINE OF DRINKING

When we eat out, we may order a glass of wine with our dinner,
but singulars are growing increasingly leery of drinking as a recreational sport.

"No one drinks anymore," declares a writer from Connecticut
now living in Los Angeles. "If you want to have someone to your
home, you invite him to an intimate dinner party, or you meet for
dinner out. Cocktail parties and long sessions at bars are simply
passé."

The rather rapid decline of alcohol as our primary social lubri-
cant springs from a fundamental shift in priorities. As singulars
invest more time and energy into building our bodies and our
careers, we have less inclination to undermine these efforts by
getting "wasted." Drinking means taking in empty calories, and it
often means sluggishness the morning after. What's more, dependency on alcohol cuts against the singular ideal of self-sufficiency.
We increasingly see alcohol as an addictive and menacing crutch
rather than a liberating vehicle. As we seek to take control of our
lives, we see that liquor can often control us.

When we do drink, we schedule it in. "I can give myself Friday
night to get plastered." Or, "I'll allow myself a debauch to cele-

brate meeting this deadline." Claire Haberman drinks heavily "two nights every other week," and the rest of the time enjoys a glass here and there of light beer or wine. If her boyfriend is buying, they select a fine wine at an expensive liquor store; if she's buying, "I get a big bottle of plonk [cheap wine]."

Scheduled rather than spontaneous imbibing has effectively cut down our level of consumption. The University of Michigan's Institute for Social Research annual "Survey of High School Seniors" of 1984 shows that "the use of alcohol and cigarettes has . . . continued to decline." According to ISR's report, which appeared in the Winter 1984–85 bulletin, "in 1979, 72 percent of seniors reported having used alcohol in the previous 30-day period, but the proportion had dropped to 67 percent by 1984. More important, the proportion of seniors drinking daily or almost daily decreased from 7 percent to 5 percent over the same period. And . . . there has been a decline in binge drinking among students."

Singulars prefer beverages with lower alcoholic content, like wine and beer, to the old-standby hard liquor favorites, whiskey and Scotch. The wine-cooler category, which offers an even lower alcoholic content than straight wine, has taken off dramatically in recent years, as have the sales of sparkling wines and champagnes. Superpremium "specialty" dessert and cream liqueurs also fare well among singulars, who drink to celebrate an occasion rather than to service an alcoholic appetite.

Raising of the minimum drinking age to twenty-one and the trend toward stringent university imposed standards on drinking have helped depress consumption among college students. Fraternity pledges at Dartmouth College, the University of New Hampshire and the University of Maine at Orono must attend alcohol-awareness programs in order to be initiated. And many Greek systems are voluntarily adopting nonalcoholic dry rushes. Some bars and restaurants are eliminating happy-hour drink discounts altogether, stressing their appetizer offerings instead.

Probably the decade's chic drink is water—not the kind you get out of the tap, to be sure, but the bottled and sparkling mineral varieties. A close second would be fresh-squeezed juice.

GOING "STRAIGHT-EDGE"

Taking drugs, like imbibing alcohol, has become less popular with singulars. Although Claire Haberman experimented with pot in prep school, "now I do it very rarely," she says. If it's passed around at a party, she'll smoke it, but she never buys anymore; the same goes for cocaine. She sees drugs as belonging to her "youth," not to her adult years.

When we do take drugs, singulars indulge for private pleasure, to service personal needs; we do not act out of pressure to conform or to make a political statement. To singulars, taking drugs is more an embarrassment than a badge of honor. *Not* taking drugs can be a point of pride.

"I don't drink, smoke, snort, bump or shoot up," says Vinx DeJonParrette, a personal trainer and aspiring musician. Because Vinx is a self-described "funky performer" who says he rubs elbows with the likes of Stevie Wonder on L.A.'s music scene, his teetotaler stance often comes as a surprise. "People know I'm a musician, so they always ask me where I can get drugs. I tell them, 'I don't take drugs.'"

"There's a real swing towards what's known as straight edge," says twenty-four-year-old San Francisco punk Bonni Doolittle. "Which is a lot of punks that drink nothing but Coca-Cola and don't do any drugs or smoke." Now, says Bonni, "there's more of a thing *not* doing drugs."

The use of cocaine—one of our favorite drugs—versus the use of marijuana—the leading drug of the recent past—makes for an interesting contrast. Joints expand the mind, while cocaine gives a rush that energizes the body in the short term, making one feel powerful and sometimes helping one achieve goals. Today if you snort cocaine at a party, you're much more likely to remove yourself to the bathroom alone or maybe with one close friend, making the thrill a private, not a public one. By contrast, in marijuana's heyday, passing the joint elicited a warm, communal feeling; everyone was included, every gathering was the right one, and the drug was always in plentiful supply. Cocaine is "cost-inefficient," one singular complains. "You spend a lot of money and buzz for a short time. It's one of those special-occasion kind of drugs."

A slacking off of the pressure to get high has certainly contributed to a downturn in drug use. "At one point, if you were going to be a hippie, you would smoke pot, drop acid and, maybe for a while, if you wanted to be in 'the scene,' you snorted speed or shot heroin," says twenty-eight-year-old Austin, Texas, musician Larry Seaman, who's been on the music scene long enough to remember its excesses. "But I don't think drugs are characteristic of our lifestyle now."

All of which is not to say that drugs are dead in Austin or elsewhere. When asked what mind-altering substances, if any, he and the members of his new wave band, Standing Waves, indulge in, Larry is coy. "We're into coffee and beer a lot, tea. Don't let me condemn myself here. We try to be an 'up' kind of band."

Do they ever take amphetamines?

"That's theoretically possible."

Larry's rather oblique response is in itself significant. By so answering, he seeks to put distance between himself and any association with drugs. Any self-respecting band of fifteen years ago would have done the opposite.

FANTASY PARTIES

Because we are reluctant to use drugs and liquor as a means of escape, we have had to seek new channels. Like moviegoers of the Depression era who flocked to musical extravaganzas to escape their woes, singulars draw on our fantasies in planning theme parties. We have parties that create new realities or suggest the way life was lived in other eras. We party to celebrate the sixties, the Indianapolis 500, the Kentucky Derby. The absurdists among us give galas to celebrate Groundhog Day or the color pink (in which guests are asked for sartorial participation). We do not hesitate to put on the dog, to produce "a big show," the glitzier the better. We rent furniture, have the party catered, even hire help if we can. Parties are our collective, collaborative fantasy.

We recognize that any party in and of itself is an arbitrary gathering, so we choose to underscore rather than downplay its artificial state. We make it into a fantasy rather than trying to pretend it's a nonparty. Come-as-you-are parties, at which friends nibble on finger food and cheese, today seem uninspired.

Some singulars embrace the "new formality," including such trimmings as handwritten invitations, wrist corsages and boutonnieres. If we can afford it, we stage and choreograph our parties as we would a movie. A Los Angeles woman recently opened a location-scouting business for parties and weddings and has been overwhelmed by the response. Her location roster includes everything from Hollywood mansions to a Pacific Coast lighthouse. At the upper end, the catering business is growing, as is the demand for professional party planners, who plan The Big Event from start to finish.

Michael Kagan, a twenty-four-year-old New York City writer, has been to three black-tie parties in the last four months. His purchase of a used tuxedo last year for $150 has already ranked among his best investments. Not only does it save him the $60-a-shot rental cost, but wearing a tuxedo that was made and worn in a bygone era adds a certain *je ne sais quoi* to the waltzes and rumbas. If your feet were to float off the ground, you might for an instant believe this were the Roaring Twenties.

TRAVEL TROPHIES

Exotic travel provides an extended escape from the pressures and doldrums of everyday singular life. It is a "gourmet living experience"—a condensed, superpremium slice of life—that is inherently more satisfying than the regular fare.

Every Thanksgiving Rhonda Gainer travels with her girlfriend Marlene to a new Club Med resort. Last year, the one-time college buddies went to the new club on Turks and Caicos Islands in the Caribbean. Once there, they indulged in their favored recreation:

boy-watching and boy-catching. "We like to try different clubs," says Rhonda with a wink, "so we can check out the scenery."

Travel to exotic locations provides a kind of romance that is lacking in our everyday lives. The exotic backdrop, the new people all make for a "holiday," heightened-party experience.

What's more, the gratification is instant. While we might have to save for years to afford a down payment on a house or condominium, most of us can take vacations every year. If we don't have the cash on hand, we use our charge cards.

Travel to far-off locations is much more accessible to the singular generation than it was to any other. As late as the early sixties, air travel was largely reserved for the wealthy. At that time, it was estimated that only 30 percent of Americans would fly in their lifetimes. Today the number has jumped to 95 percent.

As the cost of air travel, in real dollars, continues to drop, singulars increasingly think nothing of flying somewhere to hear a concert, attend a party or take advantage of a sale. No longer a luxury item, travel is now considered a necessary ingredient in our psychological bill of health. "I haven't been to England in seven years," grouses one young newspaper editor, feeling truly deprived.

It is not uncommon for a singular still living in his or her parents' home to rattle off an impressive list of vacation locations. We talk expansively about our plans to visit far-flung spots that twenty years earlier would have identified us as members of the jet set.

"This year I'm going to go to Lake Tahoe, do a little skiing, then go to Reno and do some gambling, and then do Martinique," says Dennis Richardson, a young salesman in Los Angeles. Last year, Dennis traveled with some USC fraternity brothers to Ixtapa, Mexico, where they partied for a week at Club Med.

Exotic vacations are our travel trophies that we compile on our life quests. One singular has climbed—and had himself photographed at—the highest point in forty-three states of the union. After he achieves his goal of climbing in all fifty, he plans to take his quest abroad. Another singular intends to sample the cruise boats of every nation that offers them.

Travel fulfills the needs of those of us who are hungry for experience. "I spend all my money on travel," admits a twenty-six-year-old sales rep for a West Coast pharmaceutical company. "I don't buy material goods. If you buy something, it sits there. An experience, you can reflect on. My friends call me the world traveler. I've gotten to the point where it's no big deal."

FUN DEPRIVATION

Call it nostalgia, living in the past or in another world; singulars seem to carry too great a burden to have much fun in the here and now, in our ordinary homes, on our regular jobs. Perhaps high expectations weigh us down, or perhaps we have not yet released the grip of yesterday to feel comfortable with what we are becoming in the eighties and, soon, the nineties. Whatever the case, the young no longer hold the corner on the fun market.

Fun is a desirable but rare commodity to most singulars, something we aspire to achieve. Even our favorite entertainers don't much help us let go. Pleasure today, like the proverbial Prince Albert, seems caught in the can, and no one is quite certain how to let it out.

Some of us work against our fun deprivation by pasting on the good times. We find a Girl Scout pin and wear it with irony, as jewelry. We anoint thrift-shop circle skirts or Hawaiian shirts as talismans of the good times. We schedule in leisure and relaxation, trying to have fun every day, the way our grandparents insisted upon taking their regular constitutionals.

But purposeful leisure is a contradiction in terms. In order to have fun, we must discover how to relax, to let go, to sit back, enjoy time and take it all in. In order to have fun, we must put aside our career anxieties, our performance anxieties, our doubts about the future and our improvement schedules. We have to accept ourselves and the world—if only for a while.

CHAPTER 10

Spiritual Singularity

AN INEBRIATED "ANGEL"

Andy Prieboy was near the end of his rope. The young punk singer had just broken up with his girlfriend of three-and-a-half years, an older British woman who had been both his lover and his mentor. And the recording contract that had lured him to Los Angeles from San Francisco had fallen through, sending him to square one in a strange new city.

Standing on the stoop outside his apartment on Vine Street in a sleazy section of Hollywood, waiting for his ride to a party, it seemed he had nowhere to turn. Going back to the Bay Area with his tail between his legs just wasn't his style. And he couldn't return to his hometown, Gary, Indiana. His best friend from high school was there earning the minimum wage renting out porno films at an adult video store, and he was lucky to get that job. Besides, if Andy didn't crack L.A. now, he told himself, he probably never would.

Perseverance, though, was not easy. It was already going on six months since the record contract had died on him, and the twenty-eight-year-old singer hadn't managed to convince anyone even to listen to his tapes. He was selling toys on Melrose Avenue just to make the rent.

And worst of all, he was beginning to feel ordinary. In this part of town, a tall, gaunt punk with flaming red hair in black leather didn't rate a glance, much less slow traffic.

On this particular evening, Andy was feeling so low that he turned to his last resort. He pressed his palms together and prayed to the high holy heavens for help; he prayed to the Almighty Creator, just as he had every morning for twelve long years at Catholic grammar school, junior high and Bishop Noll High School back in Gary.

When Andy arrived at the party, he didn't know a soul except for the girl who had given him the lift. He was making idle chatter with another punkish looking fellow when an overweight, middle-aged and slightly inebriated man wandered over. He took one look at Andy, then turned to the other guy.

"Here's your man," he bellowed. "He's just the one you're looking for. Here's your singer."

Andy had never seen, much less spoken to, the fat man. How did the man know he was a singer? What was going on?

It was even stranger when Andy learned that he'd been chatting with a member of Wall of Voodoo, a local comer of a band that was enjoying its first hit song, "Mexican Radio." The band happened to be short a lead singer. The fellow agreed to listen to Andy's tapes, and almost overnight, the band invited the singer to join up.

Andy ascribes his good fortune directly to his entreaty to the Creator (he doesn't like the word "God"). The fat man was the Creator's improbable messenger.

This minor "miracle" did not restore Andy to the Catholic faith of his youth. It did, however, underscore the nature of his idiosyncratic, self-styled faith—a faith in which angels exist but, in all likelihood, Jesus Christ the Savior does not.

SPIRITUAL YEARNING

Like many members of the singular generation, Andy feels an intense yearning for spirituality, for an abiding faith to carry him through the hard times, for a spiritual presence that he can call upon at will—but he has trouble making a connection with the standard religious fare.

Rapid and fundamental changes in the nature of our secular lives have intensified our quest for spirituality. As we put less stock in permanent relationships and are less likely to marry and have children, as we seek greater levels of emotional and financial self-sufficiency, our need for a spiritual dimension expands. As we tap into the potential of our bodies—which are the temples of our souls—it is only natural that we would want to cultivate the spirit within. A pinched world economy and a conservative political climate have further contributed to our feelings of powerlessness and disenfranchisement, which, in turn, leave us begging for a spiritual foundation.

We seek a kind of spiritual singularity, a state of faith in which we have a direct relationship with God and are not dependent on outside institutions, churches, ministers or gurus to mediate our exchange. Our particular brand of faith is self-styled, reflecting our personal values and sometimes incorporating our religious heritage.

"There's no doubt about it, religion is making a comeback among the youth," says twenty-one-year-old Michael Van Hoy, a senior at Haverford College in Philadelphia. To Michael's peers at this prestigious liberal college, "religion" translates into attaining "spiritual moments" rather than attending worship services. Neither fundamentalism, which is viewed as "mind constrictive," nor the more traditional mainline religions, which are seen as "weekend Christianity," are particularly attractive to Haverford students.

"People talk about what they call spirituality," says Michael, a practicing Quaker. "You can have a 'spiritual experience' of a great conversation with a good friend, or watch a sunset that warms your soul. You see the sunset as being spiritual. That's what people talk about as a substitute for religion—a good, wholesome feeling about yourself."

Just as the definitions of marriage, family and fulfilling work have changed with the singular generation, so too has our understanding of "religion" and "spirituality." To singulars, enjoying a spiritual dimension means having transcendent experiences that take us out of ourselves and our pressure-cooker lives. Such experiences are uplifting, mind broadening, expansive. We do not feel that in order to be authentic, spiritual experiences must take place in the context of a church or even a sacred environment. Though we may not subscribe to an organized religious tradition, we still do not deprive ourselves of a spiritual life.

At the same time, singulars have shaken off narrow and virulent secularism. Even though we may be neither committed churchgoers nor dyed-in-the-wool believers, even though we cannot guarantee our faith, we try to remain open to spiritual and metaphysical matters, seeking to avoid religious cynicism. Know-it-all atheists put us off. Just as we are not sure about what we can believe, we are also not sure about what we cannot—or do not—believe.

"I would not say, 'Yes, there absolutely is a God,' " remarks twenty-nine-year-old Margo Levine of Houston, Texas. "It's hard for me to do that. I consider myself cynical and pragmatic. In college, I studied a scientific discipline. I've always considered myself a logical person." Despite Margo's inability to take a stand theologically, she has gone out of her way to find some answers, pursuing her father's Jewish heritage during an extended stay in Israel, where she lived on a kibbutz and worked as a forester.

Throughout this country, singulars like Margo are exploring our religious roots along with new venues. We are searching, seeking something to elevate and add meaning to our lives, something to take us out of ourselves.

"There's a real strong Christian revival movement sweeping Harvard right now," says Lili Van Zanten, a twenty-year-old history and literature major from Poughkeepsie, New York. Membership in the venerable Harvard-Radcliffe Christian Fellowship reached a high of thirty to forty in the academic year 1984–85, double the size from a decade earlier; the half-dozen other campus religious groups have likewise grown. Although the college remains "secular all in all," according to Lili, many of her classmates are extremely curious about Christianity.

Nationwide, at the university level, interest in the study of religion has proliferated since the late sixties. At some colleges and universities, enrollment in classes on religion has reached the highest level in a decade, and a slew of full-fledged religion departments has sprung up in recent years to meet the demand.

"People are very fragmented right now," explains Malcolm Boyd, author of the 1965 countercultural classic, *Are You Running With Me, Jesus?* "There's a lot of rage under the form of passivity. In the sixties, the rage was expressed. People today have narrowed the larger view a lot. [They want to know] 'How do I get through the day?' "

Underneath the voluntary regimentation and organization of singular life-styles is a conglomeration of subdued but nonetheless shaky psyches. Ours is a life in which quiet desperation has replaced loud exhortation. We are a generation uncertain not only of the nature of our future but whether we have one at all.

RELIGIOUS HYBRIDS

The singular generation grew up without strong spiritual bearings or consistent religious education. We grew up during the sixties and seventies, when young adults of that time (some of whom were our parents) became disenchanted with mainline and traditional organized religion. They sharply questioned its role in society and accused it of being irrelevant, offensive, even repressive. Some pronounced God dead.

To the sixties generation, helping to win rights for blacks and minorities and fighting to end the war in Vietnam were more pressing concerns than saying prayers on Sunday. From the progressive vantage point then, organized religion was best left to the conformist fifties, when women wore straw hats and white gloves to church services.

These concerns effectively placed a damper on my generation's religious education. Today professors of religion and experts in the field complain that while students flock to their courses, most lack even rudimentary grounding in the Judeo-Christian tradition.

"Based on my informal classroom surveys, very few students went to Sunday school," concludes Karen Orren, an associate professor of political science at UCLA who teaches a course on religion and American politics. "When nobody can tell me who Jeremiah is, I'll ask, 'How many went to Sunday school?' And with a class of thirty, no one raises a hand."

"The ignorance, coupled with the isolation, coupled with the intense message from all kinds of adolescent media—their music especially and television generally—makes them [young adults] prone to certain kinds of religion that are high in intensity of experience," says Kenneth Woodward, religion editor of *Newsweek* magazine. "They are very susceptible to religions that offer them something simple. You can't get complex with them. They have no background to be complex with. My experience is, the higher up the economic ladder you go, the less they know."

"A lot of people don't know anything about the Gospel itself and what the Bible says and they're smart people," Harvard undergraduate Lili Van Zanten remarks. "One of my roommates didn't understand the character of the Old Testament Bible; she didn't understand why the Old Testament God seemed like a vengeful, wrathful God versus the New Testament God of forgiveness. Someone asked me about Jesus's role in church. She didn't understand his being the son of God."

Most singulars grew up in households defined by inconsistency and ambivalence toward religion and religious practice. As children, we may have been baptized, confirmed or bar mitzvahed. We may have attended services (often erratically). We probably celebrated holidays, and our parents may have paid lip service to God. But while most of us were exposed to religion, our parents often lacked the personal faith to serve as consistent spiritual role models.

Liz Brody's religious "education" was guided by her father, who, though he only attended services during the High Holy Days, nonetheless wanted to pass on his Jewish heritage to his three children. After attending weekly Saturday school for about four years, Liz grew weary of the "snotty" kids who were more "into being bar mitzvahed" than learning. So at age ten, Liz invited her father to attend class with her. "I said, 'Dad, you come with me, and if you think this is beneficial, I will go every time.' He came and told me I didn't have to go anymore."

Subsequently Liz attended a Quaker summer camp and a progressive Episcopal high school, which held weekly chapel services. But after she dropped out of Saturday school, her religious education virtually came to a standstill.

When the parents of singulars divorced, they tended to fall away from faith. When they remarried, often they traded the religion of their first marriage for the religion of their second; sometimes, in the changing of the guard, religion fell through the cracks.

"I don't know to this day whether I'm Lutheran or Catholic, even though I consider myself Catholic," says John Carlson of Seattle. When John's biological parents were married, he was baptized Lutheran, his father's faith. When they divorced, his mother reverted to Catholicism and enrolled John in parochial school.

"One day Father Power, the priest, called me over," John recalls. " 'Would you like to be a Catholic?' he asked. Who am I, at age seven, to argue with a priest? I said, 'Sure.' He said a few prayers, maybe a blessing, and from then on, I guess I was Catholic." When his mother's second marriage broke up, John was sent to public school, and he therefore missed his confirmation.

Like John, many singulars are religious hybrids, born of two traditions: Protestant and Catholic, Jewish and agnostic, Catholic and fundamentalist Christian. Sometimes we were exposed to several religious traditions as children and given our choice.

As a kid, Margo Levine and her younger sister had no religious training. Their father was of the Jewish faith and their mother Protestant, and so the girls' religious education "was left up to us," Margo explains. "It was said, 'If you're interested, you're free to pursue whatever you want.' "

If singulars rebel against anything, it is this emblematic confusion: having had no concrete religious tradition with which to come to terms, or to turn against. As a result, we seek to put our spiritual houses in order and create a personal unity and sense of order against the general chaos in the universe.

Despite our fierce need for definitiveness, singulars cannot really go back in time to the moral certitudes of the fifties or the moral outrage of the sixties. A reversion to the former, as in joining a religious cult or aligning ourselves with paint-by-numbers fundamentalism, rarely provides enough answers to last a lifetime. Though singulars yearn for clarity, we feel what's in store for us is greater complication and confusion, out of which we must piece together our own answers.

SELF-STYLED SPIRITUALITY

A multiplicity of religious and secular forces helps create the religious and spiritual personae of singulars. The Judeo-Christian tradition, Eastern mysticism and secular humanism all contribute to the moral ecology of our generation and of our time, and we must integrate all these strains into one cogent identity.

However, the final arbiters of our religious behavior, convictions and identities are ourselves. In *Habits of the Heart*, a team of academics concludes that Americans have been swept away by "radical individualism," even in our religious lives. Today we are witnessing "the complete interiorizing of meaning, intuition and feeling in religion," says Steven M. Tipton, associate professor at Emory University's Candler School of Theology and one of the book's authors. "People have their own little church in their own little mind."

One woman interviewed for the book defined her own personal faith as "Sheilaism—this little voice inside me saying . . . 'God is whatever I feel.' The problem with that is not only do you never know which end is up, but sometimes being a good person is hard; we don't want to do it."

Singulars are not in the habit of naming our self-styled forms of faith after ourselves, but "Sheilaism" is a useful reference point in understanding our theological perspective. In arriving at our spiritual singularity, we sometimes incorporate ceremonies and rituals that range from the sacred to the secular. We can pick and choose what appeals to us from the great denominational supermarket of America, whipping up our own eclectic blend by adding components of the religion of our youth to elements from other traditions.

As in other aspects of our personal lives, our religious freedom has never been greater. We can celebrate Hanukkah and Christmas—or neither. Margo Levine, who has chosen to align herself with Judaism, celebrates the former; but she could just as easily call herself Christian and celebrate the latter, or both.

Singulars integrate the personal philosophies of individuals who are influential for us: professional mentors, beloved family members, friends, teachers, ministers, even celebrities. In some cases, these hybrid traditions are a result of disparate religious voices within families, couples and even within one person.

Twenty-one-year-old Tim Paton is an acknowledged agnostic who grew up in a Christian family in Knoxville, Tennessee. Though he no longer attends church, he observes some aspects of his family's religious credo "I don't take the Lord's name in vain and don't like other people to," he explains.

Ian Fleishman was born into a conservative Jewish family in Los Angeles, but as a teenager he found Jesus. Now Ian and his wife worship at the Beth Ariel Fellowship, a congregation that bills itself for "Jewish and Gentile believers" in Christ. Even though they believe in Jesus Christ, come Christmas, all the Fleishmans do is say "Happy Birthday"; they do not put up a Christmas tree or exchange gifts. Instead, they celebrate Hanukkah in traditional Jewish fashion, lighting menorah candles, reciting the Hebrew blessings and telling the story of Hanukkah.

Though Liz Brody is in one respect a nonbeliever who thinks that religion is "so outdated, it belongs in museums," she senses an "eternal presence" in her life. "I'll look through my window at night, up through the trees, and I feel that something watches over me. I would never depend on it, but I feel it's like a safety. I never cater to it. I really don't think of it as a god."

Even if we join a particular religious denomination or faith, our own judgment, not church doctrine, is the final arbiter of our standards. Many American Catholics, for instance, affiliate themselves with the Roman Catholic Church but rely on their own consciences when making important moral choices. A November 1985 New York *Times*/CBS News Poll found that 83 percent of all Catholics between the ages of eighteen and thirty-nine favor "use of artificial birth control." Eighty percent of this same group favor "permitting people of your faith to divorce and remarry." A full 37 percent of those polled favor "legal abortion." Just 21 percent of those sampled approve of all the things the Pope has done.

For Maureen Fitzgerald, a Catholic from Seattle, abortion should be "a personal choice. Personally for me, I would never do it," she says, but that does not mean she would deny others the right to choose.

While Susan Markcity is fully committed to her brand of Buddhism, Nichiren Shoshu Soka Gakkai of America (or NSA), the twenty-four-year-old would not let church teachings interfere with her private life. Even though leaders have taken clear positions on such matters as abortion (they're against it), Susan would disregard their position if she were to get pregnant out of wedlock. She continues to celebrate the Christian holidays of Christmas and Easter. Like other singulars, her own conscience is her final authority.

DEVELOPING OUR SPIRITUAL RESOURCES

For singulars, self-reliance is an ideal in almost every aspect of life, and our spirituality is no exception. Singulars seek to develop spiritual inner resources to buffer us from the ups and downs of the world at large. We try to attain a spiritual even keel, to take in stride aggressive personalities and unpleasant incidents, refusing to allow them to derail us.

We take responsibility for the state of our psyches, chiseling our own spiritual realities, developing internal systems to meet our spiritual needs. "I don't look for outside rituals to give me focus," explains Liz Brody. "I look for that focus within myself. I don't know any religion that could offer me peace of mind, solace, a core to live by."

Tapping into the great lurking spirit within is not, however, a mere mechanical process, like following a carded exercise program at a high-tech fitness salon. Spiritual awareness can be elusive, especially for those of us who are strangers to spiritual life.

As in our careers, marital partnerships and leisure activities, singulars are purposeful, pragmatic and goal-oriented in the pursuit of spirituality. We meditate, pray or allocate "quiet time" in which we attempt to cast aside the worries of the world. We use visualization techniques to cultivate positive thoughts and feelings, to heal wounds, to achieve desired mind-body goals. We rejoice in small wonders and try to make time for the little things of life.

Spiritual singularity and self-help have become inextricably linked. Singulars believe that eating properly, drinking little and smoking less can help cultivate a spiritual dimension. To us, being spiritual increasingly means loving ourselves.

Both Christian and secular publishers have jumped on the how-to bandwagon. Word Publishing in Waco, Texas, issues such self-help titles as *Say Yes to Your Potential, Improving Your Serve, Dropping Your Guard* and *Strengthening Your Grip,* along with "Christian" diet books; the house's bestsellers often come from this self-help category. Campus Crusade for Christ's ace evangelist, Josh McDowell, travels the college circuit lecturing on such topics as "Maximum Sex," "Maximum Dating" and "Maximum Love."

On college campuses, among the most popular electives today are religion courses covering job- and career-related topics, courses that "have special interest for the professions, that deal with questions of religious and ethical values, such as courses in medical ethics," says Dr. F. Stanley Lusby, professor of religious studies at the University of Tennessee in Knoxville and head of a two-year study of religious education in the southeastern United States funded by the Lilly Endowment.

At the same time, there has been a diminution of interest in the study of world religions, Lusby says, and "somewhat of a decline" in what Lusby calls the "Religion and" category, such as "Religion and Psychology," "Religion and Culture." Interest was high in all these areas in the sixties.

At Harvard, the best-attended religious-oriented seminar of the 1984–85 academic year was Jesus and the Success Ethic, according to Lili Van Zanten. "A lot of students are going to graduate from here and become doctors and lawyers, and they have real questions about what should be the religious responsibility with their job, salary and high-earning potential. They want to know, 'What does Jesus tell us about wealth?' "

"SERVICING" OUR BELIEFS

Every morning at a makeshift altar in her bedroom, Susan Mark-city's daily ritual begins when she slips on her Japanese *yukata,* lights candles and incense, fills a cup with water and opens the twin doors of the *butsudan,* home for her sacred wooden scroll replica. The Los Angeles dancer and aspiring actress kneels in front of the shrine, chanting *nam-myoho-renge-kyo* over and over for anywhere from a half-hour to an hour and fifteen minutes. In the evening, she follows the same procedure. And three to four nights a week, she attends a group chanting ritual.

Buddhist chanting has given Susan a spiritual identity and at the same time managed to transform her life. Within three months of starting to chant, she says, her "dreams came true": She was hired to dance at a hotel in Japan that was near an important Buddhist temple.

"I discovered that through going to meetings and through chanting this, I was able to—not slowly and surely but quickly—I was able to elevate my life," says Susan, who was raised primarily by her mother, who "didn't have any religion she stuck by." Chanting has put Susan in touch with her own power and potential. "I feel like I can do everything. I can accomplish things instead of just dreaming about them. When you chant, it gives you a very strong, vital foundation so that all of the aspects of your outer life and inner life—everything that you feel inside—can actually happen."

Some of us ritualize the minutiae of our lives, raising to sacred heights the importance of smooth-running schedules, regular exercise programs, keeping our financial records up to date. Others randomly pursue the "spiritual moments" to which Michael Van Hoy refers.

Following traditional religious precepts such as good works, kindness and altruism can also "service" our spiritual needs, even if we do not accept, or fully understand, the theological arguments from which they derive. The key is that we look within ourselves and to our own actions to find abiding faith.

Andy Prieboy believes he's responding to internal spiritual cues when he extends the hand of friendship to those in need. "A lot of instances when I've seen people sleeping on streets, I've taken off my sweater and wrapped it around their feet," he says. In the manner of a latter-day Robin Hood, he occasionally snatches a garment from inside a stranger's car to the same end. When Andy was living in San Francisco, he used to pass a certain park that was colonized after dark by street people drawn to the protective cover of an overgrown hedge. Every night Andy would plant packages of food near where they slept so they'd find them when they awakened. This anonymous method of giving, he says, helped preserve their personal dignity. "I don't see myself acting in a religious sort of way. I try to live by a doctrine of being good to people."

Michael Van Hoy and his girlfriend, twenty-year-old Haverford junior Nell Martenis, find that giving their time to feed the homeless in downtown Philadelphia reinforces their Christianity. Once a week volunteers in groups of three go out at night to make the rounds distributing food.

Friends and acquaintances are extremely curious about their work, Nell observes. "They sort of say, 'Oh, you do that?' I tell them what a great experience it is. The homeless have all sorts of things to say. They tell you about their families. The interesting thing to me is how spiritually inclined they are. Most of them put all of their faith in God. They say, 'Whatever end's up, God's still there and he's trying to take care of people.' It may be that that's their only hope."

ESTABLISHING A PERSONAL RELATIONSHIP WITH GOD

One hallmark of spiritual singularity is the desire to develop a one-to-one relationship with God, to establish what theologians refer to as unmediated faith. "I have a very nice, casual relationship with the Creator," says Andy Prieboy.

Though we may return to our home churches or investigate new religious traditions to find the way, ultimately we want to establish a direct bond with the Almighty. If we go to church regularly, we see that weekly ritual as secondary to the main spiritual business at hand. Singular churchgoers rail against superfluous hierarchies, committee meetings and social functions, which seem to interfere with this primary exchange between ourselves and God. If necessary, we will switch denominations to cut the religious red tape.

Kevin Cusack is a twenty-eight-year-old evangelical Christian from Grand Rapids, Michigan, who left the Catholic church in his early twenties because he felt blocked out of a direct relationship with God. "The priest has always been the intermediary to the people. You go to Confession, Communion, Mass—always through the priest," he says. "[But] there's no precedent for that in the Scripture. It says, 'Only through me will you come to know the Father.' It doesn't say, 'Follow the high priest. . . .' "

Kevin joined the Assembly of God because he says it stands for a better, more accessible relationship with God. At the congregational level, church members play a significant role in developing their own faith by subdividing into "cell" groups of generally four couples or eight individuals. These groups constitute an informal family network and study group.

Likewise, Ian Fleishman found Judaism constrictive to developing his spirituality. When he was seventeen, Ian attended a weekend Shabbaton seminar with an orthodox youth group that proved to be a turning point in his spiritual life. During a lecture on kosher food, "When they were discussing which brand of ice cream was kosher and which wasn't due to small variations in the preparing process, I asked myself the question, 'Is God really that concerned about what kind of ice cream we eat?' I realized I had —not a relationship with God—but with religion. The important thing was Judaism . . . the importance of the Jewish life-style, the dangers of intermarriage and the importance of supporting Israel." In embracing Jesus, Ian feels he has eliminated the constricts of conservative Judaism and established a more purely prayerful, spiritual relationship with God.

Bill Stevens, pastor of the First Friends Meeting in Greensboro, North Carolina, notes that a good many of his young faithful refuse to join the Meeting officially. "Their attendance is superb and their commitment unquestionable," he says, "but they do not want to officially affiliate themselves with our Meeting." By not signing up, these young Quakers seek to streamline their relationships with God.

RETURN TO HOME CHURCHES

Our quest to achieve spiritual singularity brings many of us back to our home churches or synagogues. For some of us, it's just a stop along the way; for others, our home church becomes one— but not the only or the definitive—focal point in our spirituality. While we may respect traditional religious services, if they don't speak to us, they probably won't hold us.

Polling data indicates that in the eighties, young adults (typically the least churchgoing of any age group) have slowed the rate of outmigration from traditional, established religions, compared to the rate of exodus during the sixties particularly and, to a lesser extent, the seventies.

"There's no question about the fact that there's a return of young people to the church—young couples asking to be married, almost confused by their own felt need to go to the church and have that happen," says Frances Hall, associate for liturgical arts and youth at All Saints Episcopal Church in Pasadena, California. "There is a great cry for spiritual direction," adds the thirty-one-year-old Hall, herself ordained just two years ago.

All Saints, with one of the largest Episcopal congregations west of the Mississippi, is something of an oddity in a denomination that has been steadily losing members since 1965. All Saints' continued growth is due, at least in part, to its ongoing efforts to keep up with the times.

"We were just discussing in staff: What is the future of liberal

Protestantism, or liberal Christianity?" says Hall. "What is it the conservative churches offer? What is it that causes people to return to their roots?"

To help answer these questions, the church recently took the bold step of offering a healing service—the kind often associated with conservative and charismatic churches—during its main, 10 A.M. Sunday service. The service proved to be an overwhelming success. An estimated 90 percent of the congregation came forward for the laying on of hands.

Some church scholars say that the more receptive mainline churches are to the "miraculous workings of the Holy Spirit"—including such practices as the laying on of hands, faith healing and the casting out of demons—the more likely they'll survive and thrive during what they predict will be the coming wave of religiosity in the latter part of this century.

Whatever their motivation, established churches of all stripes, including the aggressive and fast-growing Southern Baptist Convention, are working hard to update their once-staid offerings in order to attract young new members and to ease the self-consciousness many singles feel around what has long been regarded as a family institution. For example, state-of-the-art "super-evangelical" churches tend to build strategically off freeway exit ramps in the major metropolitan areas, for ready accessibility to highly mobile young adults.

As in the political arena, churchgoing singulars are spiritual consumers who shop around for the best religious "buy" and hold out for our requirements. For Tracy Henry, a twenty-two-year-old who moved to Waco, Texas, after graduating from a Christian college in Arkansas, finding the right single peer group was her paramount consideration when selecting a church. Some Sunday-school classes for young singles she visited were full of divorcées and social misfits. "I hate to say this—but you could tell why they were still single." At present, Tracy has settled on a church with a class for "young professionals"; the class is composed of graduate students and people like herself just starting out.

HYBRID DENOMINATIONS

Despite efforts on the part of established churches to attract young adults, a surprising number of hybrid religions, targeting a specific sector of the churchgoing "market," have begun to emerge over the last twenty years. Many of them have managed to gain an impressive foothold. In Arlington, Texas, a church exclusively for singles opened in the summer of 1984. Metropolitan Community Church, a Christian "denomination" for homosexuals, which was founded in Los Angeles in 1968, now has a membership of over thirty thousand internationally, including a small fraction of heterosexuals. Another L.A. creation, the Vineyard Christian Fellowship, catering to young singles with soft-rock music, a casual dress code and strict fundamentalist teachings, in ten years has grown to have a presence in thirty states.

Unaffiliated "community" churches have also experienced impressive growth of late. They are smaller, more personalized and especially attractive to young adults who are uncertain and unprepared for sophisticated religious offerings.

Experts believe that while fewer young adults in the eighties may be signing up for such highly publicized cults as the Moonies and Hare Krishna (no one knows for sure, due to lack of public records), there's a groundswell of interest in small, homespun groups with cultish characteristics but secular identifications (e.g., diet groups and motivational seminars).

TOWARD THE CONDITION OF FAITH

The singular generation feels an intense yearning, a gnawing hunger, for a spiritual dimension. We long for those things that spirituality and religious identification have always promised: security, inner peace, a sense of protection, the feeling that all's right with the world, and a connection with humanity.

Many of us have embarked on a spiritual quest to quiet the panic in our souls. But do we have the determination to stick with the struggle, to withstand the doubts and confusion that every profound spiritual quest entails?

The stakes are high for us and the need is great, but the outcome is uncertain. Most singulars enter the spiritual "marketplace" without a strong specific religious identity, without having learned any particular religious language. With so little religious foundation to build on, it will be arguably more difficult for each of us to piece together an enduring and satisfying spiritual life, to find the complex answers that explain a complex world. If we give in to simplistic religious answers—to spiritual "junk food"—we may ultimately be disappointed, sinking into deeper despair.

On the other hand, having grown up in a religious polyglot enables us to draw from a wide religious net in determining our particular faith. At its very best, this offers us the advantage of integrating a remarkable diversity of religious interests within ourselves and, by extension, within the world, at a time when religious tolerance and accord have never been more urgently needed.

CHAPTER 11

The Deep Shadow

LIFE WITHOUT A FUTURE

We know the facts. We read *The Fate of the Earth*. We saw *The Day After* and *Testament* and *War Games*. We've watched mushroom bombs explode on TV documentaries and in science class at school and learned about the apocalyptic dangers of nuclear war. We know all too well that our lives and our civilization hang on a thin thread, that our species could vanish. We know that real cities are as vulnerable as papier mâché, that the power now exists to destroy all the world's cities, plunging survivors into a bleak nuclear winter night from which they might never emerge.

We've heard it all so often that our psyches have become numb to the righteous anger and horror we might otherwise feel; our senses and reasoning have given way to mental exhaustion and sensory overload that this glut of horrific information has produced.

We've heard it all before but still the fact remains: The greatest issue of our day is the danger of nuclear holocaust, and the greatest challenge, overcoming its threat. This danger overshadows all the political concerns and purposeful proclivities of the singular generation, because it has the potential to make meaningless, to sweep away every other human enterprise and achievement.

The lurking, ever-present prospect of nuclear annihilation has given shape to the character and psyche of my generation, and of our time. To singulars, nuclear danger is the great ugly spreading cancer with which we have grown up and which will not go away. It has cast what Jonathan Schell calls "the deep shadow . . . across the whole of life."

This shadow has wound its way into our psyches and stays there, festering, even if we push it to the inner recesses of our minds. It has become the great fear of our time, the great equalizer that renders us all uniform under its tyrannical yoke.

Because ridding the world of the threat of nuclear annihilation seems nothing less than a Herculean task, and because we as individuals feel ourselves unequal to it, some members of my generation have sunk into existential despair. The deep shadow can drop a heavy wedge between ourselves and our emerging self-styled identities, creating a kind of futility and passivity that are hard to combat, and can easily breed a variety of self-destructive traits ranging from malaise to suicide.

The "healthier" among us wrestle fears of a nuclear holocaust into submission, putting them out of our minds. We find that the only way to live constructively and productively is to pursue the singular course: to devote ourselves to improving and influencing our individual realms—our circles of friendship, our lives at work, to make living in the moment and living in our bodies a super-premium experience. Paradoxically, living "constructively" in this manner enhances the very danger it seeks to ignore. By doing nothing to combat nuclear proliferation, by denying its possibility, its spiralling growth continues unchecked.

Just as the inescapable reality of divorce has robbed the singular generation of faith in the institution of marriage, so has the prospect of nuclear holocaust denied us the ability to commit ourselves freely to the future. Even if we doubt that the world will ever come to an end in this unthinkable manner, we do not know for certain that it won't, and this uncertainty torments us.

"Most people my age expect a city to go up by some major terrorist bomb, or, at minimum, we expect to see a terrorist threaten a city as a bargaining tool in our lifetimes," says twenty-six-year-old Eric Horvitz. "That precedent would change the world."

The deep shadow of nuclear annihilation curbs our appetite for making lifelong commitments to other human beings, to procreation, to assuming responsibilities for causes and concerns greater than our own survival and advancement. It has accelerated our withdrawal from the collective concerns of humanity while promoting the pursuit of self-interest—in our careers, in creating strong bodies and homes that offer the illusion of safety and separateness from the rest of the world. It cuts into our ability to enjoy ourselves and has doomed us to a life of "presentism," a life circumscribed by the immediate rather than by an integration of the past, present and future.

"I don't think about the future," says Amy Langenberg, a Harvard University sophomore from Chicago. "I have no images when I think of 1994."

THE MUSHROOM CLOUD

An apocalyptic edge is everywhere apparent. Even President Reagan appears to have bought—or at least acknowledged as a possibility—the nuclear Armageddon argument propounded by Hal Lindsey, author of *The Late Great Planet Earth.* In his book *The 1980's: Countdown to Armageddon,* Lindsey writes, "The decade of the 1980's could very well be the last decade of history as we know it."

While various polls show that the entire American population is fearful of nuclear war—and has become increasingly so during the 1980s—among young adults under the age of thirty, the fear is consistently greater.

The editors of *Taking Off,* a short-lived tabloid published by Stanford University students, polled hundreds of Bay Area students in 1983, asking them to rate on a scale of 0 to 100 percent the answer to this question: "In your lifetimes, do you think nuclear weapons will be used?"

"The average answer was 80 percent, yes," says Eric Horvitz, one of the founders. "Some people said, '100 percent, there's no way we're going to escape this, buddy.' "

Typically, the young have more on our life slates than do older individuals, more ahead of us than behind us, and so, for us, the future is precious and meaningful. But the specter of nuclear annihilation effectively advances today's young to spiritual old age, confronting us with the possibility of untimely death and making us more past- and present-oriented than we would otherwise be.

As with other matters, the nuclear threat waxes and wanes in our imaginations, as society at large experiences waves of nuclear terror and remission. The most recent apex of collective tension came in 1982, when Jonathan Schell's *The Fate of the Earth* exploded its apocalyptic message on the national consciousness. In November of that year, nuclear-weapons-freeze referendums passed in seven states and the District of Columbia.

When we, as a society and as individuals, cannot tolerate another iota of sobering grimness, we relapse into a period of collective denial. "Most people go through phases when they think about it [the prospect of nuclear war] a lot," says Amy Langenberg. "Then they . . . forget about it. Because every time the fire alarm goes off, that could be it. It's hard to live that way; it's not constructive."

But underneath the veneer of denial, the image of a mushroom cloud lurks. The image may get buried, but it doesn't go away. We are *all* haunted by this image—not just the futurists, the scientists and the sci-fi freaks whose imaginations thrive on worst-case scenarios.

Eric Horvitz was strolling in midtown Manhattan on a very hot day several years ago when, all of a sudden, a bright flash illuminated the street and sky. Eric darted behind a free-standing street sign, thinking, "It's really happening now; this is the end."

Momentarily and much to his relief, it became apparent that a bolt of lightning, not the detonation of a nuclear warhead, had caused the flash. His move behind the street sign was automatic. As a child growing up in Long Island, Eric boned up on civil defense materials "that described the light and heat flash, the thermal flash," explains the Stanford University medical student. "I used to read with real attention and focus on the rules for survival. It said, 'If you see a bright light, jump behind anything to protect yourself from the onslaught.' "

Virtually every one of us at one time or other has entertained the prospect of abrupt nuclear termination when mulling over the meaning of it all. For some of us, these black thoughts come and go in waves; others experience a daily, nagging terror. "I think about aspects of the nuclear weapons problem several times a day," says Eric.

During the periods when we're possessed by terror, we can stay up nights, worrying that if we go to sleep, we may not live to wake up again. Or we might arise each morning wondering if the world will make it through another day. If these thoughts persist, we can become disengaged from our work, our relationships and even ourselves.

"I used to have nightmares, like I was in a nuclear war; I could see mushroom clouds popping up all over the place," confesses Roger Roberts, a twenty-eight-year-old graduate student at the University of California at Berkeley. "But I guess you learn to ignore it after a while and don't worry about it."

"If it's going to happen, it's going to happen," says his wife, Josie, while keeping an eye on the couple's two toddler daughters. "I just hope that if we're going to get hit by a bomb, I'd be at ground zero."

Thoughts like this have made for classroom chatter and dinner-table conversation all our lives.

"In sixth grade, when we started talking about the nuclear bomb, well, that's when we all wanted to live in space," says video game designer Rob Fulop. "We thought, 'Well, it will be okay, because we'll all live on the moon or on Mars. We'll just live somewhere else, and we don't care what happens here.' Every year I've lived has been the year It's going to happen."

But It never has. Instead, It has lingered in the air, the disquieting background noise of our generation. "I have grown up with this," says Rob. "I've talked about this countless times in my life, from sixth grade until now."

CREATIVE MODES OF ESCAPE

We did not create the bomb; we were born in its aftermath. Since we may decry—but must accept—the implications of its proliferating existence, the one sure way in which singulars can cope is by crafting our own realities; in many cases, these realities involve "escaping" the grim legacy of nuclear annihilation.

Some of us exalt the new age politicians, televangelists and other personalities who tell us what we want so much to believe: that we are swell and grand and have a great future, that we can have everything we want. We adopt their painted-on optimism and upbeat style because it walls out our innermost fears. But deep down, we do not believe them.

Others of us "escape" to the comfortable past, wearing the clothes, playing the music and mimicking the merriments of earlier times, especially the fifties and sixties. Now behind us, these "pet" decades have a solidity in the past that the present cannot guarantee: They possessed a future.

Our escape can take the form of spendthrift consumerism: Buy now, pay never. The rationalization is not actually as direct as this, but at the back of our minds, we feel we shouldn't wait till we can "afford" something before buying it because time is running out on us; if we delay gratification, we may never achieve it. So we try to acccelerate the achievement of lifelong dreams and ambitions, paying any price so that we can have them now.

Sometimes we are "extravagant" with our own lives. In 1982, Coloradans Michael and Joanne Quinn became convinced that the world was going to end; it was just a matter of time. So Michael left his job, and the couple took their two toddler sons on an extended Pacific tour.

"We just feel it's more important to go and do the things we want to do in this life if it is going to get cut short than to try to have a lot of money in the bank when you get blown up," Joanne, daughter of Iowa congressman Berkley Bedell, told the Associated Press. "I hate that kind of attitude because I've never been the kind of person who looks only to what's happening today and doesn't look at what's happening tomorrow, but that's the way I feel."

Some of us draw up "escape plans" in which we manage to elude nuclear Armageddon. We join fundamentalist churches that offer—to members only—promises of salvation from the fast-approaching end of time. We become survivalists, building end-of-the-world stockpiles in remote locales or planning to leave the country, in the hope that where we're going will offer better chances for survival than where we are now, and that any nuclear exchange will be of a limited nature.

"I tell you, I want to get out of this valley in the next five years," says Rob Fulop, referring to California's Silicon Valley. Rob plans to leave the country once the exodus begins. "I swear, if at some point the world is going towards a war, you're going to see more and more people who are going to start splitting. It might be pointless, but they're certainly going to leave the valley. I'll be one of them—I'll leave. I'd go to New Zealand; it's the place you're supposed to go."

Some singulars adopt the grim, serious masks of fatalists, living in the present but braced for the end. "If I visualize the future," Liz Brody confesses, "it blackens out in the twenty-first century in a cloud of atomic smoke." For Liz, the idea that life as we know it will cease in the coming years is a foregone conclusion.

This what's-the-use attitude is also a form of escape because it declares defeat before stepping into a battle. It is akin to the recent suicide-pill initiatives at several college campuses, in which students proposed stocking cyanide pills on campus in case of nuclear attack.

WHY IT'S SO TOUGH TO TAKE ACTION

Singulars gravitate toward the fantasyland of escapism because it is hard to find our political bearings on the nuclear arms predicament and, if we do, still harder to come up with a plan for constructive action. Confronting something so overwhelming as the extinction of life on the planet is a staggering proposition. Even those committed to group and social action can be unclear as to the best course to take to set about dismantling the multitrillion-dollar weapons systems that exist in at least five nations and are likely to spread to twenty-five in the next ten years. By contrast, it makes burning bras and draft cards and marching for civil rights look easy.

As political hybrids, singulars can see both sides of the nuclear arms argument and are torn between the impulse to trust the Russians and downscale—and eventually dismantle—our nuclear deterrent, and the impulse to mistrust them and continue playing the politics of buildup. Our pragmatic instincts argue that it makes no sense for both superpowers to devote such an enormous share of our national budgets to the military in a time of peace. But our inborn insecurity tells us that the Soviets are no saints, and we do not want to give them even a slim chance of gaining military superiority.

Some small number of us abide by the status quo, the military rationale that we are safe as long as our deterrent is in place. "Deterrence rests on a very rational principle," explains John Carlson, "that no one is going to commit an action in which the costs of committing the actions are far too high to justify the price." Nuclear war, he insists, "won't happen if the result is suicide."

But this kind of "security" ignores the ever-increasing danger of electronic error, acts of nuclear terrorism and the initiation of nuclear exchange from countries outside the spheres of the two superpowers. It is ultimately as unsatisfying as assuming that one will never be robbed because one's home is protected by a burglar-alarm system.

As we grapple for answers, the nuclear threat maintains a stranglehold over our lives. While we want to get out from under it, we're not sure how. But even if we are clear about the need to downscale our nuclear arsenal or to support disarmament, how do we begin to act?

Generally speaking, singulars are not taken with collective action, yet it's hard to imagine individual action as having much impact. "I don't go out and rally," says Amy Langenberg. "I wouldn't know how to go about it. I don't see it as being in my hands." Furthermore, Amy "can't remember any demonstrations" against nuclear arms in her two years at Harvard.

Karl Miller of Baltimore, Maryland, does his part by trying to influence those around him. "I think it's a lot more important to work on it in an individual fashion. I don't mean 'individual' where everyone goes off into the woods and meditates; it's a question of how you interact with your society."

Those committed to group and social action can follow a variety of paths. We can teach nuclear-age education. We can analyze nuclear problems, lecture on them, stage media events, write about them, join professional groups like Physicians for Social Responsibility or Educators for Social Responsibility, or organize new ones. But it is never easy going.

"You can get clobbered over the head by everyone's despair," says Jeb Brugmann, director of the Cambridge (Mass.) Commission on Nuclear Disarmament and Peace Education. If we aren't strong enough or emotionally self-sustaining, we may find it difficult to carry on.

Those few of us who, like Jeb, are working to prevent nuclear confrontation can easily become demoralized. The attrition rate from antinuclear activist groups is high, in part because of a pervading sense of futility and an overall lack of peer and social support for our work.

Twenty-one-year-old David Lambert, a UCLA senior, was involved with an ad-hoc group called the Nuclear Resistance Coalition for its brief political life in the mid-eighties. NRC had a mailing list of two hundred to three hundred but only eight to ten regulars. The group organized a few demonstrations and participated in one act of civil disobedience. But there was some internal friction, and the group folded after just one year. "We were doing a lot and trying to do a lot and didn't see too much effect," David admits.

While David's peers did not join him in his work for nuclear peace (in fact, he was the only activist in NRC from UCLA), he believes that there are many latent supporters of such efforts.

"I know there are a lot of sympathetic people out there," says David. "They feel they don't have the time, or the energy, or they're afraid of ridicule from peers or parents, or afraid of getting into trouble, or rocking the boat. When you do this kind of stuff and you're active, you have to be willing to have your photo in FBI files."

Even those willing to go more traditional routes to examine the issue face problems of apathy. Eric Horvitz and some other concerned Stanford students grouped to form an ongoing nuclear arms forum and a student-run center to do something about what they call today's biggest issue. In 1983, they found startup funding to publish *Taking Off,* a newspaper tabloid distributed on college campuses nationwide. The editorial note in the second issue read: "Many students feel powerless to affect the course of the arms race, to steer technology, to spread democratic ideals and to forge a better world." Even though the editorial and graphics were lively and original, *Taking Off* was grounded after only three issues.

A SHIFT IN THE WIND

If the political pendulum swings from its present state of gestation to greater activism, this pervasive feeling of apathy could abate in the latter part of the eighties and the nineties.

Tim Carpenter, twenty-five-year-old director of field operations for PROPEACE, the Los Angeles–based antinuclear group whose citizens' march from Los Angeles to Washington ran into financial troubles early on, sees a shift in the political wind. There was a massive denial of the nuclear threat in America from 1979 through 1981, Tim says, especially among those in his own age group. However, in November 1982, when the nuclear-weapons-freeze referendum qualified for the ballot in California, eight other states and the District of Columbia (and passed in all but Arizona), there was an "incredible floodgate opening," he reports.

"There is now a reaffirmation of commitment, a new sense of hope that I did not see in the '73 to '81 period." To support his contention, Tim cites a time when, in 1978, famed physician and antinuclear activist Helen Caldicott spoke during intermission of a Graham Nash/Jackson Browne benefit concert at the Los Angeles Forum. She was initially booed until basketball star Bill Walton came out and urged the audience to listen. During that same trip, when Caldicott was scheduled to speak at several college campuses, no more than ten to fifteen students ever attended her lectures. However, in the fall of 1984, when Caldicott spoke at California's Santa Ana College and University of California at Irvine, over one thousand people jammed into the standing-room-only lecture halls, with latecomers getting turned away.

Before joining PROPEACE, Tim worked for the Alliance for Survival in Southern California's conservative Orange County to educate elementary and high school students on peace issues and nuclear danger through school visits. "When I started in the late seventies, teachers and administrators were threatened by what I had to say," he says. "Now they're open to it and in some schools there's even a nuclear curriculum."

New-age activists are increasingly tailoring pitches to appeal to the political hybrids that singulars are. Mack Arrington, a founder of the Peace Fellowship at the University of North Carolina at Greensboro, helped organize a March 1985 Star Wars forum, pitting opposing sides against each other. Instead of simply preaching peace, Arrington arranged to have General Daniel Graham, the chief proponent and an architect of Star Wars, debate Colonel Robert Bowman, the former director of research and development for the U.S. Air Force and now an opponent of Star Wars weaponry. The forum was a decided success, attracting an audience of some six hundred. Like the retrospective symposium on Vietnam held at nearby Wake Forest University, such forums succeed by presenting both sides of an issue and letting attendees make up their own minds or, even better, borrow answers from both.

"I figured that proponents of each point of view would show up and at least have to listen to each other," explains Mack, a 1982 graduate of UNCG. "The advantages were that several people I talked with afterwards had to consider what the other side had said; what they assumed was completely wrong."

Mack's leadership role in the Peace Fellowship and his impartial stance in the forum help give him the credibility to put across his own message: support for the establishment of a World Security Authority, to regulate and enforce international laws on nuclear weapons much the way the International Civilian Aviation Organization enforces safety regulations at airports worldwide.

When pressed, Mack admits that he is at heart "one-sided" on the issue of survival. But he understands that in order to achieve your objective, you must have an open mind and be willing to take small steps. "The way you eat an elephant is one bite at a time. It's taken us years to get into this predicament and I feel it's going to take more than just a couple of more years to get out of it."

Singulars often employ sophisticated techniques and stage thought-provoking demonstrations to arouse awareness. At Guilford College, the Nuclear Arms Awareness Group recently held a weeklong seminar, including a dramatization of what would happen in the event of nuclear war. (NAAG subsequently changed its name to Students for Peace to make its image more appealing.) On the sidewalks, an artist chalked in outlines of fallen nuclear-attack "victims." As students crisscrossed campus, they invariably stepped around the figures in order to avoid touching them. Group organizers were pleased that students did not blithely step on the "bodies."

"It made me happy that people were realizing that in nuclear war, people get killed," says Natalie Dolan, a seminar organizer. "You've got to face up to it; nuclear arms aren't just a way of flexing your muscles; they aren't just toys."

Optimists point to the message of hope and the call to action beginning to crop up in popular music, in such songs as U2's pacifist anthem "Sunday Bloody Sunday." "The message, if there is a message in our music," twenty-four-year-old lead singer Paul "Bono" Hewson of Dublin, Ireland, told *Newsweek* magazine, "is the hope it communicates."

A CALL TO ACTION

To date, the singular generation has responded to our historical hand of cards with a kind of resigned denial. We bury ourselves in an avalanche of activity, overfilling our appointment books. We magnify the importance of the small picture, living in the present and, when we want to take comfort, in the past. We withdraw from the world at large and designate our bodies and home nests as our outermost emotional boundaries, reluctant to venture beyond. We focus our lens on our own lives, not planning for generations to come. We immerse ourselves in a zealous careerism that overrides every other pursuit. We hesitate to bear children and to make long-term commitments. We look brightly upon our own futures but block out with blinders the rest of the world.

When pressed, we admit that the deep shadow follows us everywhere and that we can never really elude its dark reach. Our worst fear is that it could all end as suddenly and impersonally as a computer screen going blank. But, as soon as we think these thoughts, we push them out of our minds and, along with them, plans for the future.

But it is not satisfying to live on the surface of life, to live without a future. And when we recognize this, individually or collectively, our first order of business is to take action.

Singulars have so far stopped short of grouping to take collective action, and individually, we simply feel overwhelmed. We do not act because we do not want to act until we think our voices will be heard.

Some argue that it will take a nuclear accident of some kind—like the devastation of a major city—to mobilize us into action, to dramatize the threat of a nuclear holocaust in a more graphic and real way than we can envision now.

But it is too easy to wait for outside events to lead us, and we may not have the luxury of a warning. It's true that we cannot guarantee that our voices will be heard now; neither can we guarantee that we'll have an impact. Yet singulars must fight for the survival of our species and for this fragile vessel that Buckminister Fuller named "Spaceship Earth."

We can make a start by shucking the protective coating of psychic numbness and learning the facts. By becoming better informed and learning about weapons systems and nuclear strategies, by doing our own digging, we can gain influence over decision makers in the Congress, the Pentagon and the White House who are shaping or denying us a future.

We have taken control of our individual lives and destinies, allowing nobody to encroach upon them or dictate our terms; and now we must be just as bold in securing our future. We must risk failure in order to succeed. The emotion is there, the anger and the energy. But while passionate singularity is in many respects the strength of our generation, with regard to lifting the shadow of nuclear darkness, it has so far proved paralyzing.

CHAPTER 12

Conclusion

THE SEARCH FOR INNER STRENGTH

This book is about the rapid adoption of a new mind-set, a new ideal, by the latest generation of young Americans. It is about my generation's determination to explore and express our singular identities, crafting them from a variety of sources and influences.

The drive to define ourselves from within and on our own terms is largely a response to the conditions under which we grew up. The singular generation came of age without strong ethical, religious or political foundations and, in many cases, without much in the way of a secular tradition. The only source of stability came from what already seemed obsolete: that is, the social and religious mores and institutions of our parents' youth.

Megatrends author John Naisbitt calls the eighties "the time of parenthesis, the time between eras," and as far as singulars are concerned, he's right. We feel a yearning for the old but an identification with, though not generally a delight over, the new. Without a foundation or tradition on which to model ourselves and against which to rebel, my generation has been adrift between two epochs, belonging to neither. Singulars understand that the ideologies and belief systems that stabilized the past, while attractive in hindsight, probably outlived their usefulness for sound reasons; as for the future, with its medley of terrifying prospects, it is simply too uncertain to lay much faith in. So singulars are stuck with the present, an epoch defined by dislocation, disconnection and loss of meaning, an epoch in which each of us has had to grope for our own answers.

Singulars have turned inward, becoming protective rather than expansive: homebodies, not adventurers; hobbyists, not public servants; pragmatists, not idealists. We think that the most satisfying and dependable structure around which to organize our behavior and our priorities rests inside each of us, and that it is different for each of us. We borrow from different traditions and different teachers in creating our eclectic identities, from new-age technology and age-old customs. We revere tradition and have no need to defy it or take it to task because tradition lacks an oppressive grip on us. If my generation rebels against anything, it is chaos and confusion.

Inner strength has become a virtue—and a necessity—for singulars. We lead increasingly fragmented lives, have more transitory relationships, shorter attention spans and therefore need an anchor inside to hold us. Our internal pace has quickened to meet the quickening pace of the world. With no reason to expect any slowdown in the future, we brace ourselves for further, and perhaps accelerated, change.

We are a generation better prepared for endings than beginnings. When singulars start or enter into something, we reflexively consider how it might end rather than expecting it to go on forever. This is true for relationships, jobs, homes, life, the world. We are routinely bombarded with grim facts and forecasts. Experts issue a stream of statistical predictions for the probability of the world avoiding nuclear war for another five years, ten years, till the year 2000. In the name of relaxation, the average television viewer, by age sixteen, has watched 50,000 murders on the tube; by the age of thirty-two, he or she has seen 100,000. Our minds are filled with mayhem, and our unconscious begins to expect it.

Singulars have successfully adapted to this problematic social landscape and, equipped for change, we've come to thrive on the turnstile life-style. We are all-purpose animals who pride ourselves on being able to land on our feet. We seek to be emotionally self-sufficient, not to be dependent on peers, superiors, friends, lovers, family—on anyone except ourselves.

We are a generation of free agents who, like our professional analogues in big league baseball, lack overriding loyalty, even to the team that currently suits us. Singulars' affiliations are with ourselves and with those we might include inside our singular circles.

Entrepreneurs are our heroes on the job and off, because they behave in work as the rest of us would behave in life. They piece together a new reality from a disparate set of elements, the more innovative the more admirable.

We are what we do, and those who do nothing at all or who cannot find meaningful work or connect with the work they have have a hard time gaining and maintaining self-esteem. Work is the central obsession of my generation because it is the key to our identities and our means of escape. Through work, we try to defy the downward mobility that plagues our times. Careers are independent, living entities in lives that otherwise might seem limited.

A GREATER RANGE OF PERSONAL OPTIONS

Our lives have been constricted by the haunting lack of a secure future and the real possibility of having no future at all. Singulars live in a world of diminishing resources, a troubled economy domestically and internationally. We live in a world made smaller through overpopulation and more vulnerable through worldwide terrorism. Being an American no longer adds to one's sense of security but increasingly seems to jeopardize it.

As the outside world becomes more dangerous, our singular worlds open up with countervailing intensity. Singulars enjoy unprecedented options in the personal realm, having cast off the prefabricated roles of yesterday in favor of those of our own making. In virtually every aspect of our personal lives, we assume a greater range of options than has any generation before us. We can marry, divorce or remain single; we can have children or choose to remain childless. We can negotiate a relationship of our choosing with a member of the other sex, or a member of the same sex. We can affiliate ourselves with religious institutions or remain unattached.

What's more, we have for the most part released our dependence on conventions to tell us how our personal lives should be conducted. As parents, marital partners and sexual friends, we negotiate the terms that make sense for us as individuals and that fit into our schedules.

We are a tolerant generation on questions of personal freedom. We try to judge others on the basis of their singular identities, not on the basis of their ethnic and religious heritage, race, gender or sexual preference. As the social sanctions against exercising one's personal freedom diminish, singulars assume greater responsibility for our actions.

While we enjoy unparalleled social freedom, our personal lives are actually playing lesser roles than ever before in the scheme of things. We invest greater than ever emotional energy into our careers. Our bodies, once mere corporal vehicles to tote us around, have now become instruments for self-expression.

WHY I AM A SINGULAR

Because I write in the first-person plural, readers know that my perspective throughout the book has been as a member of the singular generation. This does not mean that I view uncritically the singular generation's habits and aspirations, fascinations and fixations. I do, however, feel a deep connection to the singular experience. I am a product of the forces that created the singular impulse, and I share with my generation a search for security, for a home, for spiritual grounding. I have a drive to succeed in my work and a deep-seated fear of nuclear war. I am taken with tradition, and I hold a pragmatic philosophy of life.

Mine was an unsettling, itinerant childhood. My family moved from place to place at a clipped pace, and eventually came apart. I am what is known as a "fac brat," having grown up on the college-campus circuit where my father and later my mother were members of the faculty. I was born in South Bend, Indiana, when Daddy taught at Notre Dame. We lived in Cleveland, Ohio; Buffalo, New York; Macomb, Illinois; Lexington, Kentucky; and Orono, Maine, before I graduated from high school. I once calculated that by age eighteen, I'd occupied nine different homes—two years a stop.

My parents were divorced in 1965, a shattering experience for all of us but never one I thought to be wrong. As early as junior high school, I turned my attention to excelling at school and planning my career, not party-hopping and chasing boys.

Senior year in high school, I was interviewed for *Seventeen* magazine's "Young America Today" series in an article entitled "Growing Up in a Broken Home." The interviewer questioned me at length about marriage. I remember telling him that I had no strong feelings about marriage, at least as it related to me personally. I was neither pro nor con, but felt that marriage did not hold the key to my future. The best of what I could do—and become— lay in my own hands, in a career, in something that I could fashion myself.

At twenty-three, when I fell in love for the first time, when marriage lurched to the front of my mind, it quite took me by surprise. Where did it come from, this wanting to be wed?

Only later did I realize that my attitude toward marriage was the product of a hybrid background and conflicting belief systems. Until age nine, I'd been a child of a traditional family, with a homemaker mother, a breadwinner father and a sister twenty-one months my senior. After the divorce, I became a child of a single-parent household, a poor relation in society. Childhood innocence was a luxury we could no longer afford.

UNFAIR ALLEGATIONS

The frequent criticisms of the singular generation fall on deaf ears with me, perhaps because I take them personally and dismiss them just as quickly. These criticisms come most frequently from members of the sixties generation, and they usually center on the alleged materialism and selfishness of our generation, the fact that we have "sold out" without ever having rebelled, that we seem to be politically conservative and that, in general, we lack spine.

A year or so ago, sixties radical (and eighties stockbroker) Abbie Hoffman once again spoke out for his peers by turning a twist on his old maxim. Nowadays, he proclaimed, you can't trust anyone *under* thirty. He went on to accuse today's young of ushering in an "era of designer brains." His witticisms made the wire services, and they made me wince.

Singulars reflect the tenor of our times and the mood of the whole society, just as members of the sixties generation did during their heyday. The sixties generation rebelled against the Establishment and drew up a "better plan." They had their gurus who had the answers; there was right and wrong back then. In their definitiveness, they were inadvertently reflecting the strength and self-confidence shared by both the government and the society as a whole.

Singulars have more modest goals, reflecting the spirit of a nation whose economic prowess has been shaken and whose economic, political and military position in the world has diminished. Singulars don't expect to effect our agenda—when we have one—overnight; all we try to do is take small steps. Some members of the sixties generation who cherish their memories of 1968 (but who have by now joined the Establishment) cannot fathom why singulars do not behave as they did when they were young. They cannot understand why singulars start compiling our résumés while we are still in college, or why we don't dress in rags, or how we can possibly hang on the words of our parents and teachers.

The answer is simple: The world has changed, and singulars have not had to rebel against the conformity that confounded members of the sixties generation. We have different sore points, many of them rising from the chaos that came in the wake of that generation.

In this ongoing tension between the sixties generation and the singular generation, there are no rights and wrongs; both generations are products of their times. And though our styles may differ, we are, nonetheless, legacies of the sixties generation, just as surely as they were legacies of the GI generation and the spirit of victory in World War II.

THE DECLINE OF YOUTH CULTURE

The arrival of the singular generation represents more than just the changing of the generational guard. The singular impulse also signals the breakdown of youth culture and youth power that reached its apex a generation ago. The credo of the sixties youth culture held that to be young was inherently superior to not being young, and often, that older people were beyond the reach of new-age values. The decline of youth culture is also a result of the aging of the Baby Boom and the lessening of the economic clout—and numbers—of the young.

For singulars, being young is no particular credential or achievement in and of itself. Since we are what we do, it stands to reason that the longer we live and the more experience and insight we gain, the more seasoned and singular we become.

In the sixties, young people tended to be the only ones who had much freedom to experiment and who were not shackled to convention. Today all of society has gained or can gain this privilege. While young Americans provide the seedbed for the germination of the singular phenomenon, it is a growing reality in every age group.

DOES SINGULARITY HAVE A FUTURE?

Throughout this book, I have laid out the case for the singular mind-set without commenting on its growth potential or longevity, without examining the legacy the singular generation is likely to leave our descendants and where singulars, as individuals, may wind up twenty years from now.

It is, of course, difficult to look into a crystal ball at a future that may never come. It is especially difficult when prognosticating the lives of singulars, who are almost impossible to fit under one umbrella.

Singulars seek answers individually, and when we find them, we understand that they work for us alone; we do not try to apply, or impart, those answers to others. By the same token, our generation is notable for its lack of prophets, of spokespersons, of single and unifying voices that speak for and to us all. We instinctively mistrust the easy answer and the one-sided solution. We are, after all, a generation of hybrids, shaped by several different eras, nostalgic for a past that we can never retrieve and fearful of a future that lies in peril.

Nevertheless, I would like to suggest that singularity has a life cycle and that it contains the seeds of its own obsolescence. Singularity is a conscious and sometimes self-conscious impulse, a reaction to a confusing, transitional epoch. If conditions change (and, to our way of thinking, improve), singularity could prove to be a temporary condition.

The desire to be singular derives from a number of primary needs: the need to find an inner core that is protected from the outer chaos and conflicting messages given by society; the need to cast off the prefabricated but dated roles that society has accepted for so long, and often still slips into when in doubt; and finally, the need to find a positive new model that is widely acceptable.

When these unmet needs are filled, or are no longer compelling, and when the singular impulse becomes second nature rather than self-conscious, people will be free to fight new battles, to enjoy new passions. Once singularity becomes implicit, not learned, the great social freedoms that we now enjoy will extend even further, multiplying our options for human interaction and joyful exchange. This would parallel the evolution of gender and racial equality from self-conscious adoption by the sixties generation to implicit acceptance by the eighties generation.

WRESTLING WITH OUR FUTURE

To date, the strongest vital sign of the singular generation has been our will to succeed in life via pragmatism and a nondogmatic approach. We pride ourselves on our ability to pull ourselves up by the bootstraps in the world of work, and on being realists rather than idealists. We comfort our consciences by saying that realists are more likely to achieve their goals than are pie-in-the-sky dreamers.

Mired in presentism, singulars often say that we cannot imagine what the future will bring. (The truth is, we can imagine only too well.) But we cannot forever deny the greatest issue of our day—the threat of nuclear annihilation. It has a choke hold on us, in the literal, megatonage sense, with existing weapons poised to blow up the world. In another, less direct way, this unresolved threat undermines our quality of life. It lingers in the background noise of my generation; by ignoring it, we confine ourselves to the inherently unsatisfying condition of living life only in the present.

Only by confronting the hideous prospect of the nuclear threat can we wrestle into submission the fears that have a grip on us. Even if—God forbid—we fail in our mission, the process, the fight, would help to free our lives. It would give us a common purpose and would help rid us of the stifling dislocation, disconnection and loss of meaning that are endemic to our time.

There is hope. Because we devote so much time and effort to mining and expressing ourselves, we may come to a satisfying understanding of who we are as individuals, thus enabling us to apply our specific talents for the benefit of the community—the global community.

We have choices to make if we want to fight for a future. And we have choices to make if we want to take command of our era, as the young have traditionally done. These choices involve moving beyond the narrow self-interest of individual singulars and of the generation as a whole. We must get to, and then build upon, the common interests of all generations. Survival is our starting point.

Singulars are saddled with the greatest challenge of any generation, and we are playing for the highest stakes. We will be nothing less than heroic if we succeed.